<deconstructing web graphics.2>

■ Words: Lynda Weinman
and Jon Warren Lentz
■ Design: Ali Karp

■ deconstructing web graphics.2

**By Lynda Weinman
and Jon Warren Lentz**

Published by: New Riders Publishing
201 West 103rd Street
Indianapolis, IN 46290 USA

©1998 by New Riders Publishing
Printed in the United States of America 1 2 3 4 5 6 7 8 9 0
Library of Congress Cataloging-in-Publication Data
CIP data available upon request
ISBN: 1-56205-859-2

Warning and Disclaimer

This book is designed to provide information about web design and web publishing. Every effort has been made to make this book as complete and as accurate as possible, but no warranty or fitness is implied. The information is provided on an "as is" basis. The author(s) and New Riders Publishing shall have neither liability nor responsibility to any person or entity with respect to any loss or damages arising from the information contained in this book or from the use of the discs or programs that may accompany it.

Trademark Acknowledgments

All terms mentioned in this book that are known to be trademarks or service marks have been appropriately capitalized. New Riders Publishing cannot attest to the accuracy of this information. Use of a term in this book should not be regarded as affecting the validity of any trademark or service mark.

Publisher:	Jordan Gold
Brand Manager:	Alan Bower
Managing Editor:	Brice Gosnell

This book was produced digitally by Macmillan Computer Publishing and manufactured using computer-to-plate technology (a filmless process) by GAC/Shepard Poorman, Indianapolis, Indiana.

■ credits

Deconstructing Web Graphics

Executive Editor
Beth Millett

Development Editor
Jennifer Eberhardt

Project Editor
Katie Purdum

Copy Editor
Michael Brumitt

Technical Editor
Robert Reinhardt

Team Coordinator
Carol Ackerman

Manufacturing Coordinator
Paul Gilchrist

Book Designer
Ali Karp "alink newmedia"
alink@earthlink.net

Cover Designer
Bruce Heavin
bruce@stink.com

Director of Production
Larry Klein

Production Team Supervisor
Brad Chinn

Production Team
Carol Bowers
Mona Brown
Ayanna Lacey
Gene Redding

Indexer
Christine Nelsen

About the Authors

Lynda Weinman is the author of the best-selling *Designing Web Graphics.2*, *Deconstructing Web Graphics*, and *Coloring Web Graphics.2*, as well as the recently published *Creative HTML Design* (all by New Riders Publishing).

She is renowned for her ground-breaking research into web design issues and ability to communicate and teach digital design techniques in an easy-going and relaxed writing style.

Lynda is a featured columnist on—web design, video, animation, and screen-based design for many periodicals, including *Web Techniques, How Magazine, Step-by-Step Graphics*, and *MacWorld magazines*. Lynda has trained some of the best digital design talent in the industry and has taught at many institutions, including the highly regarded Art Center College of Design in Pasadena CA, and San Francisco State Multimedia Studies program.

Jon Warren Lentz is a graduate of the Classical Studies program at the University of California at Santa Cruz. A freelance artist and author, Jon's images have been featured in the 1997 Graphis Poster Annual, *Mac Art & Design Magazine* (Sweden), and *IdN, The International Designer's Network Magazine* (Hong Kong).

Jon regards the photodigital realm as a medium well suited to the creation of art works of serious abstract intent. His Internet web gallery is at http://www.uncom.com. Prior to entering the photo-digital frontier, Jon achieved notice as a sculptor working with sand-carved glass, which he helped to define as a fine art medium (http://www. uncom.com/jwlpsi/html/art/art.htm).

Jon has lectured on digital design and technology at many venues. Most recently, he conducted seminars in Web Page Design and Intro-ductory Interactive Multimedia at the Maine Photographic Work-shops/International Film & Television Workshops in Rockport, Maine. In 1998 Jon will present seminars at the Thunder Lizard Photoshop Conference, New Media 98 Toronto, Maine Photographic Workshops, and the Palm Beach Photographic Center.

Lynda's Acknowledgements

I would like to thank my daughter **Jamie**, who always brings a smile to my heart, and my husband **Bruce** who is so generous with his love and support, even when he misses seeing much of me.

Thanks to **Jon Warren Lentz** for putting his heart and soul into this project, and for putting up with my stubborn ways. I am proud of what we created together.

Thanks to **Ali Karp**, who after seven books with me can now finish all my sentences. Thanks to Barak, her fiancé, for understanding that designing books usually requires an unreasonable amount of time.

Thanks to **Jennifer Eberhardt**, our trusted development editor, who has helped us realize our vision for this and many other books. We love ya!

Thanks to all the **web designers** who allowed themselves and their projects to be profiled in this book. It took a lot of work on their parts, and they deserve a huge amount of credit for making this book the generous and helpful resource that it is.

Jon's Acknowledgements

This book is dedicated to my family: my mom and dad, **John E. Lentz** and **Mildred Lentz**, and to my son **Rob**. It's especially dedicated to my wife, **Roanne Rogers**... although it took me 40 years to find her, she is the one. Without her love, support, and subordination of her own interests, I never could have done this. I love you, darling.

I would like to thank two steadfast friends, Larry Susnow and Sharon James. Thanks also to Katrin Eismann for her constant support, encouragement, and tireless belief in my work. Thanks to Dianne Fenster for her smile, her friendship, and the inspiration of her art. Other friends, influences, and collectors whom I must acknowledge are: Jim Beshears, Steve Kenyon, John Kent, Jerry Ratch, Gregg Palin, Gary Miles, Norman O. Brown, Glen Carter, Susan Kurtz, Greg Soucy, Eric and Lori Greenfield, Rainey Strauss, Martha Weinstein, Marco Chiavacci di Lucca, Bill Slatkin, Les Cowan, David Pope, Robert Altman, Robert Reinhardt, Mark Mannheimer, and Nancy Conte.

Special thanks to Ali, our favorite obsessive compulsive book designer, whose dedication to quality is unsurpassed and totally invaluable!

"Real surfing is far superior to surfing on the web." Photo of John shot by his equally enthusiastic surfing son, Rob.

Co-author Jon Warren Lentz's Image Gallery

Berg: Sand-Carved glass sculpture, circa 1987, collection
Dr. Leo Steinberg, NY, NY.

Commissioned by the Port of San Francisco to promote
SF as a cruise destination, this was selected for the 1997
Graphis Poster Annual.

Selfscape: The first in a suite of abstracted self-portraits.

Ulysses@Hades: One of a suite of images that references
Jon's personal experience of the myth of Odysseus and
Ulysses as told by Homer and Joyce.

■ contents at a glance

Introduction 13

| Qaswa 19

3 Bosch Power Tools 73

4 National Geographic 105

5 Akimbo Design   125

6 @tlas   157

Web Graphics Appendix   189

Introduction
by Lynda Weinman

- **Qaswa**
- **Cooper-Hewitt**
- **Bosch**
- **National Geographic**
- **Akimbo**
- **@tlas**

We chose to focus this book on the jewels of the web:
the few and far between inspiring examples of what the
medium is truly capable of. We profiled the artists and
programmers who created each site, dissected their work,
got into their heads to find out what inspired them, frus-
trated them, challenged them, and rewarded them. This
book, if you will, uses a voyeuristic method of studying a
subject of immense diversity and new challenges—the
field of web design.

Deconstructing Web Graphics.2

The world of web design is very different from other digital (and analog!) design mediums. It contains a host of workarounds, frustrations, variables, and barriers. Those who excel in this field are really pioneers, working with their individual goals in mind, while fighting the technical obstacles that block their way. It behooves anyone interested in web design to understand why and how successful sites work. The best way, in my opinion, to learn is to ask the people who made them.

You might hear the hype of how great a new web technology is, or how easy a new web tool is, but nothing compares to getting the real lowdown on what works and what does not. This book is not about hype or promises. It's about real sites, real tools, real problems, and real solutions.

My co-author, Jon Warren Lentz, and I spent hundreds of hours interviewing web designers we admired to produce a chronicle of their techniques, tips, and lessons. Along the way, we assembled a tremendous amount of very helpful information that we poured back into our manuscript.

When Jon Warren Lentz approached me about wanting to work together, I was thrilled to find another writer who was interested in collaborating with me on this sequel. Much of what you see in this book is Jon's writing and research, injected with a healthy dose of my teaching skills. I could not have done this book without Jon and am indebted to him for his belief in this project and efforts in bringing it to print.

When browsing or reading this book, you might be stunned by the amount of work that went into a single graphic or bit of code. Many books might tell you how easy authoring web content is, but in order to have an exemplary site, you have to truly care about every pixel and closing tag. This is a book about people who care deeply about making the best possible web site. It is not about quick fixes or shortcuts, but about real challenges and innovative solutions.

As a teacher with eight years of experience teaching digital design, multimedia, animation, and now web design and over 18 combined years of professional experience in these various fields, I have strong ideas about how people best learn a new subject. My book series, which is listed in the back of this book, offers a number of different teaching approaches. I believe there are different types of learning systems, and that some people learn best by "doing," others by "studying," and others by "observing." This book takes the observation approach, as I believe many of us learn best by studying what others have done "in context" of real world projects.

We based the choice of sites on many factors, not the least of which was the consideration of which site would teach which technique the best. The overriding purpose of this book was not to simply show a gallery of impressive sites, but to also teach our readers how they might implement some of the techniques profiled here. Accordingly, we had to carefully edit each site's chapter so it taught something new and valuable. For example, many of the sites here might have used the same technique well, but we edited the chapters so each technique was only presented once.

When I wrote the first edition of this book, my book designer Ali Karp commented about its time-sensitivity and how someday it would probably be regarded as a history book instead of a web design book. Her prophetic words are true; today only a handful of the first set of sites from the original *Deconstructing Web Graphics* are online anymore. For this reason, we chose to archive many of the sites in this sequel edition on Jon Warren Lentz's site: http://www.uncom.com/decon2/.

It is with great excitement that we send this book out into the hands of web designers everywhere. We wanted to make a truly useful and educational resource to help raise the bar of design on the web. Our hope is that this book will enable you to see web design in a new light and help inspire you to develop more satisfying web sites of your own. We owe the artists in this book our respect, admiration, and extreme gratitude for their generous spirit in sharing the inside details about how they do their work so freely. Thanks to all of the people who agreed to be featured in this book and to our loyal audience, who makes this effort possible.

■ Lynda Weinman

What Are the Differences Between the Two Editions of This Book?

For those of you who own the first edition of *Deconstructing Web Graphics* or are debating about which edition to purchase, this chart outlines the differences between the two books. I recommend them both, but I am biased <grin>. Actually both books contain tons of useful information, and though many of the sites are no longer online from the first book, many of the techniques used are still as inspiring now as they were then.

Deconstructing Web Graphics	Deconstructing Web Graphics.2
■ Aliased Graphics	■ Multimedia Versus Web
■ Converting Print Graphics to Web Graphics	■ Shockwave Design
■ Forms Processing and CGI	■ Innovative Background Tiles
■ Customizing Type in Photoshop 3.0 and Illustrator 6.0	■ Interfaces in Photoshop
■ Browser-Safe Colors	■ Museum Design on the Web
■ Hybrid-Safe Colors	■ Building Community
■ Custom Photoshop Brushes	■ Using Color for Hierarchy and Navigation
■ Creating Clean Transparent GIFs	■ Adding Value to the Web
■ Creating Seamless Tiles	■ JavaScript Rollovers
■ Animated GIFs	■ 3D Animated GIFs
■ ASCII Art	■ Acrobat
■ Black and White Techniques	■ Imagemaps
■ LOWSRC Tricks	■ Creative Process
■ Using Tables for Alignment	■ Hub and Spokes Architecture
■ Client-Side Imagemaps	■ Information Architecture
■ Designing for Frames	■ Use of Real Audio
■ Copy Editing for the Web	■ Designing with Flash
■ Quark HTML Conversions	■ Designing with Frames
■ Invisible Objects	■ DHTML
■ Client Pull	■ Cascading Style Sheets
■ Server Push	■ Photoshop 4.0
■ Copyrighted Images	■ DreamWeaver
■ Human Interface Design	■ BBEdit
■ Java for Animation	■ GifBuilder
■ Guestbooks with CGI	■ JavaScript Browser Detection
■ Scanning Techniques	■ Storyboarding Web Sites
■ Movie and Audio Formats	■ Using QuickTime and Premiere
■ HTML for Audio and Video	■ Using Illustrator for the Web
■ VRML	■ Using Screen Captures

■ what the chapters cover

Do I Need to Understand HTML to Read This Book?

Sometimes I wonder if anyone truly understands HTML. It has been a moving target until now, and since it has settled down a bit, there are now many new moving technologies to take its place. This book does its best to "deconstruct" HTML and other types of code, but it does help to understand a few basics.

HTML Basics

- The HTML language includes "tags," and the tags require brackets around them like this, < & >.

- Many tags require a closing tag, which means that directions must be turned "off." For example, the HEAD tag <HEAD> must be followed by the END HEAD tag </HEAD>, where the "/" is the character that tells the browser to stop the HEAD. This type of opening and closing tag is also referred to as a container.

- Attributes that modify the function of a tag are placed inside the brackets, < & > of the tag. For example, the element <FONT FACE> includes the <FONT> tag and the FACE attribute.

- Variables are values specified to control an attribute. For example, the element <FONT FACE="verdana"> includes a tag attribute, and a value, which is "verdana."

- The body of an HTML document is initiated by the <BODY> tag and ended by the </BODY> tag.

- When used as an attribute for <BODY>, BGCOLOR calls a color of the HTML document, and the variable specifies the value of the color. Thus, in this code: <BODY BGCOLOR="FFFFFF"> ...content... </BODY>BGCOLOR is the attribute of <BODY and "FFFFFF" is the variable, expressed in hexadecimal color. Hexadecimal color is discussed in the Web Graphics Appendix at the back of this book.

For a better and more thorough understanding of HTML, I recommend *Creative HTML Design* (http://www.htmlbook.com), written by myself and and my programmer brother, William Weinman. It includes a step-by-step tutorial for learning HTML and includes a reference appendix in the back of all the current HTML 4.0 tags and attributes. Information

■ note

Contacting the Authors

The web site for this book will be located at http://www.lynda.com/decon2/ and http://www.uncom.com/decon2/. You will find additional resources, addendums, surprises, and errata at both these sites. If you would like to contact us, try the following places:

Lynda Weinman
lynda@lynda.com
http://www.lynda.com

Jon Warren Lentz
jwlpsi@uncom.com
http://www.uncom.com

We welcome your feedback about this book.

Qaswa
Design and Function

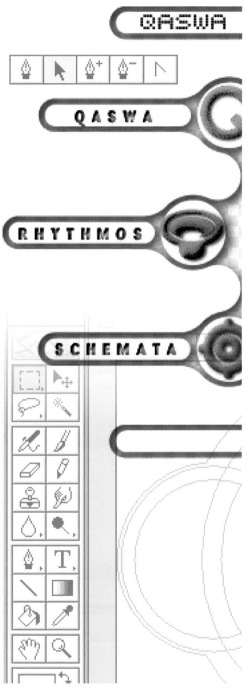

- ■ **Multimedia Versus Web**
- ■ **Creating Interfaces in Photoshop**
- ■ **Background Tiles**
- ■ **Shockwave Design**

http://www.qaswa.com/ Qaswa is a one-person web development company specializing in finely designed, easily navigable web environments. The Qaswa site started originally as an ongoing experimental project, and resulted in a leading edge portfolio for its creator, Ammon Haggerty. Although the site was originally created in 1995 and still retains much of its original look, Qaswa endures as one of the finer design destinations on the web. This chapter covers Ammon's background in design and multimedia, and how he turned it into a foundation for his strong web design convictions. His clever use of Photoshop and Macromedia Director are also reviewed.

Web Design Firm: Qaswa, San Francisco, California

Client: Qaswa, San Francisco, California

Type of Site: Company Demonstration Site and Portfolio

Original URL: http://www.qaswa.com

Archived URL: http://www.uncom.com/dcwg2/

Server: Sun Station

Operating System: UNIX

Server Software: Stronghold 2.0

Host: Virtual Sites (v-sites.net)

Producer/Webmaster/Digital Designer: Ammon Haggerty

Art Direction/Illustration/Animation/Sound: Ammon Haggerty

Development/Production Platform: Macintosh Quadra 650

Software: Adobe Photoshop, Adobe Illustrator, DeBabelizer, PhotoGIF, Infini-d, Shockwave, Amapi, GIF Builder, Sound Edit 16, Macromedia Director

Qaswa's History

When Ammon Haggerty started Qaswa, he never dreamed that someday his client roster would include Couloir Skiwear, Intranet Partners, Orion Pictures, Tonic Domain Registry, Argos Adriatic Corporation, Creation Spirituality Network, Warner Interactive, SOL | Snowboarding Online, and Axis Consulting. When he started on the web, no one could have predicted how powerful this venue would become for a self-promotional design portfolio.

In college, Ammon studied business, electronics, and computer science but then "dropped out to become a professional snowboarder." He received his art knowledge from his mother, who is an Asian art teacher. He shared, "She's a master Thanka painter (traditional Tibetan painting), which has been an influence on my design." His interest in art and computers wasn't rekindled until after college, when he began working with a snowboard clothing company and suddenly found himself creating graphics, ads, and catalogs. Ammon worked with "a couple of incredibly talented designers" who ran the clothing company. "Neither could use a computer, but both had a seemingly endless source of creativity. Working with them inspired me to design and to feel good about my work."

This inspiring work led to a brief freelance graphics career until he landed a job at Colorscape, a startup multimedia company in San Francisco. During his tenure at Colorscape, Ammon said that he produced content for CD-ROMs. "For many projects, outside artists were hired to create the interface. Since I was the one implementing the design, I worked with these artists directly. I quickly realized that these artists knew nothing about interface design because they didn't understand the functionality of the medium. So I began to design interfaces and ultimately replaced the outside contractors."

But before he replaced those outside contractors, Ammon paid some dues. He learned Photoshop from countless hours of production work. "When I first started to learn the program, I was given an assignment to cut out 150 complex images with the Pen tool. It took me three months."

Two years later Colorscape folded, and Ammon started his own company. It took three months of searching and experimenting with names until Ammon found one. "I was skimming through a book called *The Prophet Mohammed*. Qaswa caught my attention because the word sounded so sweet, yet it didn't have any English meaning. I read that Qaswa was the Prophet Mohammed's camel and that Qaswa was also recognized as a messenger of decisions and frequently made important choices for Mohammed (either by not moving or not stopping). So Qaswa represented a vehicle for a message, both a high and strong back from which the message could be delivered and also a purveyor of important decisions."

Now, at the wizened age of "nearly 26," Ammon is recognized as a pioneer of design on the web. When Ammon built the first Qaswa site, back in 1995, he relied upon his experience of interface design and intuition that it should be possible to create a more interesting experience by introducing an illusion of space and depth to the interface.

CD-ROM Multimedia Versus the Web

When Ammon started his own company and turned to the web, he arrived with skills and concerns that he'd developed through his work in multimedia. Although the web is a form of multimedia, it differs significantly from CD-ROM-based multimedia:

- CD-ROMs do not have their content downloaded over lowbandwidth connections.

- The limitations of the color palette are not as extreme on CD-ROMs as on the web.

- CD-ROMs can be authored and delivered via sophisticated authoring tools—most notably, Macromedia's Director. Web authoring tools are still very primitive—at best. Even when an HTML authoring tool is used, the most advanced sites almost always require some manually authored code.

- The world of interactive CD-ROMs is rooted in the game culture—which involves entertaining movement, color, and flash. By contrast, the web was originally devised for the distribution and communication of data within the scientific and engineering worlds that was often presented without concern for aesthetics or entertainment.

- Unlike the world of CD-ROM, the web audience has greater control over how they view the final output. This control includes browser choice, screen resolution, font selection and size, the option to turn off images, and the choice to either use or ignore plug-ins.

Ammon began by trying to integrate what he already knew from CD-ROM-based multimedia into the web medium, but one of the problems he came up against was frustration from the lack of tools. "I was used to great tools, like Macromedia Director, in my work with CD-ROM multimedia development." This time in web development pre-dated animated GIFs, or any software that was dedicated to web design needs.

Another problem that concerned him at the time was the lack of other competent designers on the web owing, perhaps, to its scientific origins. "There was nothing, or almost nothing, inspiring to look at or bounce off of." One of Ammon's goals for designing Qaswa was to inspire good web design and to attract more designers to the web medium.

The Qaswa Interface Design

Unlike many web designers who migrated from print, Ammon's designs are derived from what he wants the site to do. "I design based on functionality. It's not ruled by design. I'm primarily interested in what and how the site is supposed to work, so my shapes spring from these considerations, either from what I want it to do or from what it needs to do. The driving design force is this functionality." Ammon's focus has led him to build interfaces that not only work well but are original and beautiful.

This interface is a near-perfect example of simple organization. Although nearly 50 destinations can be reached either within or through the Qaswa site, a visitor arriving at the site is not overwhelmed by an ugly profusion of listed options. Instead, the visitor is presented with a balanced, beautiful menu bar from which all other destinations may be reached. This menu bar is created from a basic shape that is repeated down the menu to house the signature icons and symbols for each discrete area of the site. These icons and symbols are, in turn, reused to develop a reassuring and consistent sense of place as the visitor moves within the site. The result is that visitors do not become lost or bewildered here. Rather, there is an experience of anticipation and delight as the icons and symbols are developed within each area of the site.

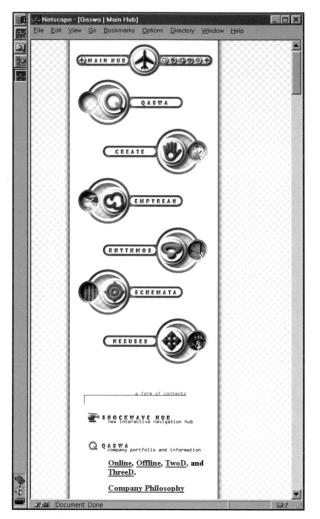

The Qaswa Main Hub is a masterful balance of function, beauty, and dimension. There's also an overt reference (an homage, if you will) to the creative environment of Adobe's Photoshop, in use of the default checkered Photoshop transparency layer for the background of the Qaswa Main Hub. "It was actually an accident," Ammon explained. "I was working on a border and clicked the visibility button revealing the Photoshop transparency layer below. I thought the gray and white checker created a great contrast to the shadow."

Ammon has divided the Qaswa Main Menu into six primary categories that lead to logical subcategories: Qaswa, company portfolio and information; Create, an artists environment; Empyrean, a VRML environment under construction; Rhythmos, a music-culture zine; Schemata, a web-tools discussion area, also under construction; and Nexuses, links to other sites.

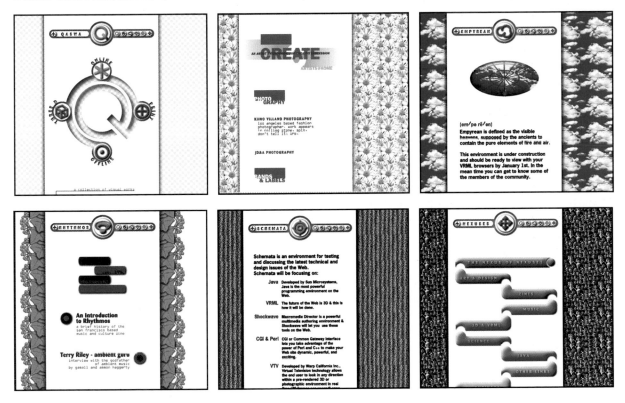

The Six Primary Categories of Qaswa

There are conflicting edicts for the maximal number of "choices," or clickable index, items on an interactive page. Depending on which authority you consult, this number seems to hover between six and 10. Certainly, anyone who has spent time on the web has encountered both extremes: Those that work despite their departure from the general rule, and those that fail despite their observance of the rule. So what is the final criteria? Navigability. The Qaswa site has extensive depth. If all the clickable destinations within this site were graphically indexed on one page, it would be perplexing and useless.

The key is organization of information into meaningful primary categories that either lead to secondary index pages or to final destinations. The optimal number will be a result of ideal functionality based upon the particulars of the information being organized. This is called information architecture.

■ note

Information Architecture?

The word "architecture," together with the concept of "being an architect," is derived from the ancient Greeks. Unlike many of these old words, the meaning has remained constant through its adoption into Latin and modern English. The word and concept have survived intact because they are fundamental aspects of human experience: humans build and inhabit space.

Then, as now, to be an architect is to design, contrive, supervise, and direct the structure of anything—most especially buildings and edifices—and usually with some regard to aesthetic effect.

How does this relate to information? To be an Information Architect is to devise, contrive, and construct a hierarchy of information so that it can be navigated spatially. Why spatially?

A book, for example, is an arrangement of information that appears within the space of its covers—it is devised to present information in both a reliable and meaningful way. The structure usually dictates that the end follows the beginning and that chapters follow in numerical order, in which information presented in Chapter 2 is either subordinate to or dependent upon Chapter 1. This ordering implies space. In a book, the ordering occurs in space. Furthermore, any deviation from this customary order may have a meaning. (It would be possible for an architect to design a functional house with an open-air bathroom on the roof, but what would that mean?)

In as much as humans want to move through the space of books and houses with some sense of reliability and meaning, we also hope that a web designer will devise a meaningful, reliable construct within which the information (or content) of the site is presented. Innovative web designers will meet this goal, as well as interject a pleasing aesthetic for the experience. They will create a look and feel of space, an ordered informational hierarchy, and it is a "place" of beauty—like a Greek temple.

If you're interested in studying more about information architecture, here are some of our favorite books:

Web Concept and Design ■ Crystal Waters ■ New Riders ■ ISBN 1-56205-648-4

Interactivity by Design ■ Ray Kristof and Amy Satran ■ Adobe Press ■ ISBN 1-56830-221-5

Multimedia Producer's Bible ■ Ron Goldberg ■ IDG ■ ISBN 0-7645-3002-X

Designing Business ■ Clement Mok ■ Adobe Press ■ ISBN 1-56830-282-7

Building the Qaswa Interface

Ammon began the design process for the Qaswa interface with rough sketches that he subsequently developed into pleasing interface shapes in Adobe Illustrator. Here, you can see the original concepts that led to both the original Qaswa Main Menu and the Portfolio Hub.

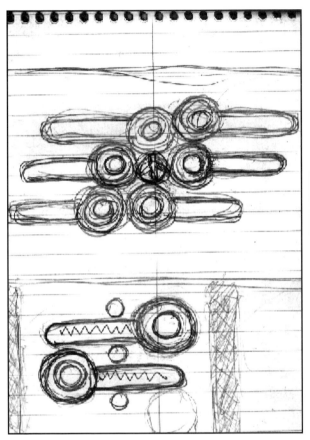

Concept sketches for the original Qaswa main menu.

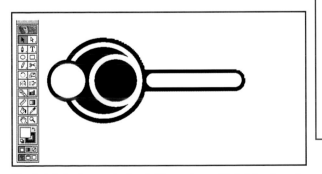

The final design for a navigational object to be used in building the main menu. It was created in Adobe Illustrator from the concept sketch.

When asked why he uses Illustrator Ammon answered, "I usually start with Illustrator to work on concepts because it has such a flexible design tool, fine type control, and very small file sizes. Geometry, symmetry, and balance have always been good starting points for me. Once an idea/shape has been formed, it's easy to change the shapes into more organic or asymmetrical shapes while still maintaining the balance. Playing and experimenting is a good way to maintain a high level of creativity and inspiration."

The creation of the final visual elements was done in Adobe Photoshop by building up successive shapes in individual layers. The shapes were derived from paths origin-ally drawn in Adobe Illustrator and pasted into Adobe Photoshop. Each Photoshop layer was derived from a discrete individual path. The shadow layers were duplicate layers of the original elements, which were offset slightly and then blurred.

■ **note**

Pixels Versus Paths

Photoshop is a pixel-based program; Illustrator is a vector-based program. What does this mean? Images from pixel-based programs are described by pixels, which means they are composed of square shapes. Illustrations and drawings created in vector-based programs are defined by paths, which are like lines between points, and are saved as compact mathe-matical descriptions. Often, designs are created in Illustrator and the finished Illustrator paths are then pasted into Photoshop for development as pixel-based imagery. This is because it is easier to create curved, mathematical shapes in a vector program, and easier to create organic-style imagery (such as glows, textures, and shadows) in a pixel-based program.

Although the two most popular web formats—GIF and JPEG—are pixel-based, designers can take advantage of the benefits of vector programs (such as paths and the ability to draw perfect mathematical curves). The artwork is then passed through Photoshop, which turns those vector images into pixel-based imagery for use as web graphics.

■ step-by-step

Converting Illustrator Paths to Photoshop

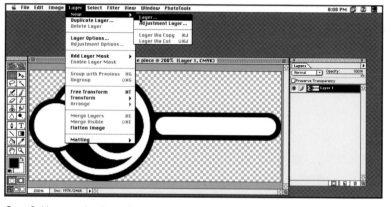

Step 1: Ammon started by opening the Illustrator file into Photoshop so it could provide a reference while he worked with the paths. To bring an Illustrator file into Photoshop, you must first save it in the Illustrator file format. When Photoshop opens an Illustrator file, this Rasterize Generic EPS Format dialog box appears, which presents options regarding how the information is to be converted from vectors to pixels.

Step 2: Here are the shapes from Illustrator converted to a pixel-based image. Ammon used these shapes as a reference layer. He created a new layer to place above this one and filled it with white, providing a new canvas upon which to work.

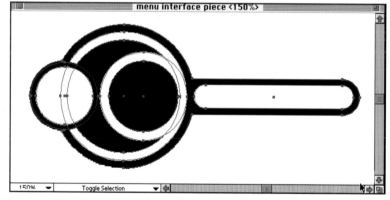

Step 4: Back in Photoshop, the paths were pasted into the image with Edit: Paste. This invoked the Paste paths dialog. Since paths were desired in this instance, the default Paste As Paths was accepted.

Step 3: Leaving Photoshop open, Ammon launched Illustrator so he could access the "paths." Here's the Illustrator file with all paths selected via Edit: Select All. Next, all the paths are copied into Photoshop with Edit: Copy. This concludes the work to be accomplished in Illustrator.

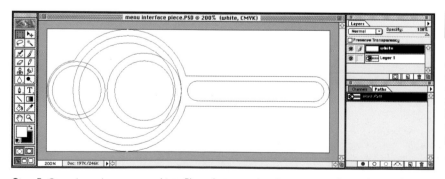

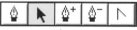

Step 6: The Pen tool variants are available by holding your mouse down on the Pen tool (within the tools palette) while dragging to the right. The highlighted arrow here is the paths Direct Selection tool, which can be used to select individual paths.

Step 5: Once the paths were pasted into Photoshop, note that they appear as thin outlines and are grouped into a single layer, called "WorkPath," in the Paths Palette.

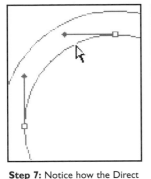

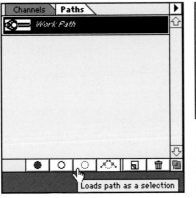

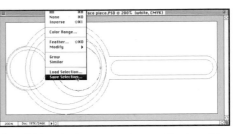

Step 7: Notice how the Direct Selection tool accesses the curves of the path. This tool allowed Ammon to edit and tweak the curved shapes in Photoshop.

Step 8: The selected path was loaded as a selection by clicking the Load Path as Selection icon at the bottom of the Paths Palette.

Step 9: The selection was saved as an alpha channel (see glossary) via Select: Save Selection: New. By saving this selection as a permanent alpha channel, Ammon was able to reaccess this shape whenever he needed to, without going through all the labor of the preceding steps.

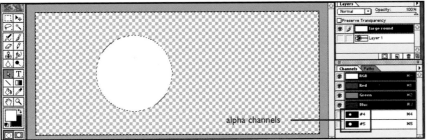

alpha channels

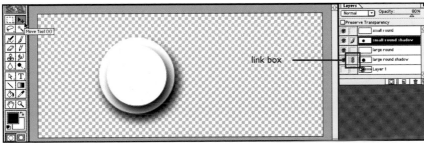

Step 10: Ammon chose Selection:Load Selection and was able to access the shape again (stored in the alpha channel) to create a round filled circle that registered itself to his original Illustrator file. The selection he loaded was inverted with Select: Inverse and the Delete key was pressed, leaving a large round white diameter. The white layer hadn't served much purpose until now, and it was renamed by double-clicking its layer bar, "large round."

Step 11: He repeated the process with the smaller circular path and created another layer called "small round." Both the large round and the small round layers were duplicated by dragging each layer bar down to the duplicate layer icon of the Layers palette. These duplicate layers were renamed "small round shadow" and "large round shadow," and were positioned beneath their respective partners. He filled the shadow layers with black, and chose Filter: Blur: Gaussian Blur: Radius 5.

link box

Step 12: By highlighting each shadow layer and adjusting the Opacity slider at the top of the Layers palette, the shadows were softened by changing the opacity to 80 percent. He positioned the shadows by highlighting a white layer, and clicking the link box of its respective shadow layer. The link function is indispensable for creating accurate and consistent offset shadows. Finally, with the Move tool selected, the arrow keys were used to nudge the linked shadow layers into place. Each click of any arrow key moved the layer one pixel (Shift + arrow key = 10 pixels). These shadow layers were offset at seven pixels down and four right.

The Double Border Background Tile

When Ammon began to design Qaswa, in the middle of 1995, the web was far less developed than today. "There were no frames, no tables, no WYSIWYG authoring tools and nearly all the other sites were aligned either left, right, or center." Ammon had ideas for things that simply had not been done. "I was playing with new ideas. So the site wasn't as difficult technically as it was conceptually." One concept that Ammon believes he may have originated is the "double border" background tile.

The source tile for a background tile is smaller than the browser window.

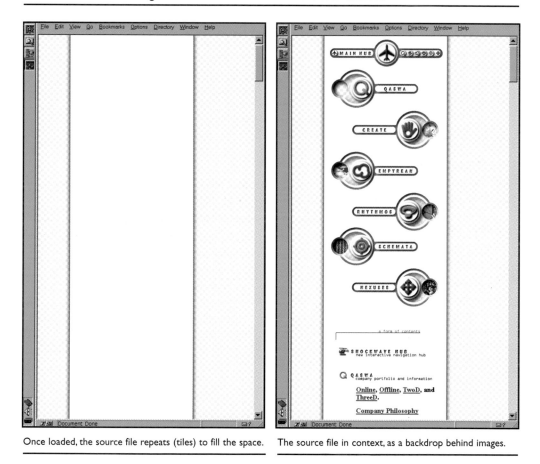

Once loaded, the source file repeats (tiles) to fill the space.   The source file in context, as a backdrop behind images.

A background tile is loaded into a web page by creating a small image that is referenced in the BODY BACKGROUND element of an HTML file. When the web browser encounters an image that has been specified this way, the image is automatically repeated across and down the page like "tile" behind the content. Images for use as background tiles can be either in the JPEG or GIF format.

Ammon's idea was to make a wide, thin background GIF that would be as wide as the browser window, so that it could only repeat down the page. This would result in the appearance of a border running along either side of the page, with an area for content in a long column running down the center page. The content would be held in place (over the center column) by the TABLE tag in HTML.

Deconstruction: Double Border Tile Code

The HTML code required to implement the double border background tile is pretty simple. The trick lies in setting up a bar-shaped, thin GIF image that is at least the width of a default browser window (approximately 640 pixels).

Because the tile ("main.gif" in the code below) is wider than the browser window, the tile stacks vertically.

```
<html>
<head>
<title> Qaswa ¦ Main Hub </title></head>
```

■ **1** `<body background="tiles/main.gif" bgcolor-"#ffffff">`

■ **1** The BODY tag with the BACKGROUND attribute indicates that whatever image is specified (GIF or JPEG) is repeated or "tiled" over the size of the browser window.

■ step-by-step

Ammon's Double Border Photoshop Technique

Ammon utilized many features of Photoshop to achieve his double border effect, such as screen capturing, working with layers and drop shadows. The following step-by-step deconstruction follows his process.

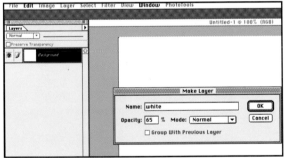

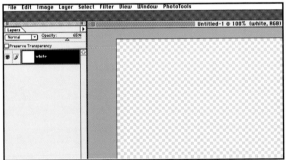

Step 1: Ammon began by creating a new, untitled Photoshop document with File: New and entering the dimensions: 600 pixels by 600 pixels at 72 pixels per inch. Double-clicking the Background Layer bar in the Layer menu brought up the Make Layer dialog box. Ammon renamed the default Background Layer to "white," in order to adjust the layer's opacity.

Step 2: Ammon adjusted the "white" layer tot 65 percent opacity and created a "softened," or "screened back," appearance to Photoshop's default checkered pattern. Next, he took a screen capture of this screen while it was open at 100 percent scale. A screen capture was made on the Macintosh, using the key combination Command+Shift+3. (On the PC, you can take a screen capture with the F12 key.) This procedure was necessary in order to obtain the softened checkered pattern as reusable artwork. This process was necessary because the default checkered pattern in Photoshop is part of the program and is meant to signify transparency. As such, it is NOT a layer that can be printed, copied, or otherwise used, UNLESS it is first stored via a screen capture.

■ step-by-step cont...

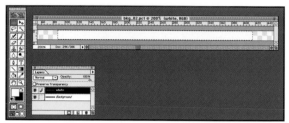

Step 4: Ammon cropped the bkg.pct image to the exact height of two squares (16 pixels), while maintaining the full width of 600 pixels. This work was saved with a new name, "bkg_02.pct," to prevent inadvertent loss of the original. Next, Ammon created a New Layer from the menu, Layer: New. This new layer was named "white." He activated the Rulers from the menu, View: Show Rulers and drew a selection from top to bottom, between pixels 85 and 415, with the Marquee Selection tool. The Rulers helped him position the selection precisely. Then, confirming that white was the top most (Foreground Color) chip in the Color Chips on the Toolbar, Ammon proceeded from the menu, Edit: Fill: Foreground Color: 100%: Normal. The active selection was filled with white and appeared on the "white" layer above his softened checkered background.

Step 3: Ammon opened the screen capture in Photoshop. Note that this is a new image, derived from the screen capture he just took. He carefully cropped off extraneous image material, so it measured precisely 600 pixels by 600 pixels. This new image was the source for the double border background GIF tile. It was also used as a tool to "mock-up" ideas when he built the pages for other areas of the site. He saved and named this image "bkg.pct."

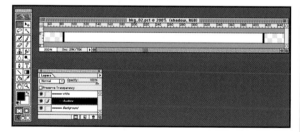

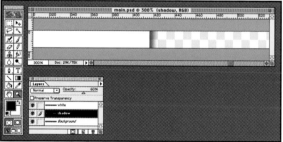

Step 5: Ammon added another new layer between the "white" and the "background" layers. He named the new empty layer "shadow", set it at 100% Opacity/ Normal, and made sure it was positioned above the "Background" layer. With "shadow" as the active layer, Ammon drew out another marquee selection from top to bottom so that it extended beyond either end of the white bar in the "white" layer by five pixels. Then he filled this selection with black and saved the image.

Step 6: Ammon used the Zoom tool to get a closer view of the of the shadow effect as he worked on it. With "shadow" still the active layer, he blurred the edges of the "shadow" layer, using: Filter Menu: Blur: Gaussian: Radius: 1.5 Pixels. Then he adjusted the Layer Opacity to 60 percent. By pressing Command+F (or Control+F on the PC), he repeated the Gaussian Blur Filter (at those same settings) until he obtained the desired softness effect. The image was saved as a layered Photoshop document (to allow him to rework this double border GIF tile, if necessary, for other interface components, without having to rebuild it from scratch) and was named, "main.psd" before he made an indexed color GIF.

■ step-by-step

Using PhotoGIF for Speedy Graphics

Ammon used a third party Photoshop filter called PhotoGIF to optimize his images. Optimization is a process that reduces file size of images. PhotoGIF is a Photoshop plug-in that produces files that are generally far more compressed than files created by Photoshop alone, while still maintaining superior image quality. In fact, it boasts the best GIF compression available. PhotoGIF is available from BoxTop Software, Inc. at http://www.boxtopsoft.com.

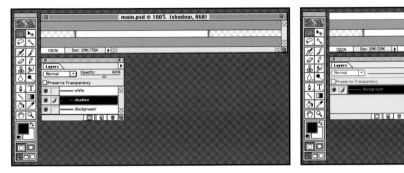

Step 1: The layered Photoshop document, "main.psd," prior to converting it into an indexed color GIF.

Step 2: Ammon "flattened" the layered Photoshop document and converted it into an indexed color image by selecting from the Image Menu: Mode: Indexed Color (the Indexed Color dialog box is shown here.) He selected Adaptive Palette with 22 colors. Because he wanted a smooth gradation throughout the shadows, he chose the Diffusion Dither Option. Clicking OK changed the image to indexed color, but it still had to be saved as an indexed color GIF in order for it to be used as a background tile on the web.

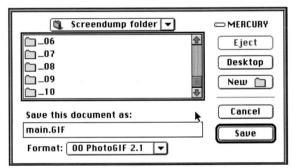

Step 3: Next, Ammon saved the image, selecting from the File Menu: Save As, with the file format setting of "00 PhotoGIF 2.1." Note that this format is grayed out if you have not properly changed your image to indexed color. Also note that, before clicking the Save button, Ammon entered the new name, "main.gif," in the dialog box headed: "Save this document as." Otherwise, the original layered file could be inadvertently overwritten and lost.

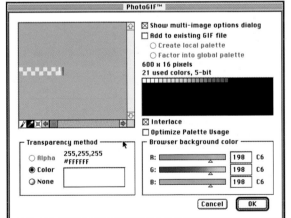

Step 4: You can see the power of the PhotoGIF plug-in in the PhotoGIF dialog box. Here are options for controlling animations (Show multi-image options dialog), palette optimization schemes, interlacing, and transparency. To use PhotoGIF simply to obtain maximal compression at the default settings, Ammon unchecked "Show multi-image dialog box" and clicked OK. Now "main.gif" is prepared properly to fly across the web at optimal speed!

Qaswa2: The Shockwave Hub

About a year after Ammon completed the original Qaswa (hereafter referred to as Qaswa1) Macromedia released the Shockwave file format, making it possible to deliver interactive web content that has been authored within Macromedia Director. Through his work with interactive CD-ROMs, Ammon had become quite adept with Director. You may recall his lament regarding the early lack of web authoring tools on a par with Director, so it was natural for him to create a second—Director authored—Shockwave sibling for Qaswa1.

When Shockwave first appeared, Ammon immediately created a "shocked" home page because Macromedia Director was already a familiar tool for him. He got a lot of response from the Shockwave piece because, in the web world at that time, it was extremely technical. Ammon even admits that Director for the web was a piece of cake compared to his experience with the world of multimedia. This "Shockwave piece" became known as the Shockwave Hub.

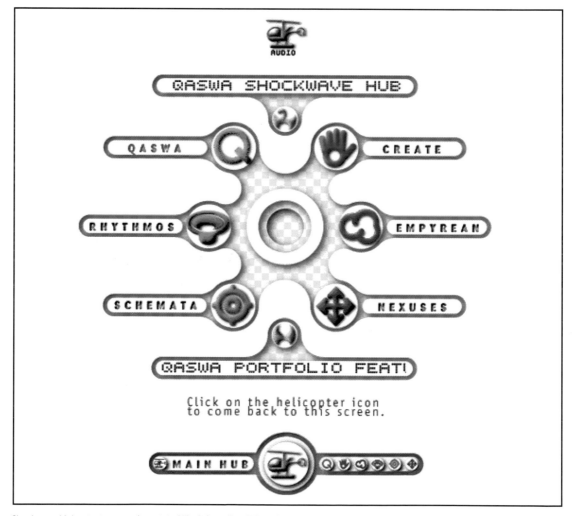

Shockwave Hub reinvigorates the original "Link Icons" and "Link Symbols" with a reorganized look and feel, developed from the look and feel of the original Qaswa1 Main Menu. The Qaswa2 Shockwave Hub features sound, rollover buttons, and scrolling read-outs for each icon.

■ note

What Is Shockwave?

In order to understand Shockwave, one must first understand what
Macromedia Director is and why it's important.

In his preface to "Shockwave Studio," Marc Canter says that he created
Director because he "wanted to create wacky, interactive 'experiences'
that allowed users to change music, art, and the overall environment.
We wanted to make room for teachers, designers, and creative folks to
experiment. It didn't seem fair that only programmers could do cool,
digital things."

Director is built around the metaphor of a stage wherein all elements of
the production are referred to as cast members. Technically, it combines
the strengths of a scripting language with a timeline-oriented score.
Functionally, it enables nearly everyone to create digital interactive productions. These productions are generally referred to as "movies" and
may include animation, video, and sound, and can be authored to permit a
greater or lesser degree of user interaction. Movies may range in complexity from the most highly structured game, to a simple educational
manual, or a plain button bar.

In order to deliver Director movies over the web, movies are first prepared for export within Director, which then compresses and writes
them as streaming Shockwave files. Streaming in this context means
that the movie can begin to play or run once the first few frames have
been downloaded. Macromedia has recently provided a Shockwave
plug-in that installs itself via a Java applet (see Glossary), which will
make the plug-in installation process less painful for those who have
Java-enabled browsers.

When Ammon added the Shockwave Hub to Qaswa, he needed a new splash page that would function as a device to separate the Shockwave-enabled visitors from the others. He arrived upon the idea of Qaswa Air, which would offer his viewers a mechanism to choose between Qaswa1 and the new Qaswa2, or Shockwave Hub. How did he get this brainstorm? "The airplane metaphor just happened. Like most ideas for me, they just happen." The addition of Qaswa Air to the site also provided Ammon with a means for preparing visitors for the site by giving them cues regarding optimal browser settings, plug-ins, and, the optimal browser of that era, Netscape Navigator 3.

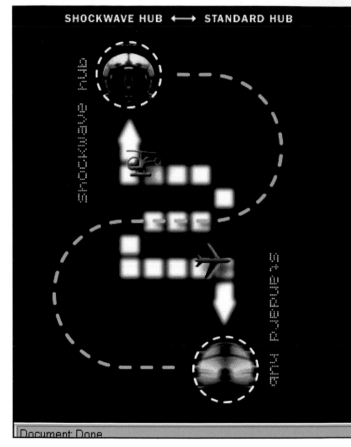

This is the new Qaswa Splash Page. Note that the helicopter becomes the symbol (sound) of the Shockwave Hub, while the airplane becomes the symbol of the Standard Hub.

Here, the passageway to Standard Hub cautions passengers to adjust their viewing window and to have the "right stuff" before continuing. Below, offscreen, is a direct link to Netscape for passengers desiring to upgrade their ticket.

Similarly, the passageway to the Shockwave Hub also cautions passengers to adjust their viewing window before continuing. Also below, offscreen, another direct link to Netscape for passengers wanting to upgrade their ticket.

Examining the Shockwave Hub

The Shockwave Hub was created as a Director movie and later exported as a Shockwave file for delivery on the web. This movie was composed of 70 cast members (stored art, animation, and sound elements). The following images document Ammon's production methodology for creating the Shockwave Hub. This section will familiarize you with Director's interface and some of the programming techniques required to integrate Director/Shockwave content into the Qaswa web site.

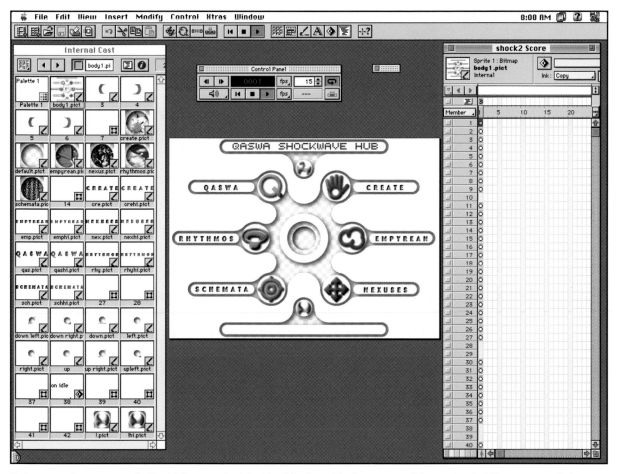

Each cast member appears in the Shock2 Score on the right side of this figure. The Score is one of the ways in which Director controls the behaviors of cast members. In this movie the Score uses a single frame, whereas animations can have thousands of frames with cast members making multiple appearances and different behaviors through the duration of the movie. Since this screen is not a "movie", but an interactive "still" screen, there is only one frame used in the Score. Every actionable part of the Qaswa2 Hub is a discrete cast member that has been dragged into position on the stage. The final Director file was then exported into Shockwave format and the resulting Shockwave file "embedded" within an HTML container. An explanation of the code follows later in this chapter.

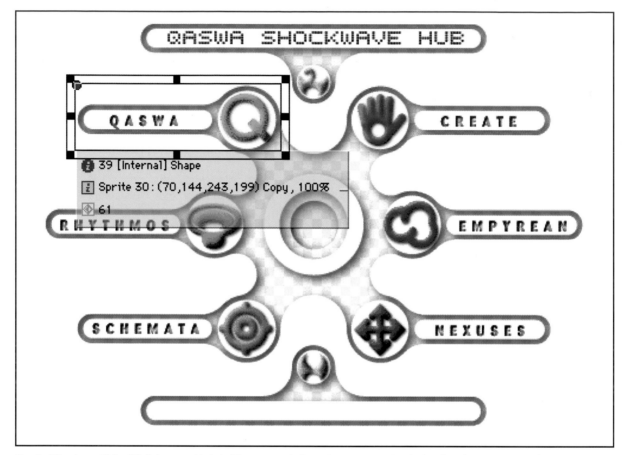

Detail of Shockwave Hub, while being assembled. In Director terminology, when a cast member is placed on the movie stage, it becomes a sprite. Sprites can be interactive. This figure shows the Sprite Overlay for sprite/cast member number 30. A Sprite Overlay displays information about each sprite, making it easier to identify and edit the behaviors of individual sprites.

Lingo is Director's scripting language used for controlling the behaviors of sprites, which are, as mentioned above, any cast member once it has been placed upon the Director stage. Most of the behaviors in this movie are controlled by Lingo in combination with functions from the Director Behavior Library. The Lingo scripts are built of "if-then" statements and related conditions. For example, if there is no mouse over the Qaswa button on the upper-left of the hub, then nothing happens. But if the mouse moves over the Qaswa button, a running text message appears in the bar below the hub and an image appears within the round central window of the hub. If the mouse is then pressed, an "if-then" statement initiates a "NetLingo" command. This NetLingo command sends the browser to the destination URL. A more detailed explanation of Director can be found in books devoted to this subject.

```
on mouseUp
    GotoNetPage "http://www.qaswa.com/qaswa.html"
```

■ note

Director and Shockwave Resources

The best place for the most current information about Macromedia Director and Shockwave is the Macromedia Site at http://www.macromedia.com/. This site includes tutorials, updates, and other information.

The following are three of the more highly regarded current books regarding Director and Shockwave:

■ **Inside Macromedia Director 6 with Lingo** ■ Lee Allis, et al. ■ New Riders ■ ISBN 1-56205-728-6. This is an excellent reference because of the breadth of real-world authoring experience from this team of nearly 10 contributing authors. It's everything one wants from an aftermarket reference.

■ **Macromedia Director 6 and Lingo Authorized** ■ Elley, McCarter and Tucker ■ Macromedia Press ■ ISBN 0-201-69629-0. This authorized text is impressive. The authors have delivered a wealth of valuable information that is not included in the manuals. Includes CD.

■ **Shockwave Studio, Designing Multimedia for the Web** ■ Bob Schmitt ■ O'Reilly ■ ISBN 1-56592-231-X. Unfortunately, this excellent book is already somewhat out of date. It covers Director 5, so either learn to interpolate or look for an revision for the new Director 6. Includes CD.

Deconstructing The HTML Container

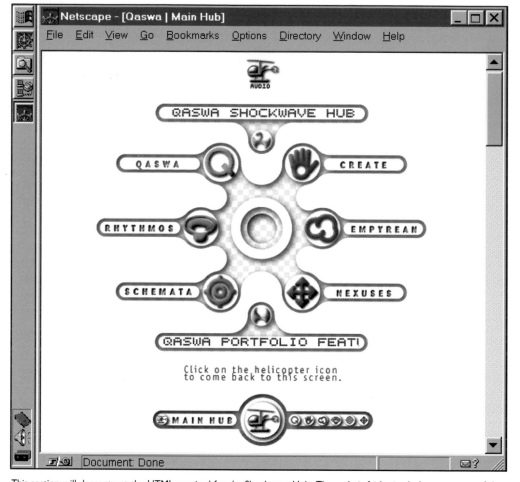

This section will deconstruct the HTML required for the Shockwave Hub. The code is fairly simple, because most of the interactivity is contained within the Director movie itself. Although Shockwave has enabled amazing interactivity on the web, the unfortunate result of this is that it makes it more difficult for newcomers to learn how to create great designs by looking at the source code.

■ code

```
<html>
<head>

<title> Qaswa ¦ Shockwave Hub </title></head>

<body  bgcolor="#ffffff">

<center>
```

■ 1
```
<embed width=64 height=64 border=0
src="shock/audio.dcr">
```

■ 2
```
<img border=0 hspace=2 vspace=5
src="images/dot_clear.gif"><hr>
```

■ 3
```
<embed width=464 height=340
src="shock/shock.dcr">
```

■ 4
```
<img border=0 hspace=2 vspace=10
src="images/dot_clear.gif"><p>

<img border=0 src="shock/iconmess.gif">

<img border=0 hspace=2 vspace=10
src="images/dot_clear.gif"><p>

<a href="http://www.qaswa.com/maps/navbar.map">
<img ismap border=0
src="shock/shockHD.gif"></a><br>

<img border=0 hspace=2 vspace=10
src="images/dot_clear.gif"><br>

<a href="http://www.qaswa.com/qasinfo.html">
<img src="standard/bar1.gif" height=37
width=106 border=0></a>
<img src="standard/bar2.gif" height=37
width=108 border=0>
<a href="mailto:qaswa@hooked.net">
<img src="standard/bar3.gif" height=37 width=47
border=0></a>

</center>

</body>
</html>
```

■ deconstruction

■ **1** The EMBED tag is used to insert the Shockwave content. The attributes and variables are stated exactly as with standard HTML in regards to images: src="shock/audio.dcr" is nearly the same as the standard HTML, img src="xxx.xxx." Note: WIDTH and HEIGHT attributes are required for the EMBED tag, and without them the tag will not work. This EMBED tag is for the tiny helicopter logo at the top of the page that controls the sound.

■ **2** This element uses a transparent GIF spacer to create space within the design. A transparent GIF is usually composed of a single pixel, set to transparency using the GIF file format, which acts as a spacer (see the Web Graphics Appendix for more information an GIF transparency). Note the <BR> tag is used to ensure that this GIF resides between the blocks of content, rather than in front of the subsequent EMBED tag. (You may also note, however, that no <BR> appears after the first EMBED tag. Therefore, the image called in the IMG tag is next to, not below, the first embedded object.)

■ **3** This EMBED tag is for the Shockwave document that contains all the rollover icons, rollover scripts, and interactive effects. The hypertext links to the rest of the site are also contained within this Shockwave file, "shock.dcr."

■ **4** The rest of the code involves the use of images and imagemaps which are discussed elsewhere in the book. For more information about imagemaps, see Chapter 2, "Bosch Tools," and Chapter 4, "National Geographic."

■ tip

The Forgiveness of Browsers Is Vanishing

As the primary browsers continue to evolve, they are becoming far less forgiving of minor HTML syntactical errors. Although Qaswa works perfectly in both Netscape Navigator and Internet Explorer up to and including version 3, the alignment of tables and text begins to fall apart in Navigator 4. Current browsers are especially unforgiving about the failure to enclose variables in TABLEs with quotation marks.

What's worse? The Shocked Hub of Qaswa2 routinely crashes Navigator 4. These are problems that could not have been anticipated in 1995.

The solution? Invest in a reliable HTML style book.

HTML The Definitive Guide, 2nd Edition ■ Musciano and Kennedy ■ O'Reilly & Associates, Inc. ■ ISBN 1-56592-235-2. You can see the book reviewed, in this context, at http://www.uncom.com/!/o23.htm.

Creative HTML Design ■ Lynda Weinman and William Weinman ■ New Riders ■ ISBN 1-56205-704-9. Another definitive resource.

What Would Ammon Redo?

When asked what, if anything, he would redo now, Ammon responded, "Hmmm... well, since you asked, I'll have to be honest. I want to redo the entire site. There are so many little things to be fixed, but it's not going to happen because I'd much rather design an entirely new, parallel site instead, which is what I'm working on right now. I'd like to think that the site that exists today will simply remain unfixed as a legacy of kinder, more forgiving browsers."

■ note

Ammon Recommended Links and Books

Here's a listing of some of Ammon's favorite sites of inspiration and resources for learning web design.

Macromedia's Shocked Site of the Day (http://www.macromedia.com/shockzone/ssod/) features the latest work in interactive technologies.

High Five (http://www.highfive.com/) reviews the best sites and interviews the best designers.

Project Cool (http://www.projectcool.com/) has developers' resources to help you make great sites.

Antirom (http://www.antirom.com) features experiments in online interactive media.

Frogdesign (http://www.frogdesign.com) where industrial design meets web design.

Planet (http://www.planet.dk/) features designers from Denmark.

Information Architects ■ Richard Saul Wurman ■ Graphis ■ ISBN 3-85709-458-3. "The best book on Information Architecture"

Elements of Web Design ■ Darcy Dinucci, Maria Giudice and Lynne Stiles ■ Peachpit ■ ISBN 0-20188-594-8. "The first book to really explain web design in designers' language."

Experience ■ Sean Perkins ■ Booth-Clibborn Editions ■ ISBN 1-87396-820-5. "A visual documentation of ideas."

Process ■ The Tomata Group ■ Thames and Hudson. "An experimental book."

Interrupted Projections ■ Neil Denari ■ Atsushi Sato, Japan ■ ISBN 4-88706-142-0. "Mixes three-dimensional space with graphic design."

Inspiring CDs

According to Ammon, "CD-ROMs can show what's in the future of web development." Check out: **Circumstance and Om Records** (http://www.circumstance.com) (http://www.om-records.com)

■ site summary

Qaswa

Qaswa proved to be an effective vehicle for the debut of Ammon Haggerty's solo web design studio. Although Ammon recently brought in another artist to help him with some of the work, this should not dilute to strength of Ammon's vision. Rather, one should expect that a synergy could only improve the designs emanating from Qaswa.

- One of the earliest examples of fine web design still remains an exemplary balance of form and function today.

- Although some of the tools are similar today, there are important differences in developing for CD-ROM as opposed to developing for the web.

- Adobe Illustrator can be used as an effective design tool prior to development of the designs in Photoshop.

- The use of icons and symbols, together with well-planned double border GIF backgrounds can add enhanced visual interest to a web site. Adobe Illustrator, coupled with Adobe Photoshop, are the programs of choice for creating such elements for a site.

- The PhotoGIF plug-in for Photoshop helps web designers to create designs that can download in nearly half the time.

- Creating content within Macromedia Director and delivering that content as a Shockwave file with the EMBED tag has brought new opportunities to the web for interactive design and function.

Cooper-Hewitt
Museum on the Web

- **Community Building**
- **Tables for Optimization**
- **Color Branding**
- **Background Tiles**

http://www.si.edu/ndm/ The Cooper-Hewitt National Design Museum (part of the Smithsonian Institution) is based in New York City and recently celebrated its 100th year of collecting. Elisabeth Roxby was working in the exhibition department at Cooper-Hewitt when the Smithsonian called to say they needed a web site, and she volunteered to meet their two-week deadline. Totally self-taught as an exhibition designer, webmaster and web designer, she has shaped their web presence into one of the most compelling museum sites online. This chapter covers her thoughtful design concepts, her quest for simplicity and purpose, and her thoughts about how web space can add value to the museum space.

Web Design Firm: http://www.roxx.com

Client: Cooper-Hewitt, National Design Museum, Smithsonian Institution

Type of Site: Educational/Informational—Design Museum

Original URL: www.si.edu/ndm/

Server: Silicon Graphics Origin 200 server

Server Software: Netscape Enterprise Server v 2.13

Producer: Elisabeth Roxby

Creative Direction: Elisabeth Roxby

Art Direction: Elisabeth Roxby

Programmer: Rollin Crittendon (special projects)

National Design Museum Webmaster: Elisabeth Roxby

Smithsonian Institution Webmaster: Peter House

Mixing Messages: Curator: Elen Lupton

Technology: Dynamo Developer's Kit 2.0, Art Technology Group

Design for Life Co-curators: Gillian Moss, Susan Yelavich

Website Editor: Julie H. Keisman

Development and Production Platform: Macintosh

National Design Museum Website Coordinator: Barbara Livenstein

A Self-Taught Designer

Elisabeth Roxby graduated from Princeton with a degree in history long before "web designer" was a known profession. She credits the fact that Apple Computer made a sizable donation of Macintoshes to Princeton in the late 1980s for landing her the job at Cooper-Hewitt. It turns out that the museum's computer crashed and Cooper-Hewitt was in desparate need of someone who could troubleshoot system failures, knew Pagemaker, and could produce labels for an impending exhibit. Ironically, her Princeton-honed Mac skills probably paid off more than her history degree in landing her the job with Cooper-Hewitt.

Elisabeth worked for Cooper-Hewitt from 1990 to 1995, where she worked as an exhibition assistant and label maker to eventually trying her hand at exhibition design, graphic design, and web design. She had experimented with HTML a little, using her own free web space (which came gratis with her first email account) when she found out the Smithsonian needed a web page in two weeks and volunteered for the job. Smithsonian asking her if she could design their web site in two weeks. They must have been a happy client, since Elisabeth has since developed two large scale web-based exhibitions for them and continues to work with them even though she has since left her full-time job to pursue a career as an independent designer working out of her own studio.

Elisabeth views the web as a similar medium to the museum space. "Both experiences involve 2D and 3D design, the use of varied paths to the same destinations, and servicing different levels of interest. The web is truly amazing, because you can experiment with exhibit issues with a lot more flexibility and freedom than in a physical museum."

As a self-taught graphic designer, Elisabeth took maximum advantage of the amazing opportunity she found herself in at Cooper-Hewitt, which exposed her to some of the best design in the world. After teaching herself HTML and web design, she decided to go back to school to study those disciplines. A few months into school, she changed her mind and decided she was capable of learning more on her own. Returning to work as an independent graphic and web designer, she has proved herself correct and has since produced some of most interesting design work found on the web today.

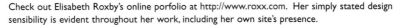

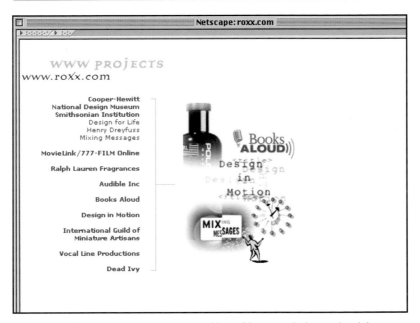

Check out Elisabeth Roxby's online porfolio at http://www.roxx.com. Her simply stated design sensibility is evident throughout her work, including her own site's presence.

Her portfolio links to many other interesting and beautiful projects she has produced that were not covered in this book.

Mixing Messages Exhibit

The Mixing Messages exhibit at Cooper-Hewitt took place from September 16, 1996, to February 17, 1997. The exhibit included over 300 examples of graphics; from posters to electronic media, which showcased design in urban culture, corporate culture, and design culture. A decision was made to create a web-based museum exhibit to display this work, as well as create an area of the site devoted to the online design (which Elisabeth developed).

The show, curated by Ellen Lupton, was the first major web-based museum exhibition for Cooper-Hewitt. "It takes a huge amount of capital and time for a museum to launch a major exhibit like Mixing Messages," Ellen explained. "It takes years of research, writing, documenting, scanning, and database development. Typically, from a show like this, the final product we create would result in a printed book and a physical exhibit. It was thrilling to us to be able to take the same content we worked so hard to produce and publish it on the web. Our product is information about design, so the web was a perfect way to extend our efforts and reach more people."

If you take into account that the web site was visited by 500,000 people, when only 50,000 actually attended the show, and only 10,000 books were sold, you can easily understand Ellen's enthusiasm. Ellen's book, *Mixing Messages*, became the Essay section of the site. From a content point of view, the work she completed for the show and book was able to be easily repurposed for the site. She and graphic designer Jen Roos gave Elisabeth text and images from their book and reworked the copy so it would fit better within a hypertext environment. Elisabeth set up the hyperlinks between the text documents, so they would create a non-linear experience of searching within the writing and linking to outside resources.

■ note

Books by Ellen Lupton

The book created for the Mixing Messages exhibition, written by Ellen Lupton, is available in bookstores. She has also written a number of other excellent design books.

Mixing Messages: Graphic Design for Contemporary Culture ■ Ellen Lupton
■ Princeton Architectural Press ■ ISBN 1-56898-098-1 ■ $35.00

The Bathroom the Kitchen and the Aesthetics of Waste: A Process of Elimination
■ Ellen Lupton ■ Princeton Architectural Press ■ ISBN 1-56898-096-5 ■ $24.00

Design Writing Research: Writing on Graphic Design ■ Ellen Lupton, J. Abbott Miller
■ Princeton Architectural Press ■ ISBN 1-56898-047-7 ■ $45.00

Letters from the Avant-Garde: Modern Graphic Design ■ Ellen Lupton, Elaine Lustig Cohen
■ Princeton Architectural Press ■ ISBN 1-56898-052-3 ■ $24.95

Mechanical Brides: Women and Machines from Home to Office ■ Ellen Lupton
■ Princeton Architectural Press ■ ISBN 1-87827-197-0 ■ $19.95

Show Identity

The design for the Mixing Messages site was first established by the design for the exhibit and the book. Since the book had been produced electronically, all the text and image files already existed in digital form.

The book and program for the exhibit, Mixing Messages, had already been designed before Elisabeth created the site.

The front page to the mixing messages site, which is archived at http://www.si.edu/ndm/exhib/mixingmessages/start.htm, was greatly influenced by the print material.

Interacting with the Show

Elisabeth carries a strong philosophy throughout her work. She believes it is not enough to simply have an online presence, but that a web site must offer some added value in order to justify its use. With this in mind, she sought to identify the possibilities that a web site would offer that differed from attending the exhibit in person.

"First of all, I do believe that there is no substitute for seeing real artwork in a museum space," she stressed. "The idea is not to replace the experience of seeing physical objects, but to produce an experience that cannot be replicated in the museum alone. In effect, the experience of attending a gallery opening is partially a social experience. You might notice, for example, that a room is filled with artwork, but that everyone is gathered around one display case. This can greatly influence your experience of the show. The process of being in the space with friends and artists is part of the experience. We thought about how to take the experiential, social aspect of this exhibit out of the museum space and into the web space where it could be further cultivated."

The site was driven by "Dynamo 2," a Java-based application server developed by Art Technology Group (Boston), which was donated for purposes of creating enhanced social interaction. The Dynamo application server offered what ATG has termed "relationship commerce." Mixing Messages used the Dynamo application server to support chat, threaded discussion groups, and interactive dialogues. It is a Java based application that works with a Microsoft Information Server, both of which were donated on loan for the Mixing Messages project.

The Dynamo 2 server was used extensively in the Dialogue section of the site. The web site is now archived, so none of the live community-building measures are currently in effect. Examples of screen shots from when the site was active follow:

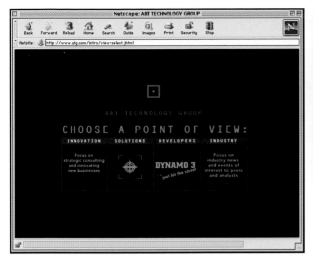

To learn more about Dynamo, visit http://www. atg.com.

http://www.si.edu/ndm/exhib/mixingmessages/dialogue/start.htm is where some of the community-building dialogues are archived from when the site was live. This level of interactivity was made possible through Art Technologies, Dynamo Application Server. If you look in the upper left corner of this page, you'll see a list of "recent visitors." The Dynamo system would default to using visitors' IP address numbers, though it also allowed users to create their own personal name handles.

The term web-o-gram (see upper left corner of this screen) was an "instant" messaging system that Dynamo enabled, which allowed visitors to the web site to communicate with each other while they were on the same page.

Elisabeth developed the Dialogue area of the site that focused on online design. It gave her a chance to showcase some of her favorite web sites and create a dialogue on the site about online design itself. Her role in this project went beyond web designer, as she actually shaped this section of content on her own, under the direction of Ellen Lupton.

Color and Style

The Mixing Messages site had three distinct areas: Essay, Dialogues, and Activities. The color themes for these areas were developed with thought to the purpose of each section. The Essay area was laid against a white background, because it needed to support a lot of text and be easy to read. The Dialogue section was designed against a black background, with bright green text to emulate the look of a computer terminal. The Activities section, which supported "workbook" style exercise activities, was a friendly yellow, to emulate notebook paper.

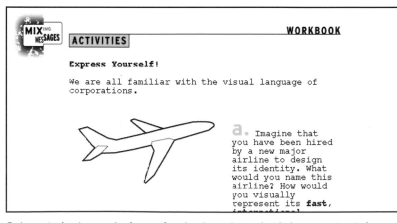

Each area in the site contained a specific color theme designed with the content in mind.

Type was specified in HTML to use the <TT> tag, which usually results in the display of Courier on Macs and Courier New on PCs. At the time this site was designed, the use of the FONT tag was not yet fully supported. The FONT FACE element did not yet exist, which enables the ability to specify fonts other than those that are preset in the end user's preferences.

```
The World Wide Web is a design in progress. In the past few years, it has
evolved from a text-based environment used primarily by physicists to a rich
visual environment shared by millions of individuals, special interest groups,
corporations, and institutions. It is an evolving landscape of many voices
seeking to create a presence or identity in an elusive and unpredictable medium.
It is also a growing community of voices looking to interact with each other.
Graphic design on the Web has provided a dynamic visual language to give shape
to this mix of voices and context to their communities.
```

The <TT> tag causes the HTML type to appear in a monospace font.

The World Wide Web is a design in progress. In the past few years, it has evolved from a text-based environment used primarily by physicists to a rich visual environment shared by millions of individuals, special interest groups, corporations, and institutions. It is an evolving landscape of many voices seeking to create a presence or identity in an elusive and unpredictable medium. It is also a growing community of voices looking to interact with each other. Graphic design on the Web has provided a dynamic visual language to give shape to this mix of voices and context to their communities.

If used the <FONT FACE> element would have caused the type to appear in a specified font assuming the end user had the font installed in his or her system. The HTML for this would look like: <FONT FACE="verdana">.

Image Optimization

Elisabeth wanted the focus of Mixing Messages to be the content, not the downloading speed. For the front page's graphic, she took design direction from from the promotional brochures and materials that supported the museum show. Once she arrived at the final graphic in Photoshop, she experimented with reducing the file size through testing with GIF and JPEG file formats. After much trial and error with trimming file size, she determined that regions of the graphic were better suited for GIF compression and other sections of the image for JPEG. She got the idea to cut apart the image and optimize each cut-apart section separately.

She realigned the images using HTML tables in BBEDIT, the HTML editor by Bare Bones Software. What follows is a deconstruction of the graphic page elements and the code.

This image shows the various regions of the HTML table.

Here are the separate images and their file sizes.

h_chm.gif ■ 1.6k

h_essay.jpg ■ 12.4k

h_dialogue.gif ■ 8.5k

h_act.gif ■ 16.8k

h_microsoft.gif ■ .08k

h_dynamo.gif ■ .05k

h_chmweb.gif ■ 1.4k

■ code

```html
<html>
<head><title>Mixing Messages</title></head>
<body bgcolor="#000000" text="#ffffff" link="#ffffff" vlink="#ffffff"
alink="#ffffff">
<center>
<p><br>
```
■ 1
```html
<table cellpadding=0 cellspacing=0 border=0 width=515>
<tr>
```
■ 2
```html
<td colspan=2 valign=bottom><img border=0 src="art/h_chm.gif" width=515
height=40></td>
</tr>
<tr>
<td rowspan=2 align=right><a href="essay/start.htm"><img border=0
src="art/h_essay.jpg" width=238 height=326></a></td>
<td align=left><a href="dialogue/start.htm"><img border=0
src="art/h_dialogue.gif" width=277 height=159></a></td>
</tr>

<tr>
<td align=left><a href="activ/start.htm"><img border=0 src="art/h_act.gif"
width=277 height=167></a></td>
</tr>

<tr>
<td colspan=2 valign=top><img border=0 src="art/h_microsoft.gif"
width=515 height=35></td>
</tr>

<tr>
<td colspan=2 valign=top><a href="atg.htm"><img border=0 src="art/h_dynamo.gif"
width=515 height=16></a></td>
</tr>
```
■ 3
```html
</table>

<p><br><br>
<a href="http://www.si.edu/ndm/"><img border=0 src="art/h_chmweb.gif"></a>
```
■ 4
```html
<br><font size=-1 color="#444444">The Mixing Messages Web Site is designed
and produced by Elisabeth C.  Roxby
<br>
```
■ 5
```html
&copy; Copyright 1996 Cooper-Hewitt National Design Museum
<p>
```
■ 6
```html
<a href="credit.htm">[credits]</a></font>

</center>

</body>
</html>
```

■ deconstruction

■ **1** The TABLE tag includes the attributes cellpadding=0 cellspacing=0 border=0, which define that the table regions will be invisible. The width attribute instructs the table to be 515 pixels wide.

■ **2** The TD tag stands for Table Data and instructs the table to create two columns with the colspan=2 attribute, and a vertically aligned bottom image with the valign=bottom attribute. The image is set with no border because of the border=0 attribute, and the width and height measurements of the image are supplied so that the table will load more quickly, since the browser doesn't have to calculate the image size.

■ **3** The closing container </table> is required, or the tables will not function properly.

■ **4** By setting the FONT SIZE attribute to size=-1, Elisabeth was able to create smaller type than the default size HTML type.

■ **5** The entity &copy was used to create the copyright symbol.

■ **6** The closing container for the FONT tag ends the request for smaller type.

Table Tags, Attributes, and Values

Caution: Table tags must be created symmetrically. Always begin by defining the table, then the row, then the cells contained within that row. Each and every tag must be matched by a closing tag. A cell must be closed before a new one is defined, and a row must be closed before a subsequent row can be defined.

<TABLE><TR><TD></TD></TR></TABLE> are Table tags.

Other items found in TABLE elements are either attributes or values. In this example, WIDTH=77, WIDTH is the attribute and 77 is the value. This is consistent throughout HTML.

HTML	Description	HTML	Description
<TABLE>	Defines the beginning of a TABLE.	COLSPAN	Number of COLUMNs the CELL spans.
<TR>	Defines the beginning of a ROW.	NOWRAP	Don't wrap contents of this CELL.
<TD>	Defines the beginning of a CELL.	CELLSPACING	Thickness of border between CELLs.
BGCOLOR	Specifies color of the TABLE, ROW, or CELL.	CELLPADDING	Space between CELL walls and contents.
WIDTH	TABLE, ROW, or CELL width in percent or pixels.	HSPACE	Defines pixel space left and right of contents, HSPACE="0" prevents space.
HEIGHT	TABLE, ROW, or CELL height in percent or pixels.	VSPACE	Defines pixel space above and below contents.
BORDER	BORDER thickness in pixels (0=invisible).	</TD>	Closes a CELL.
ALIGN	Horizontal, can be left, center, right.	</TR>	Closes a ROW.
VALIGN	Vertical, can be top, middle, bottom.	</TABLE>	Closes a TABLE.
ROWSPAN	Number of ROWs the CELL spans.		

■ warning

Gaps in Tables

Creating a seamless table with invisible borders is easy, if you do it correctly! A common problem with this type of table occurs when TABLE tags are not terminated properly. Notice in Elisabeth's code that the closing container for the TD tag is on the same line as the opening TD tag:

```
<td colspan=2 valign=top><img border=0 src="art/h_microsoft.gif"
width=515 height=35></td>
```

If you produce a carriage return in your HTML for the closing container, it will result in single pixel gaps within the table, which will ruin the illusion of a seamless reassembled set of images.

```
<td colspan=2 valign=top><img border=0 src="art/h_microsoft.gif"
width=515 height=35>
</td>
```

An example of an improperly terminated table. The background color is intentionally left off so you can see the visible breaks in the table.

Favorite Tools and Techniques

Elisabeth claimed that "learning to program HTML was easy. I prefer BBEdit (http://www.barebones.com) to WYSIWYG editors, because I always spend most of my time cleaning up the incorrect code that those products automatically generate. It's also important to me to understand what I am doing, and not let a program shield me from the true process I'm using." She looks forward to the day when there's a "QuarkXPress for the web," but in the meantime HTML is not that difficult for her to work with, and the code hasn't stopped her from doing what she's wanted.

Elisabeth also avoids imagemaps when she can and chooses instead to cut up images and reassemble them in tables. "It avoids the problem of using client-side or server-side imagemaps," she said, "and it's less time consuming to create simple hyperlinks for individual images."

A prime example of cutting apart an image is found on the opening page for Mixing Messages. Elisabeth created a 16-layer Photoshop file, which she later cut apart for reassembly using a table.

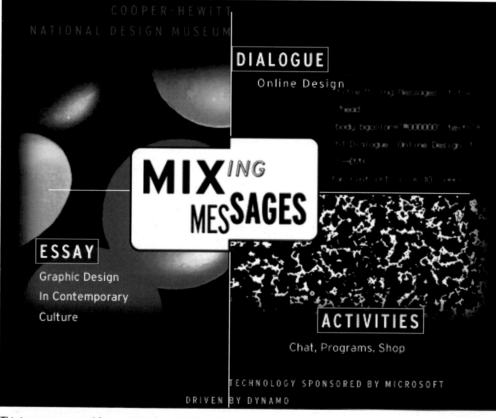

This image was created from multiple layers in Photoshop.

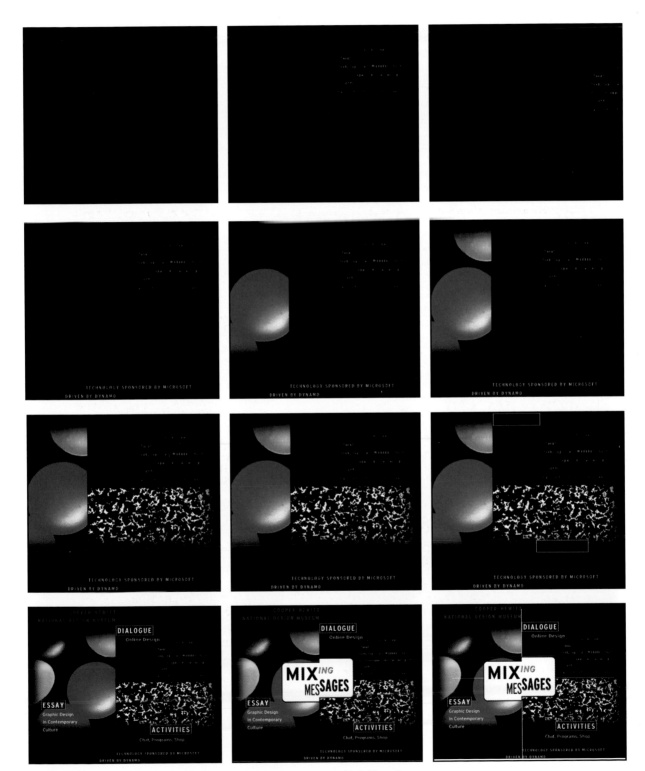

These layers show the construction of the Mixing Messages main screen graphic in Photoshop.

Design for Life

Elisabeth's latest piece for Cooper-Hewitt was to design the web-based presence for their exhibition called Design for Life, a celebration of the museum collection's 100th birthday. She used this opportunity to redesign the main Cooper-Hewitt site which served as an introduction portal to the Design for Life exhibit.

The redesign of the Cooper-Hewitt site involved the use of frames for navigation, as well as a splash screen that announced the current exhibition. The clock shown above was from the collection and was programmed by Rollin Crittendon to read the current time using a Java Applet.

Storyboarding the Site

Elisabeth used a novel approach to storyboarding, in that she made photocopies of a template depicting the browser window and drew her sketches inside the window area. She presented the entire Mixing Messages site in this manner, and much of what she originally sketched did not change too far from the final result.

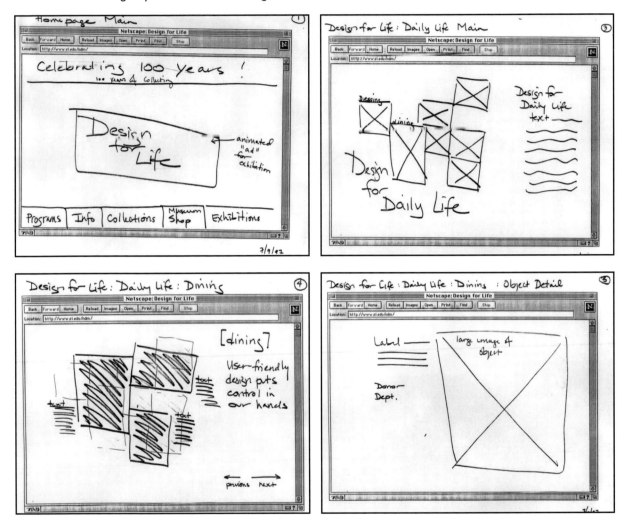

Frames

Elisabeth didn't have the technical support from Microsoft or Art Technology Group that she had on the Mixing Messages site, and this site was much larger in terms of graphics and separate HTML pages. Elisabeth chose to keep it simple and relied solely on her own HTML skills to get the job done. When she designed this exhibit, she introduced frames into the site for navigation purposes. (Frames programming is covered in detail in Chapter 5, "Akimbo.")

"I decided to use frames so the site would have cohesive navigation between all the exhibits, past and present," she cited. "I felt very strongly that our site needed to be accessible to everyone, even those on older browsers, and for this reason I avoided plug-ins and HTML 4.0 tags intentionally. I chose to use frames because they enable navigation on every page. I did get some complaints from some users with non-frames-compliant browsers, but the benefits still seemed to outweigh the disadvantages. It never feels good to exclude anyone, especially since our goal is to make our site visible to as many people as possible, so adding frames was a hard decision for me. Even with the few complaints we've received, I still stand behind this decision as the best solution for the site."

The Cooper-Hewitt site used frames tastefully, which was accomplished in two ways. First of all, Elisabeth created a very small, unobtrusive sized frame and always positioned the frame at the extreme top or bottom of the site, which caused it to occupy as little screen real estate as possible. The second consideration was to create a framed site that worked aesthetically with current and past exhibits. Elisabeth chose to fill the frame with neutral grays, whites, and blacks, which allowed her to develop color themes for areas of the site without any color clashing.

Note the subtle use of a frame on the bottom of this page. Because neutral colors were used, the frames do not detract from the main content.

Color Branding

Color is used throughout the Design for Life site as a mechanism to brand, create hierarchy, and support navigation. The three areas of the exhibit included Daily Life (green), Shaping Space (blue), and Communicating (yellow). Most of the colors used were browser safe (see Web Graphics Appendix).

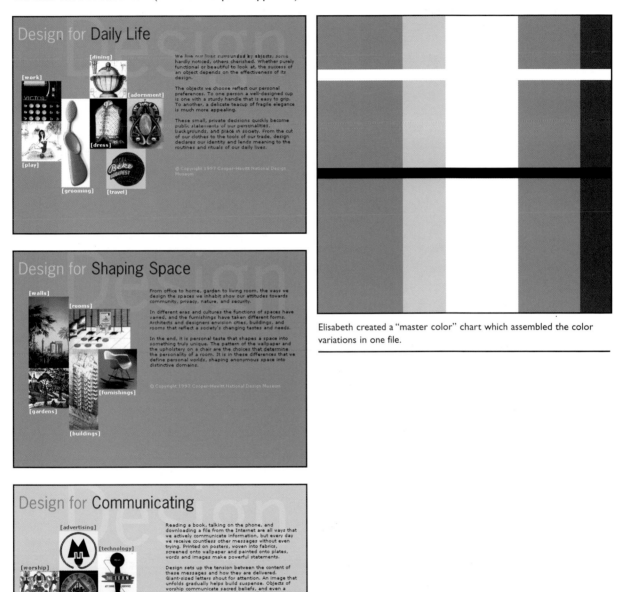

Elisabeth created a "master color" chart which assembled the color variations in one file.

The three colored catagories of the site.

Awareness of Shape and Composition

The horizontal scrolling aspect of this design was appealing to Elisabeth on a number of levels. "I think vertical scrolling is overused and predicatable," she commented. "I like the horizontal scrolling because it creates a sense of place, like the walls of a gallery. This metaphor fit the gallery experience better than a vertical page."

Once you click into each catagory, you see how the color branding reinforces the navigation of the site. Elisabeth gave thought to form and composition as well. Notice how the abstract shapes change as you click deeper into the site.

With each click deeper into the site, the composition changes. However, the color palette remains the same, which lets you know you're still in the desired section. The compositions work to create deeper and deeper intimacy with each subject.

Scaling Stripes

The front page of the Design for Life site uses color bands, which were created through the use of a striped background tile. The three horizontal bands were created by using a striped background tile.

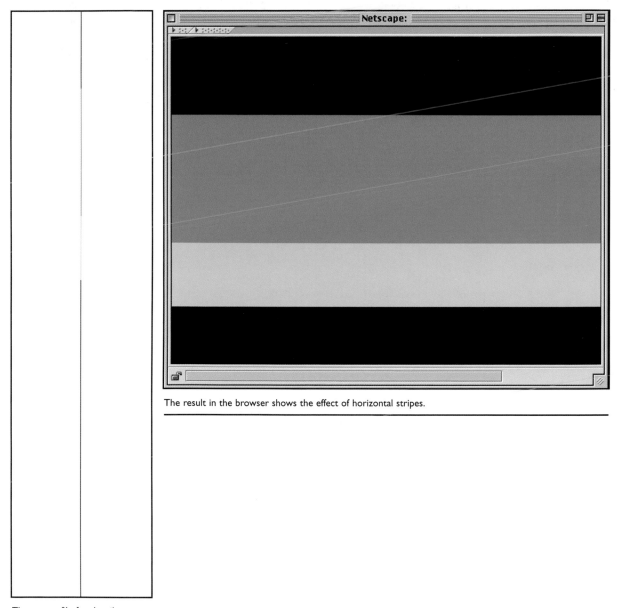

The result in the browser shows the effect of horizontal stripes.

The source file for the tile was very tall and skinny and weighed in at less than 1k!

Giant Background Tiles

A further navigation aide to this site has to do with the subtle screened words in each section. This effect was created through the use of giant background tiles. Elsewhere in the book we looked at background tiles that were small, but filled the browser window once they were tiled. Elisabeth chose a different tack to make the image quite large so it would fill the browser. This might seem irresponsible from a downloading speed, but as you read further you will see the image is actually quite small in file size.

The finished page with the bacground tile as the backdrop to images and text.

The background alone. The dimension is 900 x 800 pixels. When inserted into the BODY BACKGROUND element of Elisabeth's HTML document, this graphic filled the page on most monitors. Even though the background is quite large in dimensions, it was only 4.8k.

The large background tile was used in the HTML, like this:

```
<BODY BACKGROUND="designback.gif">
```

Because the large image was saved as a GIF file and contained large areas of solid color, it compressed beautifully down to 4.8k. See the Web Graphics Appendix for more information on GIF compression.

Digital Photography

Keeping in tune with Elisabeth's philosphy of adding value to the web site, she decided to take advantage of the opportunity to show things on the site that couldn't be shown in the exhibit. Through the use of digital photography and her Sony Mavica camera, Elisabeth was able to capture elements of the show that wouldn't have been visible any other way.

By clicking on the word "index" in the bottom right of the navigation bar, this screen appears. All the items that have asterisks next to them include images Elisabeth shot with her digital camera.

■ note

Sony Mavica Camera

One of the things that Elisabeth really likes about the Sony Mavica is the fact that it uses a floppy disk to store the images. Many digital cameras require that you plug the camera into a computer to transfer the images. Because the Mavica uses a disk, Elisabeth was able to take it out in the field easily and, with a good supply of floppies (instead of film) could take as many images as she wanted.

She did say that the images generally turned out darker than she liked, so she later brightened and adjusted their contrast in Photoshop. The resolution is fine for the web (640 x 480) but wouldn't work for print or other media well.

This shoe catalogue, dated from 1885, was part of the exhibit, though it was under glass. Elisabeth took her digital camera and shot the various pages, which offered the web audience a chance to peek inside its pages.

Ray and Charles Eames designed these cards in 1952. They were in a museum case in the exhibit, but Elisabeth made them come alive by shooting various configurations of the card deck with her trusty Sony Mavica digital camera.

An Alice in Wonderland pop-up book, designed by Jenny Thorne, after John Tenniel in 1980, was brought to life through a QuickTime movie. Elisabeth imported the still JPEG frames from the camera into Adobe Premiere and made small 160 x 180 QuickTime movies for the web.

What's Next

Elisabeth is one of the rare individuals in web design who wants to keep her design company small on purpose. "Even though I know I could take on a lot more work than I currently do, I choose to remain small," Elisabeth stated. "I want to spend my time designing, not managing people. I would far rather have one big project with a great client, than all the headaches of running a larger design firm."

She's not that hot on HTML 4.0, Dynamic HTML, Flash, Shockwave, or plug-ins, either. "The purpose of the web is to communicate, and my designs are created around communication issues, not new technologies," she said. "I love the economy of the web, and the fact that you can create something powerful and big with so little. It's almost as if someone in print said, here's $500 and two colors; now go create something amazing! I like the challenge of working within the limits, rather than pushing the envelope and in the process pushing your audience away."

With a museum, it's important to work with basic technologies. Elisabeth would rather use an animated GIF than a plug-in. "People should be able to get at the information with as little effort as possible," she said. "We are not in the entertainment or gaming business; we are in the information business."

When she recently spoke at a conference, Elisabeth was shocked to see how few museums are taking advantage of web technology. "You wouldn't have believed that most of the exhibition designers were showing their work on overhead projectors!" she exclaimed. "I didn't realize we were as cutting edge until attending that conference!"

Be sure to visit Elisabeth's web site to check out her work. It not only contains portfolio samples, but also a thought-provoking essay on web design called Design in Motion (http://www.itp.tsoa.nyu.edu/~review/current/focus/Roxby1.intro.html).

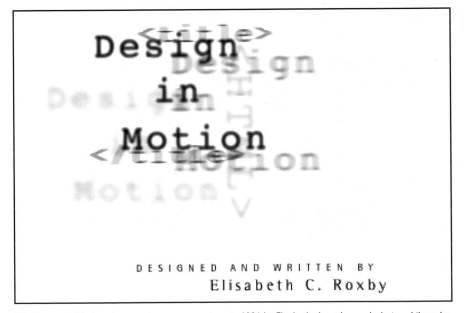

The Design in Motion site contains an essay written in 1996 by Elisabeth about her web design philosophy.

■ site summary

Cooper-Hewitt

Elisabeth Roxby has demonstrated with her Cooper-Hewitt site that artistic and tasteful use of color, composition, and navigation can call maximum attention to important content. Her use of basic HTML and dedication to bringing added value to the museum experience has set the bar in web-based exhibition design that others will have reach. Some highlights of the lessons covered in this chapter follow:

- Color can be used to create a sense of space, hierarchy, and branding. Think about your site design from the perspective of color regions, and you will enhance the usability and aesthetics.

- Even the most seemingly simple HTML enhancement, such as frames, can keep visitors away. Before you add that Shockwave, Flash, plug-in, or DHTML, make sure it's appropriate for your audience and enhances what your site is trying to communicate.

- Tables can be used for alignment and reassembling big images. Through the use of cutting up an image and optimizing each section of it with appropriate JPEG or GIF compression, it is possible to put larger images on the web and effectively deliver a huge graphic with a small download time.

- Think about how the web as a medium can add value to the medium you are representing. Elisabeth's consciousness about user experience and added value made her site designs take advantage of the web to its fullest and best potential.

http://www.si.edu/ndm/

3

Bosch Power Tools
Well-Tooled Elegance

of bosch.rds:1 at 00:00:00

BOSCH

OUR TOOLS

WOODWORKING

THE TRADES

PROJECTS

SWEEPSTAKES

OUR GEAR

WHERE TO BUY

SERVICE

WHAT'S NEW

E-MAIL US

e Line of bosch.rds

■ **Color Theme and Variation**
■ **Rollovers**
■ **3D Animated GIF**
■ **Acrobat**
■ **Imagemap**

http://www.boschtools.com This award-winning site is noteworthy not only for its simple clarity and strength of organization, but also for the manner in which the site successfully conveys the personality of Bosch Tools. There is no technological overkill here, just information presented with a well-designed, consistent interface where every detail has been crafted with exemplary care. This chapter describes behind-the-scenes techniques for color themes, JavaScript rollovers, 3D animated GIFs, and imagemap creation.

Web Design Firm: Cramer-Krasselt Interactive

Client: Bosch Tools (S-B Power Tools Company)

Original URL: http://www.boschtools.com

Archived URL: http://www.uncom.com/dcw2

Type of Site: Catalogue, Brochure, Added-Value for the Brand

Server: Wintel Platform

Operating System: UNIX

Server Software: Apache

Webmaster: Heath Greenfield

Account Executive: Heath Greenfield

Management Supervisor: Greg Reifel

Creative Director: Marshall Ross

Art Direction: John Taylor, Stuart Cohn

Writer: Bob Volkman

GIF Animations: John Taylor, Stuart Cohn

HTML and Programming: Cramer-Krasselt Interactive and Associates

Photography: Jim Arndt

Development and Production Platforms: UNIX/Windows

Design Software: Adobe Photoshop, Adobe PageMill, HomeSite

Downloadable Project Files: Adobe PageMaker, Adobe Acrobat

Programming: CGI, JavaScript, Java

Bosch Tools' Goals

Bosch Tools originated in Germany and is renowned in Europe, where it is considered the Mercedes-Benz of powered hand tools. Here in the U.S., Bosch tools are prized for their balanced ergonomic design, comfortable grip, sturdy manufacture, and rugged dependability. From a design perspective, the tools themselves are quite beautiful. These are premium tools for master woodworkers and serious tradespeople who know the wisdom in buying the best. These tools help them to accomplish their best work.

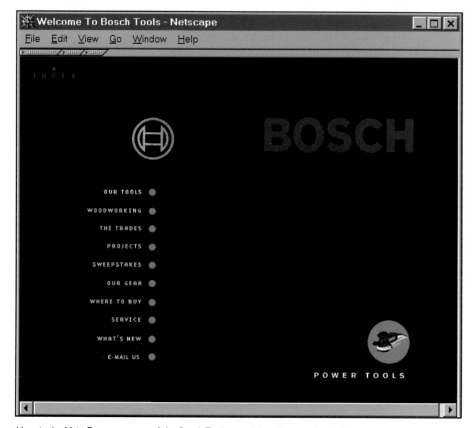

Here is the Main Directory page of the Bosch Tools site. Note the appealing balance of form, color, and space that is established here and remains consistent throughout the site. This page has a link at the upper left "INDEX" that expands this graphical directory into an index of the site in outline format.

The purpose of the Bosch site is to provide a web-based added value campaign for current and prospective users of Bosch Tools. The different areas of the navigation clearly reflect the site's purpose; there is information about the tools, features of current tools, updates on new tools, information on where to purchase tools, where to obtain tool repairs, and how to find customer service. Plus, there's considerable value in the form of downloadable tips, tricks, plans, and projects—all delivered in PDF format.

Bosch also wants to use the web to build relationships with their customers. As part of their plan to add further value to the site by initiating a dialogue, the site includes a web-based sweepstakes to win free Bosch Tools. In order to enter this sweepstakes, the visitor surrenders information. Thus, Bosch is registering both their loyal and prospective users. This registry will also be used to develop web-based forums for their various client trades as, for example, a "Woodworkers Forum."

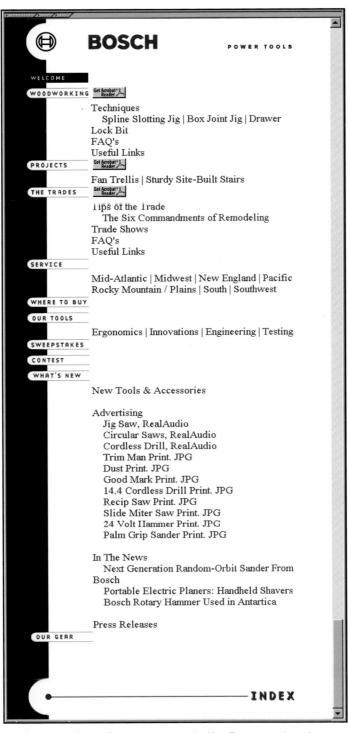

The Bosch Tools "INDEX" page compliments the Main Directory with an alternative means of navigating the site. We are all familiar with the concept that different people are predisposed to different learning styles. The same is true of visualizing information. The "INDEX" page helps visitors who aren't comfortable with a graphical approach, or for those who want to quickly peruse the entire contents of the site.

The Bosch Creative Team

The look and flow of the Bosch site was developed by two designers, John Taylor and Stuart Cohn, who came to this project with respectable digital abilities, but no real HTML or web experience.

John Taylor attended the design program at Iowa State University, where he received his BFA in '92. Upon graduation from ISU, John moved to Chicago where he landed a job at Imageland. While on the job, he taught himself Photoshop and Illustrator and learned to "play with lots of high-tech toys." In 1994, he moved to Cramer-Krasselt, a Chicago advertising agency where he worked on the Bosch site, and recently relocated to freelance in San Francisco. Regarding the expertise which he brought to this project, John Taylor said, "My main emphasis is in print. I really don't do a lot of web stuff. In fact, while I can look at HTML and figure out how someone got something to work, I don't write it myself. I'm mainly just the 'art guy.'"

Stuart Cohn is a Chicago native who obtained his art training in an unlikely way. He enered a "Draw Tippy" contest (like you see on the inside of a matchbook) and won. He claims, "That was enough to get me into art school and that's where I got my basic art and design training." Like John, Stuart is self-taught Photoshop and, also like John, he confesses, "Of HTML, I do not know a thing. No coding here. I'm strictly the design and art direction guy."

Stuart started right out of school, in mid '89, as a digital comp-artist at DDB Needhan Chicago. "Back then," he said, "I really had to push digital comping and design in the office. People in a big agency environment didn't know how to use the technology yet. At the time," he continued, "I had been on the Mac for less than a year. I hadn't learned how to use a computer in school. I talked my way in the door and learned on the job. Basically, I went to the art directors and said, give me your stuff, I'll make it look good. From there it took off." Over time, Stuart built himself into a one-man design department. His success at DDB Needhan led to an opportunity to move over to Cramer-Krasselt, "Where," he says, "it's been non-stop ever since. I'm working on everything from corporate ID programs to web design to television."

The point of describing both of these designer's backgrounds is that they were—and, to a large degree still are—neophytes to the technical side of web site creation. The success of their site is largely attributable to two things: the excellence of their design sensibility and their ability to clearly communicate and collaborate with the people who actually implement their designs.

The technical team was headed by the account executive, Heath Greenfield, who, like his design associates at Cramer-Krasselt, had no experience with HTML or web code. Heath was recruited In June of 1996 to function as the intermediary between the in-house designers and the outside contractors and associates who were contracted to assemble the site. The ultimate contractor, Level 9, was primarily responsible for the final functionality of the site. Level 9 entered into a business arrangement with Cramer-Krasselt and, as such, is considered Cramer-Krasselt Interactive when they work on Cramer-Krasselt projects.

Design Constraints and Concerns

The Bosch site has a very organized and clean feel to it, much like its printed brochure. The look and tone is consistent with the current Bosch advertising campaign (also implemented by Cramer-Krasselt), as well as with the look of the tools themselves, which feature small dabs of orange and red color in their detailing and buttons. The designers determined that this familiar color scheme and the overall tone of the site helps the audience feel less intimidated about the web and the technology being used.

In a sampling from the many areas of the site, the Woodworking, Trades, Projects, Service, What's New, and Press Releases pages provide a consistent, easily navigable interface. Note how the text-laden pages, such as What's New and Press Releases, exchange white type over a black background for optimal legibility.

The designers knew that the audience for this site probably wouldn't be as technically adept with computers as they were with their sanders, routers, and radial-arm saws. They also expected that while many contemporary craftsmen would perhaps have computers, it might be ludicrous to expect them to have the high-end computer hardware.

According to Heath Greenfield, "We tried to minimize the use of high-tech programming while still projecting a contemporary, quality site." The design team anticipated that many people were going to be visiting this site through older browsers and would not have time nor the inclination to wait several minutes for pages to appear or to download many special plug-ins. The site includes a number of buttons that link to downloadable plans, projects, and articles regarding the various crafts and tools. These optional items can only be viewed with the Adobe Acrobat reader (described later in this chapter)—yet the actual site is fully navigable without this plug-in.

Chris Pfaus, VP of Marketing at S-B Power Tool, stated… "Greenfield and his team wanted to stay true to the tone and attitude of the professional tool users and their market." This is not a techno-boutique for premium tools. The copy speaks the language of tradespeople and woodworkers, and the site provides plenty of no-nonsense, useful information. The writing itself is consistent and clear. Like Bosch Tools themselves, both the graphical site and the information it delivers are intended to be a functional tool for the pro tool user.

AOL Compliance

AOL promotes its own browser which does not acknowledge many of the tags and features included in the Bosch site. A major design concern was to create a web site that would work well with Netscape Navigator, Microsoft Internet Explorer, and America Online because they felt it was important to build consistency across platforms so that the site would remain true to the corporate image for design and dependability.

The Bosch Tools Splash page is the first page visitors see upon arrival to the site. The purpose of this page is to greet visitors and to direct AOL users to resources that ensure them the fullest opportunity to access the site as it is intended to be viewed.

Welcome to the Bosch Tools Web Site!

If you are using the AOL browser to view this site, you will be unable to experience the full-quality version of this site, as we have taken advantage of many of the "advanced" design features that new browsers take advantage of. Due to this, we recommend that you view our site using a browser that is fully Netscape compatible, including Netscape and internet Explorer.

For more information on using Netscape and Internet Explorer with your AOL connection, type 'go netscape' inside AOL.

Clicking the "AOL Users!" link at the preceding Bosch Splash page takes visitors to this informational page. Here, AOL users are provided with Bosch's explanation of browser differences. It suggests that visitors take a detour to AOL's Netscape area so they can return to the site fully prepared to take advantage of advanced design features that the AOL browser does not support. This is a simple and effective solution to a problem that the designers anticipated: Much of their target audience will probably be AOL users.

■ note

Controlling the Experience

The Bosch site has provided a means for users to enter the site and obtain a browser to view the site with optimal results. Similarly, Qaswa, from Chapter 1, provided a split at the Qaswa Air page where visitors could choose to view the site with or without Shockwave. As you will see in subsequent chapters, other sites also provide a means for users to enter the site and subsequently either upgrade their browser or acquire necessary plug-ins.

This is good information architecture. The general objective is to greet the visitor with a universally accessible "splash" page or entryway, which will be sufficiently interesting to ensure that the visitor will opt for the full site experience, even if it requires plug-ins or even a browser upgrade. An effective splash should clearly delineate the objectives and style of the site and generate sufficient excitement to retain the audience.

Information Architecture: The Planning

Information architecture must be planned carefully. The Bosch site is exemplary for the way in which various areas and types of information are organized to create a "sense of place," unified with an easily-navigable interface. Early attention to this aspect of the design was a fundamental factor in the ultimate success of the site.

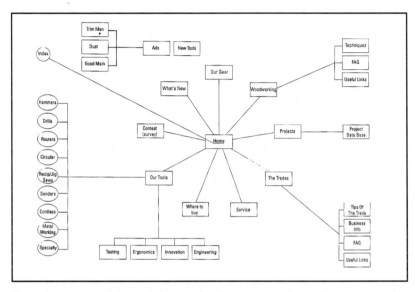

This early organizational diagram helps to explain the continuity and smoothness experienced by visitors to the Bosch site. Every area of the site (and its relationship to the rest of the site) is clearly delineated within this diagram.

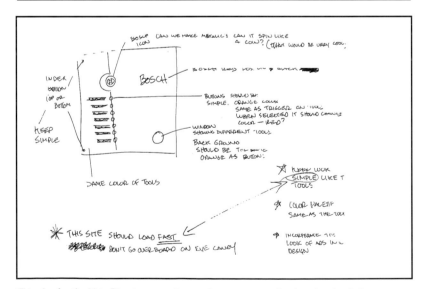

This plan for the Main Directory page is one of many concept sketches that the designers used to communicate their design sensibility to the HTML and programming team at Cramer-Krasselt Interactive.

Design Consistency

Whoever says that designers have no control over their designs on the web should take a good look at the Bosch Main Directory. Great attention was paid to establish a graphic identity and color identity throughout the site. The navigation design was integrated seamlessly with the visual design.

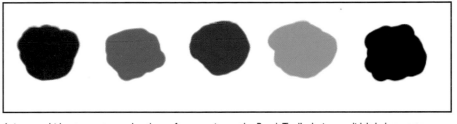

It is a good idea to create a color theme for your site, as the Bosch Tool's designers did. It helps create consistency and continuity.

The color theme was chosen for its relationship to the colors of the Bosch Power Tools and was consistently maintained throughout the site. Browser-safe colors were chosen because they reproduce consistently across platforms and browsers. (Browser-safe color is discussed in the "Web Graphics Appendix" at the back of this book.)

Color was a powerful component of the overall visual interest of the site because the colors were varied relative to the function of specific types of pages. For example, the dramatic dark blue-green and black background of the splash and home pages is exchanged for a white background wherever text-laden pages occur. On these pages, the original left-side black band becomes blue-green, the text background is white, and the text is black. This scheme creates optimal legibility and generates an unspoken visual vocabulary that enhances the information.

Rollovers Are HOT

Visitors love interactive rollover buttons (also called changing state buttons or mouseovers). These types of buttons change visually as the end-user's mouse touches them. Rollovers signify interactivit and lend a lot of added vitality to static "normal" buttons.

The Shockwave Hub of the Qaswa site in Chapter 1, for instance, accomplished its rollovers via Shockwave. Other chapters explore the use of JavaScript and Flash rollovers. Choosing which rollover technology to use is a personal decision, which should be based on the goals of your site, and the projected sophistication of your audience.

The Bosch Tools site used JavaScript for its rollovers. JavaScript is scripting language, developed by Netscape, that is included within HTML and is executed by web browsers. It offers a means of creating interactive content on a web page and is used for many purposes including rollovers. JavaScript should not be confused with Java applets (see "Glossary"). Unlike a Java applet, JavaScript is included within the HTML code for a web page and is easily viewed within the browser. For this reason, JavaScript is much easier to learn than Java.

The JavaScript scrolling text that appears in the status window at the bottom of Bosch Main page was accomplished through a JavaScript from Nick Heinle and Athenia Associates (downloadable at http:www.webreference.com/javascript). The HTML deconstruction of this technique, and the rollover technique, follow in the next section.

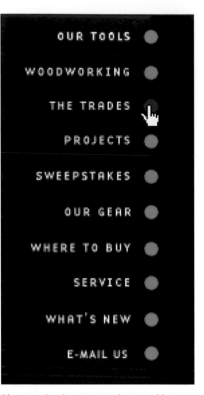

Here are the changing state buttons. Note how the button has turned red in response to a mouseover. These buttons were created in Photoshop and required two images for each button: one orange dot and one red dot.

■ note

JavaScript Resources

Designing with JavaScript ■ Nick Heinle ■ O'Reilly
■ ISBN 1-56592-300-6

JavaScript Interactive Course ■ Arman Danesh ■ Waite Group
■ ISBN 1-57169-084-0

JavaScript for Macintosh ■ Matt Shobe, Tim Ritchey ■ Hayden Books
■ ISBN 1-56830-278-9

Nick Heinle's online tutorial, "The Definitive Rollover Script"
http://www.webcoder.com/howto/article.html?number=6,length=4, demo=1,source=1

Deconstructing the Bosch Main Directory

Note: due to space constraints, the code for this page is not presented in its entirety. It has also been edited both for clarity and minor errors of HTML syntax. The full, original code is archived at http://www.uncom.com/dcwg2/bosch/html/WELCOME.HTML. To see the code—once the page has loaded into your browser—choose View: Source from Explorer or View:Page Source from Navigator.

Nested HTML tables are used to layout and order the contents of this page. The advantage of tables is that they permit complex alignment of multiple kinds of elements. This nested table contains two GIF animations, two static GIF images for large type, and 10 rollover buttons—all superimposed over a tiling GIF background.

As the Bosch Main Directory loads into the browser, the separate areas of content, established by nested HTML Tables, are visible as blocks.

■ code

```
<html><head><title>Welcome To Bosch Tools</title>
```

■ 1
```
<SCRIPT LANGUAGE="JavaScript">
```

■ 2
```
<!--
// To pause the scroller when the mouse is over a link, use:
//  <A HREF="url" onMouseOver="scrollerPause()">linktext</A>
```

■ 3
```
var POSITION = 100      //  how wide is the scroller?
var DELAY    = 40       //  milliseconds between shifts
```

■ 4
```
var MESSAGE  =
"Coming soon to the Bosch Power Tool web site - a bulletin board forum"
+ " designed for tradesmen and woodworkers eager to hear from their peers"
+ " on topics such as power tools, woodworking projects, construction and other related subjects."
+ " Check back soon for details."

var MESSAGE2  = ""
            + ""
var LINK_PAUSE = 2000   //  how long will a link pause the scroller?
//----------------------------------------------------------
```

■ 5
```
function statusMessageObject() {
    this.msg = MESSAGE
    this.out = " "
    this.pos = POSITION
    this.delay = DELAY
    this.i    = 0
    this.reset = clearMessage
}

function clearMessage() {
    this.pos = POSITION
}

//----------------------------------------------------------
```

■ 6
```
var scrollID = Object
var scrolling = false
var killScroll = false     // set this to true to kill the scroller
var pauseScroll = false    // set this to true to pause scroller
//----------------------------------------------------------
```

■ 7
```
var scroll = new statusMessageObject()

function scroller() {
  //
  //  check to see if the scroll should be stopped.
  //
    if (killScroll) {return}
  //
  //  if a link has the mouse over it, pause the scroller.
  //
    if (pauseScroll) {
      scrollID = setTimeout('scroller()',scroll.delay)
      return
    }
  //
  // add spaces to beginning of message
  //
  for (scroll.i = 0; scroll.i < scroll.pos; scroll.i++) {
   scroll.out += " "
  }
```

■ 8
```
//
// if you're still have leading spaces, just
// add custom string to tail of message
// OR else if the string is running off the
// screen, only add the characters left
//
if (scroll.pos >= 0)
scroll.out += scroll.msg
else scroll.out = scroll.msg.substring(-scroll.pos,scroll.msg.length)

window.status = scroll.out

// set parameters for next run
scroll.out = " "
scroll.pos--

// if you're at the end of the message,
// reset parameters to start again
if (scroll.pos < -(scroll.msg.length)) {
scroll.reset()
}

scrollID = setTimeout ('scroller()',scroll.delay)
}
```

■ 9
```
function scrollerPause() {
pauseScroll=true
setTimeout('pauseScroll=false',LINK_PAUSE)
}

function scrollerStop() {
killScroll=true
scrolling=false
window.defaultStatus=''
var killID = setTimeout('killScroll=false',DELAY+1)
}

function scrollerSetup() {
if (scrolling) {
// if (!confirm('Re-initialize scroller?'))
// return
killScroll = true
scroll.reset()
if (scrollerSetup.arguments.length == 1) scroll.msg = scrollerSetup.arguments[0]
var killID = setTimeout('killScroll=false',DELAY+1)
}
scrolling = true
scrollID = setTimeout('scroller()',DELAY+5)
}
```

■ 10
```
This code is Copyright (c) 1996 Nick Heinle and Athenia Associates,
* all rights reserved.  In order to receive the right to license this
* code for use on your site the original code must be copied from the
* Web site webreference.com/javascript/.  License is granted to user to
* reuse this code on their own Web site if and only if this entire copyright
* notice is included.  Code written by Nick Heinle of webreference.com.
*/
```

■ 11
```
browserName = navigator.appName;
browserVer = parseInt(navigator.appVersion);
     if (browserName == "Netscape" && browserVer >= 3) version = "n3";
     else version = "n2";

     if (version == "n3") {
```

■ 12

```
toc1on = new Image(42, 197);
toc1on.src = "../gifs/buttons/toolson.gif";

toc2on = new Image(42, 197);
toc2on.src = "../gifs/buttons/woodon.gif";

toc3on = new Image(42, 197);
toc3on.src = "../gifs/buttons/tradeson.gif";

toc4on = new Image(42, 197);
toc4on.src = "../gifs/buttons/projectson.gif";

toc5on = new Image(42, 197);
toc5on.src = "../gifs/buttons/sweepon.gif";

toc6on = new Image(42, 197);
toc6on.src = "../gifs/buttons/gearon.gif";

toc7on = new Image(42, 197);
toc7on.src = "../gifs/buttons/buyon.gif";

toc8on = new Image(42, 197);
toc8on.src = "../gifs/buttons/serviceon.gif";

toc9on = new Image(42, 197);
toc9on.src = "../gifs/buttons/newon.gif";

toc10on = new Image(42, 197);
toc10on.src = "../gifs/buttons/emailon.gif";
```

■ 13

```
toc1off = new Image(42, 197);
toc1off.src = "../gifs/buttons/tools.gif";

toc2off = new Image(42, 197);
toc2off.src = "../gifs/buttons/wood.gif";

toc3off = new Image(42, 197);
toc3off.src = "../gifs/buttons/trades.gif";

toc4off = new Image(42, 197);
toc4off.src = "../gifs/buttons/projects.gif";

toc5off = new Image(42, 197);
toc5off.src = "../gifs/buttons/sweep.gif";

toc6off = new Image(42, 197);
toc6off.src = "../gifs/buttons/gear.gif";

toc7off = new Image(42, 197);
toc7off.src = "../gifs/buttons/buy.gif";

toc8off = new Image(42, 197);
toc8off.src = "../gifs/buttons/service.gif";

toc9off = new Image(42, 197);
toc9off.src = "../gifs/buttons/new.gif";

toc10off = new Image(42, 197);
toc10off.src = "../gifs/buttons/email.gif";
}
```

```
■ 14    function img_act(imgName) {
              if (version == "n3") {
              imgOn = eval(imgName + "on.src");
              document [imgName].src = imgOn;
              }
         }

■ 15    function img_inact(imgName) {
              if (version == "n3") {
              imgOff = eval(imgName + "off.src");
              document [imgName].src = imgOff;
              }
         }

■ 16  // -->
      </SCRIPT>
      </head>

■ 17  <body background="indxbgr2.gif" vlink="#cc9966" alink="#cc6600" link="#980000"
      onLoad="scrollerSetup()">

      <!--begin container table-->

■ 18  <table border=0 cellpadding="0" cellspacing="0" width="603">
      <tr><td nowrap align=left>

      <!--begin graphics-holding table for topthird of page-->

■ 19  <table border=0 cellpadding="0" cellspacing="0" width="603">
      <tr><td width=603 valign=top align=left nowrap>

■ 20  <a href="boschindex.html" onMouseOver="scrollerPause()">
      <img src="../gifs/home_index.gif" alt="Index" width="85" height="30" border="0"></a>

■ 21  </td></tr></table>

      <!--end graphics-holding table for topthird of page-->

■ 22  <table border=0 cellpadding="0" cellspacing="0" width="603">
      <tr><td width=603 height=5 nowrap>
      </td></tr></table>

■ 23  <!--begin graphics-holding table for middle third of page-->
      <table border=0 cellpadding="0" cellspacing="0" width="603">
      <tr><td nowrap width="85" valign=top></td>

■ 24  <td nowrap width="199" align=center>
      <center><img src="../gifs/home/bosch3.gif" alt="Bosch Tools" width="130" height="130"
      border="0"><br><p></center>
      </td>

■ 25  <td nowrap width="321">
      <img src="../gifs/logo2.gif" alt="Bosch" width="332" height="70" border="0"><br>
      </td></tr>

      <!--end graphics-holding table for middle third of page-->

■ 26  <!--begin graphics-holding table for bottom third of page-->
      <tr><td nowrap align=left>

      <table border=0 cellpadding="0" cellspacing="0" width="603">

■ 27  <tr><td nowrap width=85></td>

■ 28  <td align=left nowrap width="199">
```

■ 29
```
<a href="BTOOLS.HTML" onMouseOver="scrollerPause(); img_act('toc1')" onMouseout =
"img_inact('toc1')"><img src="../gifs/buttons/tools.gif" alt="Our Tools" width="110" height="26"
border=0 name="toc1"></a><br>

<a href="BWOOD.HTML" onMouseOver="scrollerPause(); img_act('toc2')" onMouseout =
"img_inact('toc2')"><img src="../gifs/buttons/wood.gif" alt="Woodworking" width="110" height="26"
border=0 name="toc2"></a><br>

<a href="BTRADE.HTML" onMouseOver="scrollerPause(); img_act('toc3')" onMouseout =
"img_inact('toc3')"><img src="../gifs/buttons/trades.gif" alt="The Trades" width="110" height="26"
border=0 name="toc3"></a><br>

<a href="BPROJ.HTML" onMouseOver="scrollerPause(); img_act('toc4')" onMouseout =
"img_inact('toc4')"><img src="../gifs/buttons/projects.gif" alt="Projects" width="110" height="26"
border=0 name="toc4"></a><br>

<a href="sweepstakes.html" onMouseOver="scrollerPause(); img_act('toc5')" onMouseout =
"img_inact('toc5')"><img src="../gifs/buttons/sweep.gif" alt="Sweepstakes" width="110" height="26"
border=0 name="toc5"></a><br>

<a href="BGEAR.HTML" onMouseOver="scrollerPause(); img_act('toc6')" onMouseout =
"img_inact('toc6')"><img src="../gifs/buttons/gear.gif" alt="Our Gear" width="110" height="26"
border=0 name="toc6"></a><br>

<a href="BWHERE.HTML" onMouseOver="scrollerPause(); img_act('toc7')" onMouseout =
"img_inact('toc7')"><img src="../gifs/buttons/buy.gif" alt="Where To Buy" width="110" height="26"
border=0 name="toc7"></a><br>

<a href="SERVICE.HTML" onMouseOver="scrollerPause(); img_act('toc8')" onMouseout =
"img_inact('toc8')"><img src="../gifs/buttons/service.gif" alt="Service" width="110" height="26"
border=0 name="toc8"></a><br>

<a href="NEW.HTML" onMouseOver="scrollerPause(); img_act('toc9')" onMouseout =
"img_inact('toc9')"><img src="../gifs/buttons/new.gif" alt="Service" width="110" height="26"
border=0 name="toc9"></a><br>

<a href="mailto:techinfo@sbpt.com, Bosch_Comment@c-k.com" onMouseOver="scrollerPause();
img_act('toc10')" onMouseout = "img_inact('toc10')"><img src="../gifs/buttons/email.gif" alt="Email"
width="110" height="26" border=0 name="toc10"></a><br>
```

■ 30
```
</td>
<td nowrap width=321 valign=bottom>
```

■ 31
```
<table border=0 cellpadding="0" cellspacing="0" width="321">
<tr><td align=right nowrap width=274>
```

■ 32
```
<a href="NEW.HTML" onMouseOver="scrollerPause()"><img src="../gifs/home/bschnew.gif" alt="Bosch"
width="63" height="63" border="0"></a>
</td>
```

■ 33
```
<td nowrap width="47"></td>
</tr></table>
```

■ 34
```
</td></tr></table>
```

■ 35
```
</td></tr>

<!--end graphics-holding table for bottom third of page-->

</table>
```

■ 36
```
<table border=0 cellpadding="0" cellspacing="0" width="603">
<tr><td nowrap width=85></td>
```

■ 37
```
<td align=left nowrap width="199"></td>
```

■ **38** `<td nowrap width=321 valign=bottom>`

■ **39** `<table border=0 cellpadding="0" cellspacing="0" width="321">`
`<tr><td align=right nowrap width=274>`
`<img src="../gifs/powertools.gif" alt="Power Tools" width="274" height="22" border="0"></td>`

■ **40** `<td nowrap width="47"></td></tr></table>`

`<!--end container table-->`

■ **41** `</td></tr></table>`

■ **42** `</body></html>`

■ deconstruction

■ **1** The SCRIPT tag tells Java-enabled browsers that the following code is JavaScript. This tag and the associated JavaScript content always go between the HEAD tags. Note that optimal HTML style has all HTML and Java tags typed in CAPITALS. This makes it much easier to read and edit the code because the tags stand out from the other content.

■ **2** The <!-- tells browsers that are not Java-enabled to ignore the Java contained between <!-- (here) and //--> located below at [16]. The remaining code in this section is one of many notes from the author of this JavaScript instructing how the parameters of this script may be customized. In this instance, the note regards a pause of the scrolling text (which appears in the status bar window of the browser) caused by a mouseover. Such a pause is termed a LINK_PAUSE in this script.

■ **3** Here the author has supplied an explanation after each variable declaration. The double // separates the declaration from the explanation. Note that ending double // indicates the beginning of the script. This format is observed consistently throughout the script.

■ **4** The var MESSAGE is where the scrolling message is input in the script. Usually a little experimentation with the arrangement of the text and the value for the LINK_PAUSE is required to yield the desired result.

The statusMessageObject script establishes a message object that is sent to the status bar. The subsequent entries are definitions for most of the variables described above in items [3] and [4]. Generally, these do not need to be changed, as the script will function fine as it was originally written.

■ **5** Another set of variables. The last two are essentially "off." The notes indicate how they can be activated and what they do.

■ **6** The first line of this section defines the scroll as the statusMessageObject previously described in [5]. The rest is a series of conditions that control the scroll and the author's comments regarding the implementation of each condition.

■ **7** These comments from the author of the script are solutions to troublesome messages that run with either too much leading space (space between lines) or else run off the screen.

■ **8** This section of the script contains three functions. The first regulates the Scroller Timeout (LINK_PAUSE) that occurs when the mouse is rolled over an active link. The second sets the parameters for the delay, and the final function regulates the resumption of the scroller once the mouse leaves the active link.

■ **9** Here the author of this script, Nick Heinle, exercises his copyright and stipulates conditions for use.

■ **10** This is the beginning of another JavaScript, which controls the MouseOver changing state buttons. Since Navigator 2 doesn't support ARRAYS, which are fundamental to JavaScript MouseOvers, this bit of code establishes which version of Netscape is present. If it's Netscape 3 or greater, then the Script will run. Otherwise, the browser skips the MouseOver interactivity and runs the buttons as static hypertext links.

■ 12 This is the first ARRAY, including 10 items. These items are the images for the "on" state of the changing state MouseOver buttons. toc1on signifies "table of contents #1 on," it is a new Image, and its dimensions are 42 pixels tall by 197 pixels wide. Much like a hypertext reference, toc1on.src indicates the path where the image resides. This syntax is repeated for each of the nine remaining buttons. Note that the images differ because the buttons are unique for each item.

■ 13 This is the second ARRAY, also including 10 items. These are the images for the "off" state of the changing state MouseOver buttons. toc1off signifies "table of contents #1 off." As with the first array, this syntax is repeated for each of the nine remaining buttons. Note that the "off" images also differ because the buttons are unique for each item.

■ 14 This img act FUNCTION activates the "on" state of the MouseOver, but only if the browser is Netscape 3 or greater. Otherwise, the buttons are fixed in the "off" position and act as static hypertext links.

■ 15 This img inact FUNCTION activates the "off" state of the MouseOver, but only if the browser is Netscape 3 or greater. Otherwise, as stated above, the buttons are fixed in the "off" position.

■ 16 This is the end of the JavaScript, as previously mentioned in [1]. Note the </HEAD> tag here, after the </SCRIPT> tag.

■ 17 This is the <BODY> tag together with its attributes. Note the BACKGROUND tag for the tiling background GIF, which is (as noted previously) 800 pixels wide and five pixels tall. This GIF is divided into two colors: blue-green on the left and black on the right. It stacks up vertically to create the tiling border GIF background of this page.

Here's the Bosch tiling border GIF background. For more information on background tiles, refer to Chapter 1, "Qaswa." The only differences between this and the Qaswa example are the dimensions of the GIF and the colors.

■ 18 Nested tables were used to assemble the contents of this Bosch Index Page. The advantage of using tables here is that they permit complex layouts of multiple kinds of content. This nested table contains two GIF animations, two static GIF images for large type, and 10 rollover buttons—all superimposed over a tiling double-border GIF background. Although the images and assembled content are relatively small, the table layout and background tile work together to deliver the illusion of a single large image.

This table tag defines the first container TABLE within which most of subsequent content of this page is nested. (The rest of the content is contained in another container TABLE beginning at [36].) The accompanying attributes and values of this first container TABLE determine how and where theTABLE is placed; border=0 specifies that there is no border on the table. Similarly, cellpadding="0" and cellspacing="0" specify that there is no loose space between TABLE ROWS and TABLE DATAS. width="603" specifies that the page will be precisely 603 pixels wide. <tr> opens the first TABLE ROW. td opens the first TABLE DATA, the attribute nowrap specifies that this item will not wrap with a line break if the browser is sized less than 603 pixels wide, and the attribute align=left ensures that the contents will be displayed flush left to the edge of the browser. Note the HTML author's comments bracketed between <!-- and -->.

■ 19 This is the opening statement for the first nested TABLE within the TABLE described above in [18]. The TABLE DATA tag, <td width=603 valign=top align=left nowrap> has attributes that ensure it nests at the absolute top, flush left to the edge of the table cell, which in this case happens to be the left edge of the browser window, and will not wrap.

■ 20 The contents of the TABLE [19] are described here. This is the index link that appears as item #A in diagram. Note the function call for the JavaScript onMouseOver="scrollerPause()" as discussed in [2].

■ 21 This line of code ends the TABLE DATA, TABLE ROW, and TABLE initiated at [19] above, but note that we are still within the open TABLE initiated at [18].

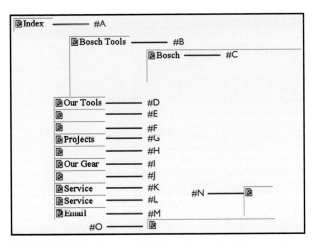

DIAGRAM I:This diagram is helpful to reference for deconstruction steps 22—32.

■ **22** Here's our third nested TABLE. This is a self-contained unit with no contents. Note the height=5 attribute. This TABLE is merely a layout device to ensure a five-pixel vertical space between items #A and #B, per diagram. Note that some browsers might not respect such an empty TABLE. One method to ensure that this TABLE does its job as a spacer (regardless of browser anomalies) is to provide contents in the form of a single-pixel transparent GIF spacer (see Glossary).

■ **23** Note the author's comment. This is the fourth nested TABLE. There is one TABLE ROW here, containing three TABLE DATA tags in a horizontal row. The first TABLE DATA tag, like [22] above, is another spacer, providing an 85-pixel horizontal space to the left of item #B, (per **DIAGRAM** I).

■ **24** The second TABLE DATA is item #B in diagram I. This second TABLE DATA is specified width="199" and centered, align=center. The content of this second TABLE DATA, the animated Bosch logo, is also centered, <center>. Because the logo is only 130 pixels wide, the additional space is distributed to either side of the logo; this is another layout device.

■ **25** This is the third and final TABLE DATA tag of this TABLE ROW, represented by item #C, (per **DIAGRAM** I), which is a static GIF image with the Bosch name. The final line includes the closing tags for this third TABLE DATA tag and also for the TABLE ROW, which was initiated at [23].

■ **26** Again, note the author's comments. The inclusion of such guideposts makes subsequent edits much easier, especially when more than one person is involved in the development of the HTML.

Now we have a new TABLE opening as a nested item within the second TABLE ROW of the TABLE that was opened at [18]. This nested TABLE has the same attributes and values as its parent.

■ **27** The only TABLE ROW for this nested TABLE [26] is a massive, sprawling chunk that performs primarily on the repeated use of the <br> tag to separate the button images, so pay attention here! The first TABLE DATA is a horizontal spacer whose function is to push items #D-M (per **DIAGRAM** I) 85 pixels to the right of the left browser margin.

■ **28** The second TABLE DATA <td align=left nowrap width="199"> contains items #D through M (per **DIAGRAM** I).

■ **30** The contents of this TABLE DATA is a stack of 10 clickable (hypertext referenced) images, associated via the arrays at [12] and [13] with the JavaScript discussed above. The images stack on top of each other because each entry ends with the <br> tag.

Note that each a href includes JavaScript function calls for onMouseOver="scrollerPause(); img act('toc1')" onMouse Out= "img inact('toc1')" as discussed in [2],[14], and [15]. Essentially what's happening is that the JavaScript instructions that were loaded between the <head></head> tags are invoked here in association with the images, hrefs, and HTML layout.

[30] The closing tag, </td>, for the TABLE DATA initiated at [28] above is followed by a third TABLE DATA. This TABLE DATA occupies the space to the bottom right of the page and it contains another nested table.

■ **31** The first TABLE DATA of this nested TABLE is item #N per diagram __. It's forced to the right by the attribute align=right.

■ **32** The contents of this TABLE DATA is the little power tool image associated with item #N per diagram __. Note the inclusion of onMouseOver="scrollerPause()" continues consistent as with all other hypertext links—this is the LINK_PAUSE of [4].

■ **33** The second TABLE DATA tag is merely a spacer that holds the empty space to the right of the power tool image. This is followed by the closing tag for the TABLE ROW and TABLE initiated at [31] above.

■ **34** These are closing tags for the TABLE which was initiated at [26].

■ **35** These closing tags, </td></tr>, are for the TABLE DATA and TABLE ROW initiated at [18]. The following TABLE closing tag closes the TABLE initiated at [18].

■ **36** Here's the second container TABLE. It's an independent entity that stacks directly beneath the prior assembly. The first TABLE DATA of the TABLE ROW is a spacer 85 pixels wide.

■ **37** The second TABLE DATA is also a spacer. It is 199 pixels wide and has an attribute align=left that forces it to align to the left.

■ **38** The final TABLE DATA has an attribute valign=bottom that forces it to align vertically to the bottom. The content of this TABLE DATA is a nested TABLE. The first TABLE DATA in the TABLE ROW of the nested TABLE is a GIF image for the text which reads "POWER TOOLS," associated with item #O (per **DIAGRAM 1**).

■ **39** The second TABLE DATA of the TABLE ROW is merely another spacer to ensure the right edge alignment of items #N and #O. The closing tags for this nested table (initiated at [38] above) follow.

■ **40** The attribute nowrap specifies that this item will not wrap with a line break if the browser is sized less than 47 pixels wide.

■ **41** These are the closing tags for the TABLE initiated at [36].

■ **42** These are the closing tags for the BODY and the HTML document.

■ note

Table Resources

A number of sites host tutorials on the subject of HTML tables. Here are several of the more useful tutorials currently online. (Note that the bellcow site has further links to more tables-related sites.)

http://www.golden.net/~steinman/html/tables/index.html

http://www.lehigh.edu/~ludoc/seminar/www_authoring_2/tables.html

http://www.usats.com/learn/tables.shtml

http://www.bellcow.com/tables.html

http://www.quadzilla.com/

Often, deciphering a table structure in HTML can seem impossible. Here's a clue: print out the code, and get a handful of colored marker pens. Start by color-coding or coordinating table opening tags with their closing tags. The table structure will then become clearer.

Another great online resource that actually checks an HTML page for table errors is:

http://www2.imagiware.com/RxHTML/

The Bosch Logo Animation

The Bosch site uses animation sparingly on its opening page (http://www. bosch tools.com/html/WELCOME.HTML). One of the surprising elements is that the Bosch logo first appears to be static, and suddenly it turns a full revolution. The following section examines the process of creating this animated graphic, which involved a 3D modeling and animation tool, and an animated GIF authoring tool.

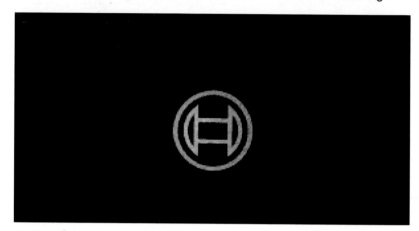

The Bosch logo is an animated GIF that was modeled as a 3D object in Ray Dream Designer. The logo object was rotated 360 degrees in 24 steps, and 24 frames were saved as separate files from the scene. The frames were optimized in Photoshop to ensure both palette consistency and optimal GIF bit depth, then placed in GifBuilder to create the animated sequencing and delay characteristics.

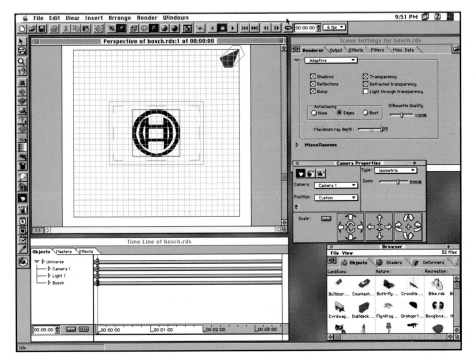

The Bosch Logo extruded from an outline drawing into a 3D object in Ray Dream Studio 5.

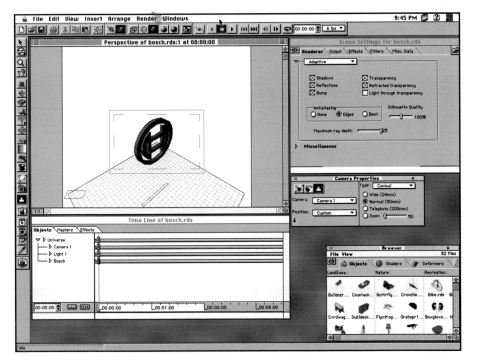

In this shot, the camera angle was adjusted in Ray Dream to a frontal view. The 3D logo was rotated 360 degrees in 24 steps and a snapshot of each step was taken for assembly within GifBuilder. Note that this new version of Ray Dream Studio 5 includes new animation capabilities, which would have allowed the entire logo animation to have been created without exporting snapshots to GifBuilder for assembly.

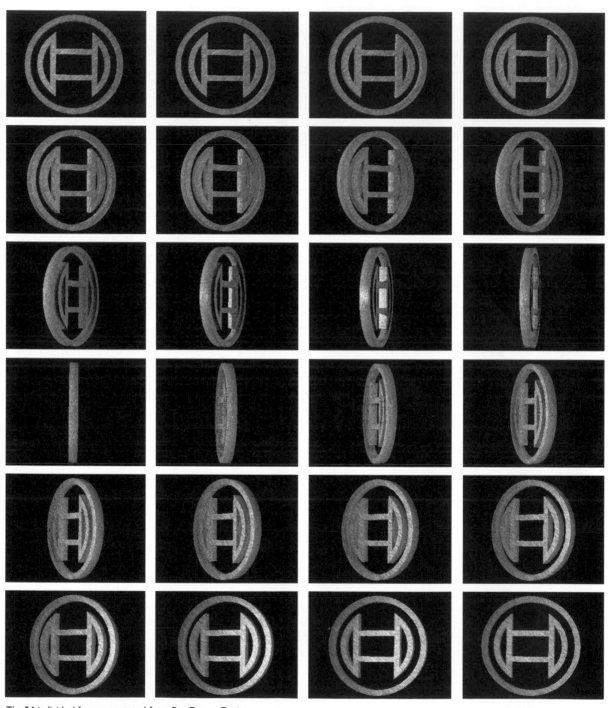

The 24 individual frames, exported from Ray Dream Designer.

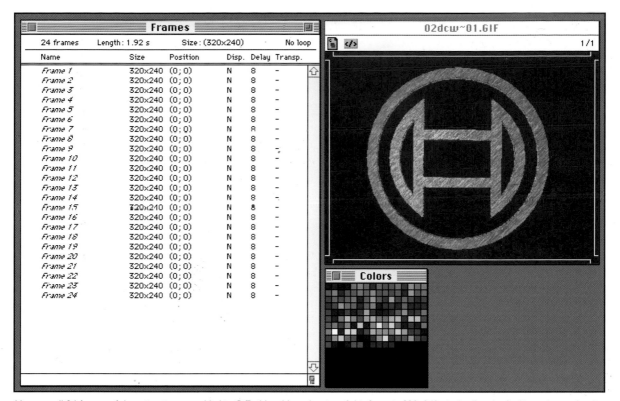

	Frames					
24 frames	Length: 1.92 s	Size: (320×240)			No loop	
Name	Size	Position	Disp.	Delay	Transp.	
Frame 1	320×240	(0; 0)	N	8	–	
Frame 2	320×240	(0; 0)	N	8	–	
Frame 3	320×240	(0; 0)	N	8	–	
Frame 4	320×240	(0; 0)	N	8	–	
Frame 5	320×240	(0; 0)	N	8	–	
Frame 6	320×240	(0; 0)	N	8	–	
Frame 7	320×240	(0; 0)	N	8	–	
Frame 8	320×240	(0; 0)	N	8	–	
Frame 9	320×240	(0; 0)	N	8	–	
Frame 10	320×240	(0; 0)	N	8	–	
Frame 11	320×240	(0; 0)	N	8	–	
Frame 12	320×240	(0; 0)	N	8	–	
Frame 13	320×240	(0; 0)	N	8	–	
Frame 14	320×240	(0; 0)	N	8	–	
Frame 15	320×240	(0; 0)	N	8	–	
Frame 16	320×240	(0; 0)	N	8	–	
Frame 17	320×240	(0; 0)	N	8	–	
Frame 18	320×240	(0; 0)	N	8	–	
Frame 19	320×240	(0; 0)	N	8	–	
Frame 20	320×240	(0; 0)	N	8	–	
Frame 21	320×240	(0; 0)	N	8	–	
Frame 22	320×240	(0; 0)	N	8	–	
Frame 23	320×240	(0; 0)	N	8	–	
Frame 24	320×240	(0; 0)	N	8	–	

02dcw~01.GIF

1/1

Colors

Here are all 24 frames of the animation assembled in GifBuilder. Note the size of this frame is 320×240 pixels. For the final iteration, each animation cell was cropped in Photoshop and re-exported at 130×130 pixels for placement within the web page layout. The background was also altered to include a black circle that, when the animation was layered over the body background tile, created the black die-cut look.

■ note

What Is Ray Dream Designer?

Ray Dream Studio 5 is a 3D modeling and animation program, which boasts an intuitive interface and a relatively easy learning curve. Although Ray Dream has been through a few name and company changes (it was first an independent product, then allied with Fractal Design which subsequently merged with Meta Tools) the product is widely used because of its power and versatility. Ray Dream is now available from MetaCreations in two configurations: the new Ray Dream Studio 5, which includes many new features, plus an accelerated renderer and Ray Dream Designer 4.1.

With regards to the Bosch logo animation, Ray Dream Studio 5 would have been a real boon for John Taylor when he modeled the logo animation, because one of the new added features is animation. This capability would have streamlined his workflow, because he could have proceeded from 3D model to GIF animation without the hassle of passing each of the 24 frames through both Photoshop and GifBuilder. It's very cool that imaging and 3D programs are starting to "get" that the web graphics market is important and requires special features. For more information on Ray Dream contact them direct at http://www.metacreations.com.

Distributing Files via Adobe Acrobat PDF

One objective of the Bosch site was to create a relationship between Bosch Power Tools and the master woodworkers and skilled tradespeople who use Bosch Tools. Bosch and the site designers knew that their target audience would be receptive to plans, tips, and tricks relevant to specific areas of craftsmanship and particular trades. The big question was how to disseminate the information.

The Adobe Acrobat **PDF** (**P**ortable **D**ocument **F**ile) format was chosen over building a web page for each document because the PDF format permits visitors to both print out and save the document to their own hard drive. Although the PDF format requires a plug-in, the designers decided that the advantages to this plug-in outweighed the drawbacks of having a plug-in requirement for this content.

To simplify things, the designers made the plug-in accessible directly from the page. According to Heath, this use of PDF files gave his content and design team the luxury of putting "project files" that were originally intended for print on the web quickly, without having to reformat them for the web. Besides the Acrobat, the basic informational content of the main site is entirely accessible without the plug-in. The Acrobat plug-in (which is downloadable from Adobe at http://www.adobe.com/acrobat) is only necessary to access the added value items such as plans, tips, and tricks, which most users would want to printout in order to make full use of them.

Adobe Acrobat PDF files can be generated directly from Adobe PageMaker, Quark Express, and MS Word, to cite a few applications. For information or tutorials on Acrobat PDF refer to these URLs:

http://www.adobe.com/prodindex/acrobat/main.html

http://www.islandnet.com/~bigblue/apr97nl/acro3.htm

http://ftp.inf.vtt.fi/pdf/lund/default.htm

http://microvet.arizona.edu/help/viewingAcrobat.html

http://www.purepdf.com

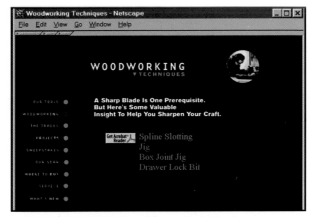

Selecting the TECHNIQUES from Woodworking Page leads a visitor to this page with downloadable Adobe Acrobat files. Those without the Acrobat plug-in can download and install it within a few minutes by clicking the "Get Acrobat Reader" button. This button is an Adobe supplied GIF, coupled with the following code linking to the Adobe Acrobat Download site: <a href="http://www. adobe.com/acrobat"> <IMG SRC="../gifs/acrobat.gif" Alt="Get Adobe Acrobat"></a>.

The "Spline Slotting Jig" required little more than a minute to download.

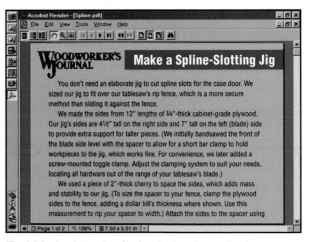

The Adobe Acrobat project file downloads and opens Acrobat over the browser. The visitor can choose to save the project to disk or even print it out.

The Bosch Service Imagemap

Imagemaps are commonly used as navigation devices on web sites. They are so called because a set of coordinates are used to map out "hot spots" on JPEGs or GIFs, which result in multiple hyperlinks associated with a single graphic. There are two types of true imagemaps, client side imagemaps, and server side imagemaps. There's a third method, which is an alternative to using an imagemap, that is actually a table built hold multiple linked images. This works because the image is cut into tiles and reassembled within a borderless table.

The Bosch site employs a client-side imagemap. Client-side imagemaps differ significantly from server-side imagemaps. A client-side map permits all the map information to be stored live within the HTML document. A server side map requires that most of this same information be created within a separate "map definition file" that must be stored on the server and accessed by a CGI script. Aside from the added complexity of creating server-side maps, they are also functionally different in two main regards: Server-side maps are slower to respond to a visitor's actions and they also provide a far less meaningful readout in the browser's status bar.

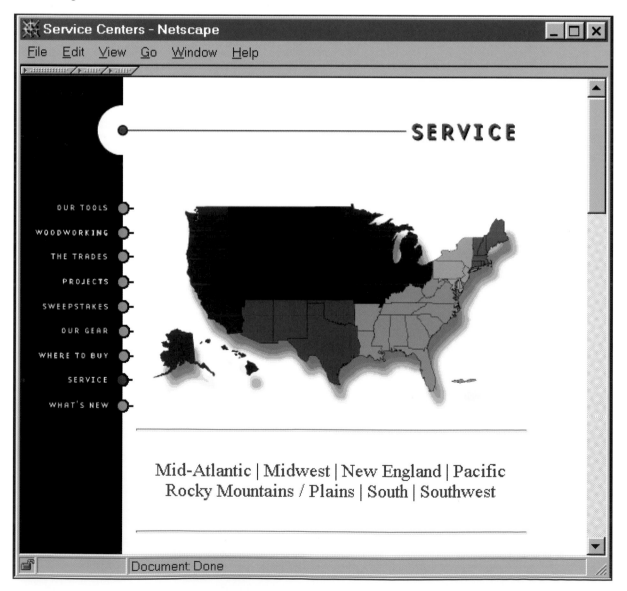

The only real drawback to client side maps is that some browsers still don't support them—(although Netscape and Explorer 3.0 and beyond do support client side maps.) Highly conscientious web designers sometimes employ a dual map that works as both a server side and client side map! For exhaustive information on either kind of map and also dual mapping, refer to Lynda Weinman's *Designing Web Graphics 2*.

http://www.cgibook.com/links.html

The status bar in the clientside imagemap yields helpful information about the link destinations.

http://www.razorfish.com/bluedot/typo/menu.map?105,70

The status bar in the server side map yields a useless set of numbered coordinates, which tell the end-user nothing about where the map directs them.

Several imagemap authoring shareware programs are available for both the Mac and PC. In addition to shareware utilities, a number of programs' latest releases have the added capability to create an imagemap, complete with URLs. So far Adobe Illustrator 7 has the most complete support for this function, although we can expect Macromedia Freehand 8 to add this feature. Most web authoring applications such as NetObjects Fusion, Adobe PageMill, and the most advanced web authoring environment, Macromedia's DreamWeaver, include complete tools for imagemap creation. There is an excellent online tutorial for Map This! located at: http://www.incontext.ca/support/spider/userguid/tutor/mapthis/mapthis.htm.

■ step-by-step

Map This! Imagemap Utility for the PC

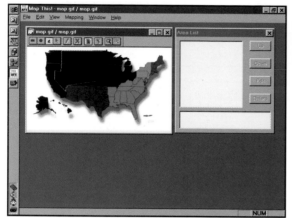

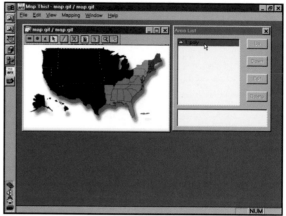

Step 1: The Bosch map.gif image is opened in Map This! and the polygon tool is used to outline the Northern Rocky Mountains and Midwestern States. You can download Map This! from http:// = www. masteringcomputers.com/masteringcomputers/util/iis/mapthis.htm.

Step 2: When the polygon is completed it appears as "1 poly" in the Area List. Double-clicking this item invokes the Settings dialog for Region #1.

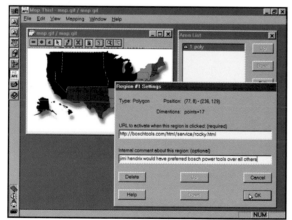

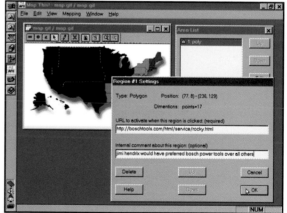

Step 3: The Region Settings dialog gives the overall coordinates for the region and provides a field for the destination URL (the web page that is accessed by clicking this region of the imagemap.) It also provides a comment field for notes.

Step 4: When all areas of the map have been described and augmented with settings as above, final information is input via Edit: Edit Map Info. The default URL is the address for the page that contains the imagemap. Functionality of the map file format is dependent on the kind of server employed to host the page. The choices are NSCA or CERN. This required fact is obtained from the webmaster who maintains the server where the site is hosted.

■ step-by-step

WebMap Imagemap Utility for the Mac

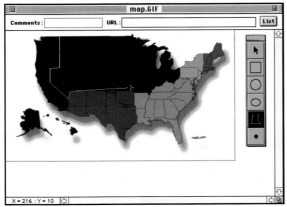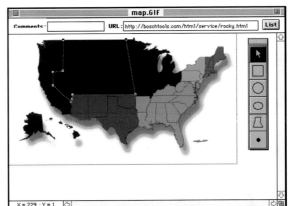

Step 1: The Bosch map.gif image is opened in WebMap and the Polygon tool is used to outline the Northern Rocky Mountain and Midwestern States. You can download WebMap from: http://www.filez.com.

Step 2: When the polygon is completed, the URL for this section of the map is entered into the URL field. Other aspects of image-map creation are nearly analogous to the procedures involved with Map-This! There are excellent online tutorials for WebMap at: http://www.uwec.edu/Info/UWECWeb/Wkshops/Imaps/webmap.htm. and at: http://hyperarchive.lcs.mit.edu/HyperArchive/Archive/text/html/web-map-101.hqx.

What's Next?

With the entire tool catalog now online, the Bosch site is being used more and more by retail customers who are looking for information on particular tools. To extend that mission, Cramer-Krasselt has many ideas in the works to make the site even more useful for their target professional and retail customers.

When asked what specific plans were in store for the near future, Heath Greenfield responded, "Aside from adding a new section for John and Stuart's baby pictures, we plan to add several new features to the Bosch web site in the upcoming year, including a retailer locator and an exclusive (password protected) distributor/retailer section. In general, we are continuing to make the site more useful to our visitors. We want to add items that have functional value and not just items that might look cool or that might be placed there purely as a gimmick."

Adding to this, John Taylor volunteered, "From what I've heard, reader response has been pretty good. Many of them want to see more projects. I would like to see the Woodworker Forum brought in very soon, as well as a threaded bulletin board system that would function as a Power Tool Discussion Forum."

■ site summary

Bosch Power Tools

Although it doesn't include any groundbreaking uses of technology, the Bosch site is a text book example of just how much more less can be. The success of this site is largely attributable to the restraint exercised by the designers in their insistence upon avoiding gratuitous effects. They have followed the advice of the Bosch copy writers: "Artists sign the bottom of the canvas. Athletes set records. Yours is a more subtle signature, but if you do it right, your legacy won't fade. And it will never be broken."

- One means of ensuring the success of a site is to clearly identify the reasons for building the site and then establishing an information architecture that supports these reasons.

- Exemplary site design can be developed by designers with little or no understanding of HTML or web techniques. The truly important issues are clarity of design, and the capability to effectively communicate these goals to the technical team.

- Precise planning is essential to effective communication of design concepts between the designers and the technical team.

- Maintaining design and color consistency throughout the site helps develop a sense of comfort and security to the end-user.

- Judicious, restrained employment of an animated GIF logo adds a touch of elegance to a well-crafted design.

- The Adobe Acrobat PDF format is an effective means of delivering content that is intended to be printed and saved by visitors to the site.

http://www.boschtools.com

4

National Geographic
Synergy of Print and Web

- ■ **Creative Process**
- ■ **Hub and Spoke Information Architecture**
- ■ **Imagemaps and Fragments**
- ■ **Use of RealAudio**

http://www.nationalgeographic.com/features/97/nyunderground/ The National Geographic Society and National Geographic Magazine don't need an introduction—they are reknowned for their high quality print publications, extraordinary photography, and mesmerizing feature stories. The magazine's approach to presenting a feature story is a proven winner, and this chapter bears witness to their equally excellent approach to online storytelling.

Web Design Firm: ContentFree, Marina del Rey, California

Client: National Geographic Society, New York, NY

Original URL: http://www.nationalgeographic.com/features/97/nyunderground/

Archived URL: http://www.uncom.com/dcwg2/

Type of Site: Web affiliate of printed magazine

Server: Sun Ultra Sparc

Operating System: Solaris 2.5 & 2.6

Server Software: Netscape Enterprise

Webmaster: Mark Powers—National Geographic

Producer: Maria Bunai—National Geographic

Assistant Producer: Mark R. Holmes—National Geographic

Photography: Bob Sacha—National Geographic

RealAudio/RealVideo of James Graseck Violinist: Mark Christmas—National Geographic

RealAudio Tour: Info North

Producer: Tim Stanton—ContentFree

Art Direction: Trevor Elliot—ContentFree

Illustration & Design: Don Foley—National Geographic. Oscar Valdez, Trevor Elliot—ContentFree

HTML Authoring: Doron Tordjmon, Shane Bishop—ContentFree

Development and Production Platforms: NT/Mac

Design Software: Adobe Photoshop, Adobe Illustrator Macromedia Director, Visual SlickEdit, Visio

New York Underground Web Site's Mission

The February, 1997 issue of *National Geographic* magazine ran a 21-page feature article, "Under New York," which was about the intensely crowded terrain below New York City. With words, diagrams, and pictures, this article unearthed some staggering statistics about this "sub-urban" landscape. For example, did you know that New York City is punctuated by 465,000 manholes? These lead to an infrastructure of sewers, utilities, communications, and transportation that ranges in depth from just beneath the street to 80 stories below.

This is the New York Underground opening splash page. By clicking the manhole cover, visitors are invited underground to explore the web site. The manhole metaphor is consistent with the rest of the site, which uses geological imagery to tell its story.

National Geographic's Strategy

National Geographic Interactive's online, editorial developmental strategy is to add value to a magazine feature subject without re-dundancy. It is against their philosophy to repurpose content; they instead strive to develop online features and stories by developing new areas that traditional (linear) media are less able to handle. This development model allows the Society to attract a new audience to its existing products, such as web visitors drawn to the magazine's content. It also enables existing members to find additional informa-tion via the web about magazine features that interest them.

Mark Holmes cited his overriding goals for their mission. "We are interested in developing content that works for as wide an audience as possible. For example, we'd like as many schools as possible to connect with us online, and we recognize that many schools simply haven't the resources to keep their workstations up to true state-of-the-art standards. So we try to stay nearer the leading edge than the bleeding edge."

Another part of the site's developmental intent is to put their best visual foot forward—with as efficient a download as possible. The Society has long been recognized as publishing world leaders in the development of photography, art, illustrations and diagrams, so their online presence could not be anything less.

National Geographic Interactive is also mindful of developing content for an international, potentially non-English speaking audience that doesn't want the main thrust of the message delivered through a text-based delivery (between 30 and 40 percent of National Geo-graphic Interactive's traffic is from outside the United States). It's a fact that most visitors on the web today don't like to read lengthy passages of text on a computer screen, so why develop that way?

The Creative Team

New York-based National Geographic Interactive hired two outside firms to collaborate on this site—ContentFree and InfoNorth, both located in the Marina del Rey area of Los Angeles. According to Mark Holmes, "Our development model has always been to pair up our inhouse editorial teams with outside new media firms. These pairings benefit both sides. They learn how National Geographic has traditionally developed stories, and we learn how to tell those stories interactively. Everyone benefits from this. Even the editorial folks here at the magazine benefit because they are learning to tell stories in new, interactive ways."

The creative direction for this site came from Tim Stanton and Trevor Elliot, founding partners of ContentFree, who worked through alliances with team members at both InfoNorth and National Geographic Interactive.

Responding to whether he had any advice for budding web designers, Tim Stanton replied: "For sure. We'd bid on three or four jobs for National Geographic Interactive and came close on a couple of cool ones, but we stayed in touch. Then Mark Holmes asked us to send in a proposal for a companion site for the "Under New York" magazine article that was coming up. He sent along some text and illustrato, Don Foley's 3D diagrams for the piece. It was easy to get into this idea and we had the contract in short order."

Foremost among the design problems that Tim Stanton and Trevor Elliot confronted in developing this site was the conundrum of, as Tim says, "showing the confusion of the underground in an non-confusing manner. There are so many amazing things down there and I still don't think we've done justice to it all." Trevor adds his observation, "With so much content and so little room, it was too easy to clutter the page. We were given total freedom, so we went overboard and then pared it down later. I focused on detail and space to ensure that every choice and detail on each image-mapped illustration was positioned perfectly."

The Creative Process

ContentFree had a unique opportunity with National Geographic Interactive. Normally the editorial process is well underway by the time web developers get to pitch projects. As Tim related, "Since this new procedure was loose, we squeezed in. This allowed us to come up with the central concept and visual theme for the website. We were able to report on the same subject as the magazine, but in a thoroughly different, complimentary way."

Responding to a question regarding how they generate design concepts, Trevor replied, "Our aim is to loosen up and get untethered in a brainstorm." In concrete terms, this means that when Tim starts a project he tosses out "lots of ideas and garbage. Then I narrow the choices from that collection. I try to acknowledge the corny, clichéd, over-used notions and let them onto the list. I know that the beginnings of new good stuff will be mixed in there. Later, I go through and gather the notions that are worth developing." For Trevor this means that, "when I start a project, I keep a sketchbook near at all times, including off-work hours. I've also found that it's really great to get away from work and have a beer with the other creative people on the team." To this, Tim chimed in, "We can often be found in this manner, practicing for when we have to be creative."

Regarding the specific process for this project, Trevor stated that "this was one of those rare projects where the final concept came quickly. We played with many ideas—going down a manhole, the point of view of a tunnel worker, the point of view of a sewer rat, an elevator going down, a direct cutaway view of the city. We were always scrolling down. Tim wanted to make the sewer the star of the show. On closer inspection, we agreed that was fun, but not what National Geographic Interactive wanted, nor did it convey the information."

They finally arrived at a concept that revolved around a navigation device that portrayed a "cutaway" diagram of what could be found in the New York City underground. This diagram was labeled the "core sample diagram"; a name derived from drilling terminology (into the earth's "core", and soil "samples"). The core sample diagram idea just stuck. Trevor reported that initially, "Tim didn't like this concept, but I just kept hammering on the idea until he got it. Then that scrolling idea started to make real sense."

Diagrams for the Web

The remarkable strength of the New York Underground site springs from the online development of an asset for which National Geographic magazine is perhaps best known: the use of diagrams. Those who are familiar with National Geographic know that most features within the magazine develop at least one particular part of the story through diagrammatic presentation. Often, such presentations are a visual elucidation of concepts or interconnections that cannot be photographed.

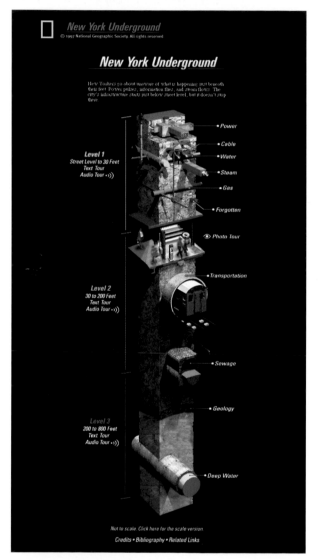

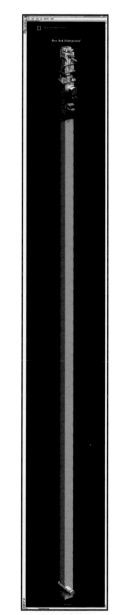

The "giant core sample diagram of the Big Apple" was adapted specifically to the strengths of the web. Note the uncluttered clarity of detail and the well-planned distribution of information. One of the finest details of this presentation is accessed by clicking the text at the bottom, "Not to scale. Click here for the scale version."

By clicking on the bottom text, "Click here for the scale version" in the previous screen, you will see an extremely long, scrolling iteration of this diagram that accurately represents the true distance between levels two and three. This is one of the most compelling examples of the scrolling capabilities of a web-based presentation found anywhere.

Because of the ability to scroll and interact with the core sample diagram, the New York Underground web site goes well beyond what the magazine has room to do on the small, static confines of its pages. While the site adheres to the central theme of the story as reported in print, it has both developed and added depth to the subject of the artwork. Unlike the magazine, the nature of a web site enables the audience to enter the diagrammatic space, to interact with the labels and to access deeper levels of information.

In creating the art for the sample main menu, the team of Trevor Elliot, Art Director, and Don Foley, National Geographic Illustrator, began with a single diagram from the magazine's feature article and developed it into the central element of an interactive feature. The first hard part was settling on this idea. The other hard part was making it work visually.

Referring to the image from the magazine article, Trevor Elliot shared this cautionary tale, "There were hours of headache spent adapting it to our core sample diagram idea. Poor Don Foley didn't know what he was getting into; the web was an entirely new medium for him. Don and I went back and forth many times on this. At first, I just explained the idea and told him to go for it. Although he made many fine attempts, there was always something off—perspective, distribution of detail, or clarity. By the time I made a detailed sketch for him of exactly how I wanted it, he was pretty well fed up with me. So in the end we did most of the finish production for the final art at ContentFree.

What did I learn from this? No matter how talented and capable an artist is, if you have a firm idea about the look and feel, detailed sketches and hands-on art direction are a must from the start of the project."

This is the initial diagram from the magazine coverage that was developed into the core sample main menu. Trevor Elliot scanned this illustration from the actual magazine article, which was already in print when the online development began. It was created by the National Geographic Illustrator, Don Foley. Although this artwork is fantastic, it had to be revised to adapt it to web space.

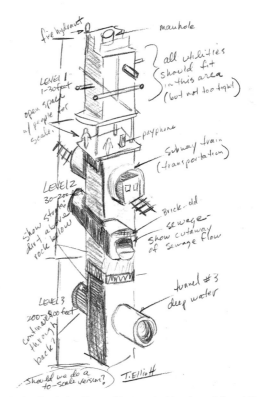

Here is the sketch that Trevor Elliot supplied for the web-based illustration of the core sample diagram. The perspective and layout were more fitting for a scrolling web page than the original magazine diagram. Why didn't he make this drawing in the first place? Probably because the groundwork hadn't yet been established to permit him to see this solution. It should be emphasized that the job of the art director is to have a hunch, an unrealized concept, and to hang onto that hunch, nudging and prodding the talent until the concept begins to materialize. With this in mind, developing multiple renditions is understood as an intrinsic part involved in obtaining the best possible art.

Hub and Spokes Information Architecture

In discussing the structure of the site, Trevor Elliot recalls that Mark Holmes of National Geographic Interactive had insisted on a "hub and spokes" model for the site's architecture. A hub and spokes model of information architecture refers to a central navigation element that serves as the "hub", with all the other branches originating from this main menu, which serve as "spokes".

According to Mark, he chose this model because he wanted the visitors to interact with the main menu as both the central design feature and the central navigational device of the site. That is, the visitor clicks one aspect of the subject, steps off the hub page to interact with that aspect, then returns back to the hub page to select another aspect to explore.

■ **note**

Information Architecture

The hub and spoke model of interactive architecture that is used in developing the New York Underground site is essentially the same scheme that is employed in organizing the Bosch Tools site.

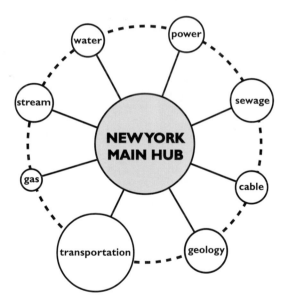

Note that although the information architecture is very similar, the experience and feel of these two sites is quite dissimilar. Information Architecture is a fundamental underpinning of good site design, but it does not necessarily predetermine the quality of the experience that the site may produce. Provided that the architecture has been well planned, it will become almost transparent, and the experiential quality of the site will, most likely, become a dual function of both the story and the art direction employed in telling that particular story.

Imagemaps and Navigation

The core diagram of the National Geographic New York Underground web site is actually composed of many small images which form the illusion of one giant diagram. This method of breaking up the images allowed the developers to make extensive use of imagemaps to implement its navigational branching (or "spokes" as discussed earlier). This chapter focuses on the HTML programming to implement imagemap data. Refer to Chapter 2, "Bosch Tools," to learn how to make imagemaps.

What was the purpose or advantage of using so many imagemaps on the National Geographic Main Menu Core page? The use of imagemaps gave the site designers complete control over the fonts used to label each navigational item on this page. If they had used straight HTML, they would not have been able to use images of fonts, but instead would have been forced to use the more limited text options that HTML affords.

Lynda Weinman's *Designing Web Graphics.2* has helpful sections on the subjects of "Graphics-Based Typography" and "Using Photoshop for Type Design." If you intend to create image-based chunks of type for web use, this book covers many techniques and procedures for creating "images of type" instead of using HTML's limited type options.

New Yorkers go about unaware of what is happening just beneath their feet: Power pulses, information flies, and steam flows. The city's infrastructure starts just below street level, but it doesn't stop there.

HTML type is fairly limited in terms of fonts and visual effects.

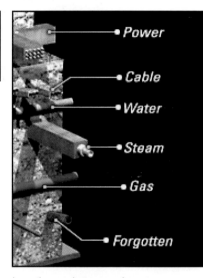

Instead, many designers make type treatments in Photoshop or other imaging programs, save the type treatments as GIF or JPEG images, and insert them into their HTML pages. This technique was used by National Geographic Interactive extensively.

Code Deconstruction: Main Menu Core Diagram

The main menu of the NY Underground site is deconstructed here for its use of imagemaps, tables and fragments. The imagemaps in this example are "client-side imagemaps," meaning they do not require an external CGI script (see glossary) or need to be executed at the server end. Client-side imagemaps are easier to code (because you eliminate the need for an external script), and easier on the server because they are executed on the client's side (the visitor's web browser). The disadvantage to using client-side imagemaps exclusively is that older browsers (anything below a 2.0 release and AOL's native browser) will not be able to access the imagemaps at all.

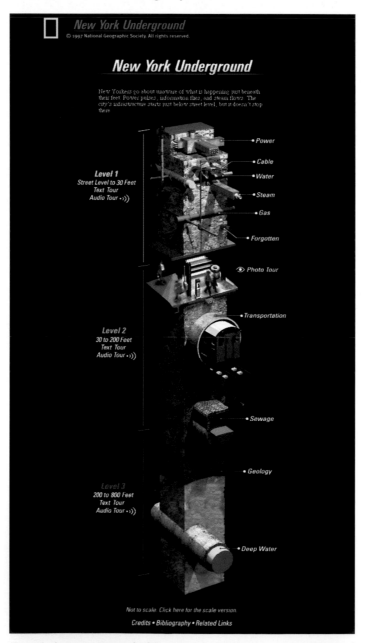

The code deconstruction on the following pages examines the use of imagemaps, tables and fragments for the core sample diagram, located at http://www.national-geographic.com/features/97/nyunderground/docs/nymain.html.

■ code

```
<html>
<!-- (c)1997 National Geographic Society.  All rights reserved.-->
<head>
<TITLE>New York Underground: Main Menu @ Nationalgeographic.com</TITLE></head>
<body bgcolor="#000000" text="#FFFFCC" link="#FFFFCC" vlink="#cccc99">
```

■ 1
```
<MAP NAME="mainmenu">
<AREA SHAPE=RECT COORDS="215,30,272,50" HREF=ny110.html>
<AREA SHAPE=RECT COORDS="218,72,270,91" HREF=ny130.html>
<AREA SHAPE=RECT COORDS="216,100,271,118" HREF=ny210.html>
<AREA SHAPE=RECT COORDS="217,133,273,158" HREF=ny140.html>
<AREA SHAPE=RECT COORDS="217,168,275,191" HREF=ny240.html>
<AREA SHAPE=RECT COORDS="207,215,277,242" HREF-old510.html>
<AREA SHAPE=RECT COORDS="184,278,277,299" HREF=pic100.html>
<AREA SHAPE=RECT COORDS="193,363,288,391" HREF=ny330.html>
<AREA SHAPE=RECT COORDS="203,562,271,589" HREF=ny230.html>
<AREA SHAPE=RECT COORDS="198,664,267,691" HREF=geo410.html>
<AREA SHAPE=RECT COORDS="187,814,277,839" HREF=wat100.html>
<AREA SHAPE=RECT COORDS="126,904,287,925" HREF=myth000.html>
</MAP>
```

■ 2
```
<MAP NAME="mainstak1">
<AREA SHAPE=RECT COORDS="32,33,86,48" HREF=ny120.html>
<AREA SHAPE=RECT COORDS="21,51,106,64" HREF="av/tour1.ram">
</MAP>
```

■ 3
```
<MAP NAME="mainstak2">
<AREA SHAPE=RECT COORDS="12,36,65,50" HREF=ny220.html>
<AREA SHAPE=RECT COORDS="3,53,85,68" HREF="av/tour2.ram">
</MAP>
```

■ 4
```
<MAP NAME="mainstak3">
<AREA SHAPE=RECT COORDS="9,33,63,47" HREF=ny320.html>
<AREA SHAPE=RECT COORDS="2,50,84,65" HREF="av/tour3.ram">
</MAP>
```

■ 5
```
<MAP NAME="credbib">
<AREA SHAPE=RECT COORDS="1,0,37,11" HREF=cred100.html>
<AREA SHAPE=RECT COORDS="45,0,113,12" HREF=bib100.html>
<AREA SHAPE=RECT COORDS="125,0,193,12" HREF=rel100.html>
</MAP>
```

■ 6
```
<MAP NAME="banner">
<AREA SHAPE=RECT COORDS="5,11,35,50" HREF=/main.html>
</MAP>
```

■ 7
```
<center>
```

■ 8
```
<table border=0 width=560><tr><td>

<img border=0 width=310 height=60 src="images/banner.jpg" alt="[Ad Banner]"
usemap="#banner">

</td>
```

■ 9
```
<td>

<a href="/event.ng/Type=click&ProfileID=2&RunID=1127&AdID=247&Redirect=
http:%2F%2Fwww.planetk-12.com%2Fnational" target="_top">
<img src="/ads/images/phillips4.gif" border=0 width="234" height="60"
alt="Ultimate Education Resource"></a>

</td></tr></table><br><br>
```

■ 10 `<img width=378 height=29 src="images/mainhed.jpg" alt="[New York Underground]">`

■ 11 `</center><br><br><center>`

■ 12 `<table width=325 border=0 cellpadding=0 cellspacing=0><tr><td>`
New Yorkers go about unaware of what is happening just beneath their feet:Power
pulses, information flies, and steam flows. The city’s infrastructure
starts just below street level, but it doesn’t stop there.

`</td></tr></table></center><br><center>`

■ 13 `<table border=0 cellpadding=0 cellspacing=0><tr valign=top><td>`

`<a name="part1"></a>`

■ 14 `<table border=0 cellpadding=0 cellspacing=0><tr><td height=20`
`valign=center></td></tr>`

■ 15 `<tr><td height=220 valign=center align=right>`

`<img width=113 height=62 border=0 src=images/mainstk1.gif usemap="#mainstak1"`
`alt="[Main Stak 1]"><br>`

`<font size=-1>`

■ 16 `</td></tr><tr><td border=0 height=44 valign=bottom align=left>`

`<font color="#000000"><a name="part2">.</a></font>`

■ 17 `</td></tr><tr><td height=297 valign=center align=right>`

`<img width=77 height=63 border=0 src=images/mainstk2.gif usemap="#mainstak2"`
`alt="[Main Stak 2]"><br>`

`<font size=-1>`

■ 18 `</td></tr><tr><td height=301 valign=center align=right>`

`<a name="part3"></a>`

`<img width=82 height=63 border=0 src=images/mainstk3.gif usemap="#mainstak3"`
`alt="[Main Stak 3]"><br>`

■ 19 `</td></tr></table></td><td>`

`<img width=289 height=925 border=0 src="images/mainmen.jpg" usemap="#mainmenu"`
`alt="[Mainmenu]"><br><br>`

■ 20 `</td></tr></table>`
`<center>`

`<a href="scale.html"><img border=0 width=214 height=10 src="images/scale.gif"`
`alt="[Full Scale]"></a>`

`</center><br><center>`

■ 21 `<img border=0 width=193 height=13 src="images/credbib.gif" usemap="#credbib"`
`alt="[Credits, Bibliography, Related Links]">`

`</center>`

`</body></html>`

■ deconstruction

■ **1** This first client-side imagemap correlates to the image, mainmenu.jpg, found later inside a table [9]. The MAP NAME element defines the "name" of the imagemap. The name can then be referenced anywhere else in the document, and will refer back to this data. You can use any name you want, but you must name the imagemap in order for it to work. See the section later in this section to on Fragments see how the NAME attribute is used for anchoring purposes. The AREA SHAPE elements describe the shape of the linked regions of the imagemap. The COORDS element lists the coordinates for the linked regions. The HREF element is where the target URL is specified.

■ **2** This second imagemap data correlates to the image mainstak1.gif, which is contained lower in the code, within a table [15]. Note that an imagemap can be generated with either a JPG or a GIF image. The only possible drawback to using the JPG format together with GIF for imagemaps on the same page is that there is a potential color-shift problem with the JPG format. Refer to the "Web Graphics Appendix" at the back of the book for further information regarding browser safe color and the propensity of JPG to shift color.

■ **3** This imagemap correlates to mainstak2.gif, which is included lower in the code within a table [17].

■ **4** This imagemap correlates to mainstak3.gif, which is included lower in the code within a table [18].

■ **5** This imagemap correlates to credbib.gif, which is contained later in the code within a table [21].

■ **6** This imagemap correlates to banner.gif, shown later in the code [8].

■ **7** This <center> tag is pivotal to the positioning of the elements that follow. It ensures that both the TABLE (which contains two images appearing side-by-side) and the main head (which stacks beneath the table) are centered on the page.

So far, we've covered the parts of code that relate to the imagemaps, images, and type color. Tables and "nested" tables were used for alignment purposes on this site, and from here on out through the end of this deconstruction you'll find the code and explanations for tables.

■ **8** Here is the opening for the first TABLE. It's borderless, border=0, and has a single ROW, <tr>. The first CELL, <td>, of this row contains the image banner.jpg. The ALT tag is being used to ensure the words "Ad Banner" will appear in the event the end user cannot view the banner image.

banner.jpg

■ **9** Here's the second CELL, <td>, of the TABLE initiated at [8] above. Note that the extensive code is merely a very long HREF for the clickable destination of the ad. Some of this code relates to CGI scripts (see glossary) which help the advertiser track cookies and data about the client. The fine point here is the element, target="_top". Clicking the ad banner causes the destination URL for this ad to open and replace the current National Geographic feature. If this code were replaced with target="new", then clicking the ad banner would open a new browser window on top of the current National Geographic feature, thus helping to ensure that visitors remain at the National Geographic site. The typical tags follow to close the CELL, ROW, and TABLE. The dual

 provides a little space between the TABLE and the mainhed.jpg that follows in item [10]. Note that this is not nearly as precise as the use of a transparent GIF spacer because different browsers implement the <br> tag with varying space allotments.

■ 10 The mainhed.jpg is centered because of the tag <center> occurring at [7].

New York Underground

mainhed.jpg

■ 11 Here's the closing </center> tag for the <center> tag at [7]. Notice that all of the CENTER tags brac-ket the TABLE containers within the HTML. Everytime a table is specified, it reuqires its own CENTER tag, if you want that element to be centered.

■ 12 The purpose of this second TABLE is to position and contain the text that occurs between the New York Underground banner and the main menu core sample assembly. Note that the color of this font is specified as an attribute text="FFFFCC" within the BODY tag at [6] above. The font size is determined by the visitor's prefer-ences as specified in their browser. Note the special code at city’s and doesn&146;t which creates a "curly" apostrophe via HTML. These special characters are called "entitities" in HTML. A list of other entities can be found online at http://www.luna.bearnet.com/iso8859-1.html. If an entity had not been used to specify the "curly apos-trophe", the HTML would have produced a straight line for the apostrophe, which is not considered proper in typographic circles.

■ 13 This is where the use of one TABLE nested within another TABLE begins to be quite interesting. The third TABLE that is initiated here is the container for the six image elements that comprise the aggregate core sample main menu. The order of these elements is ruled by the nesting of another TABLE with this one. Note that this only works seamlessly when the TABLE, ROW, and CELL are specified via attributes, which stipulate zero values for border, cellpadding, and cellspacing. The first CELL of this first ROW contains the entire nested TABLE. Also note the ANCHOR tag with the NAME attribute, <a name= "part1">. This is very useful because it permits the sublevel pages to link directly back to each subsector of this page, without scrolling. This feature is called a "fragment" and is discussed later in this chapter.

■ 14 The nested TABLE commences here. The only CELL of the first ROW of this TABLE is merely a spacer 20 pixels high, which serves to push the subsequent ROW and CELL into alignment with the adjacent elements.

■ 15 The second ROW and CELL of the nested TABLE contains the image element, mainstak1.gif. The attribute align=right ensures that this element will abut the image element, mainmenu.jpg, which appears to the right of main-stak1.gif. Note the inclusion of usemap=#mainstak1 that correlates this "mainstj1.gif" image to the map data, which resides at [2].

Level 1
Street Level to 30 Feet
Text Tour
Audio Tour •))

mainstak1.gif

■ 16 This code begins with the closing tags for the CELL and ROW initiated at [15] above. The subsequent CELL is another spacer—this time, 44 pixels high.

The next line of code is the second incidence of the ANCHOR tag with a NAME attribute, <a name="part2"></a>. It differs significantly in the manner that this is imple-mented. Here, the ANCHOR tags bracket a "." that is made to disappear by the COLOR attribute of the FONT tag (as a black dot on the black background). More information about the NAME attribute is at the end of this section.

■ 17 This code begins with the closing tags for the CELL and ROW discussed in [16] above and continues with the opening tag for the third ROW and CELL of the nested TABLE that is initiated at [14]. Note that the combined effect of the attributes for HEIGHT, height=297, and VERTICAL ALIGNMENT, valign=center coupled with the HEIGHT attribute height=63 of the image mainstak2.gif centers the image within a 297-pixel vertical space. Also note the usemap="#mainstak2.gif" attribute that correlates this image to the map data located earlier in [1-6].

Level 2
30 to 200 Feet
Text Tour
Audio Tour •))

mainstak2.gif

■ **18** The first and third line of this code is consistent with the explanation in [17], only it refers to the image and imagemap NAME for mainstak3.gif. The middle line, which is the ANCHOR and NAME assembly for the third level of the core sample main menu, is consistent with the explanation as in [13].

mainstak3.gif

■ **19** Here, </td></tr></table> are the closing tags for the nested TABLE, which is initiated at [14]. The subsequent </td> closes the first CELL of the TABLE, which is initiated at [13].

The final tag in this first line of code <td> opens the second CELL of that same TABLE initiated at [13]. This second CELL extends the full length of the assembly that is discussed in [14] through [19]. It contains the image element mainmenu.jpg.

Note that the

 tags after the image serve to extend this CELL (and the entire TABLE) downwards, generating the open space between mainmenu.jpg and the following image element, scale.gif. Cleaner HTML syntax would have placed these

 after the close of the TABLE.

■ **20** Here's the close of the final CELL initiated at [19] above and the close of the ROW and TABLE initiated at [13]. The following image item, scale.gif, is controlled merely by the <center> tag that precedes it.

■ **21** This code places the last image element, credbib.gif, on the page. Like scale.gif above, credbib.gif is controlled merely by the <center> tag. Note that "credbib.gif" is the final imagemap.

Credits • Bibliography • Related Links

credbib.gif

What Are Fragments?

"Fragments" are an HTML technique used for navigation purposes. Fragments enable you to have one long page of information that can have multiple "anchors" within it. This means that you can access the long page at multiple locations. The multiple locations are marked by "anchors" within the page. Imagine the long page as a series of stair steps, and that you could tell the browser to automatically go to stair step 3 or step 7, depending on what hyperlink was clicked. To make this more understandable, let's look at some visual examples how fragments were used on this site. Next, we will examine the HTML technique itself.

(A) By placing your mouse over the number 3 on the left-side navigation graphic, **(B)** notice the bottom readout of the browser which shows the fragment: http://www.nationalgeographic.com/features/97/nyunderground/nymain.html#part3. The "#" symbol **(C)** lets you know a "fragment" is in use.

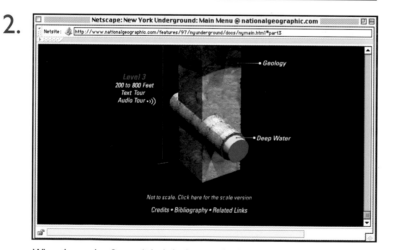

When the number 3 was clicked, the browser loaded the main navigation page, but not at the top of the page! It instead loaded the image at the number 3 level. We'll examine the HTML for this page next.

3.

New York Underground illustration

New York Underground

New Yorkers go about unaware of what is happening just beneath their feet. Power pulses, information flies, and steam flows. The city's infrastructure starts just below street level, but it doesn't stop there.

• Power
• Cable
• Water
• Steam
• Gas
• Forgotten

◉ Photo Tour

Level 1
Street Level to 30 Feet
Text Tour
Audio Tour •⟩⟩

• Transportation

Level 2
30 to 200 Feet
Text Tour
Audio Tour •⟩⟩

• Sewage

• Geology

Level 3
200 to 800 Feet
Text Tour
Audio Tour •⟩⟩

• Deep Water

Not to scale. Click here for the scale version.

Credits • Bibliography • Related Links

This is the entire document that contains the element <a name= "part3"></a>. The hyperlink requested a fragment, it loaded up in the number 3 position automatically.

■ code deconstruction

```
<MAP NAME="subnav">
<AREA SHAPE=POLY
COORDS="1,70,16,76,42,68,47,90,51,153,18,169,
5,156,5,98,1,87,11,82,11,78,1,70"
HREF=nymain.html#part2>
<AREA SHAPE=POLY
COORDS="3,66,5,5,29,4,41,22,46,45,41,66,16,
73,3,66"
HREF=nymain.html#part1>
<AREA SHAPE=POLY
COORDS="6,162,20,172,40,162,41,241,36,249,
19,254,6,245,2,215,6,162"
HREF=nymain.html#part3>
</MAP>
```

Notice the three different references, to #part2, #part1, and #part3? These are fragments. What do they do? Let's click on the number 3 to find out.

Inside the HTML for the nymain.html, there was a fragment marker that looked like this:

```
<a name="part3"></a>
```

This established an anchor with a "name". The name is the marker that the previous HTML page accessed by using the "#" symbol. The "#" symbol combined with the referenced "name" in the first document, sent the browser to the marked anchor spot in the second document.

If you're interested in learning more about how to use fragments, a step-by-step exercise with source files will walk you through the process in *Creative HTML Design* by Lynda and William Weinman.

Note: The W3 consortium's online reference is located at http://www.w3.org/MarkUp/html3/anchors.html.

Use of RealAudio

To implement audio for the site, RealAudio technology was chosen. RealAudio is a continuous or streaming sound technology from Progressive Networks' RealAudio. Streaming sound is sound that is played as it arrives. The alternative is a sound recording that doesn't start playing until the entire file has arrived, such as a WAV file. Support for streaming sound may require a plug-in player or may come with the browser.

Here's the RealAudio player that pops up in response to clicking "Audio Download." With a 28.8 modem, this audio file is delivered in less than two seconds. RealAudio is a streaming technology that performs quite well within today's limited bandwidth. Used sparingly, it adds a nice touch to what would otherwise be silent web sites.

A RealAudio player or client program may come included with a web browser or can be downloaded from the Real-Audio or other web sites. As of this printing, the latest application for generating both RealAudio and RealVideo is RealPublisher 5.0. It is obtainable directly from http://www.real.com/publisher/index.html.

Until recently, to deliver RealAudio sound from your own web site, either you or your web space provider needed to have a RealAudio enabled server. The latest application, however, no longer requires a streaming media server. All Real-Audio and RealVideo content created with RealPublisher can be streamed directly from a standard web server using the HTTP protocol. This enables site visitors to play clips immediately, without download delays.

With RealPublisher, you can add both audio and video content to web pages. Among its many features, it creates audio and video content using easy-to-use templates, generates web pages with embedded audio and video, automates content publishing to servers without FTPing, and creates compressed audio and video content from extant WAV, AU, AVI, and QuickTime files. RealPublisher also supports LIVE encoding, which means that advanced users can capture audio or video directly from the source and create RealAudio and RealVideo in real time. There's also an HTML wizard available for generating audio/video enabled web pages. A RealAudio file will have a filename extension of either xxx.ra or xxx.ram.

■ tip

Real Audio

For more information about RealAudio, consult the following independent URLS:

http://www.e-z.net/tech_support/ratut/

http://biz.yahoo.com/prnews/971210/ny_realnetworks_mdia_1.html

http://www.news.com/News/Item/0,4,14935,00.html

For information from RealAudio, with an extensive online knowledge base for their product, go to: http://www.realaudio.com/

For a tutorial from RealAudio in PDF format, go to: http://205.158.7.51/docs/ccguide50.pdf

For more information about developing, managing and delivering sound on the web, Lynda Weinman's *Designing Web Graphics.2* has an exhaustive introductory chapter dedicated to this subject.

■ note

What's Next for Underground?

From here on, the piece will reside in the National Geographic Interactive archives and remain permanently accessible. Unlike other web sites and web publishing models, New York Underground will not be improved, enhanced, or updated. It will remain the same. In relevant situations there will be active links to it from current features and it may occasionally be brought back out on National Geographic's main menu.

■ site summary

National Geographic New York Underground

The National Geographic Society's entry into web development enables it to take an asset, like the illustration from the printed feature, "Under New York," and inject new information and life into it that would have previously gone largely underdeveloped. Not that the magazine doesn't get the whole story; actually, quite the opposite is true. Each asset that the Society develops has so much more potential than can be realized in the print medium's presentation. The new synergistic model of a feature's development, which utilizes the strengths of both print and the web, is perhaps the most exciting new development to touch either media.

The following epigraph from the New York Underground Web site, "The city's infrastructure starts just below street level, but it doesn't stop there" might well be paraphrased, "National Geographic's feature development has traditionally started with print, but it doesn't stop there."

- ■ The National Geographic Society has long been regarded a leading innovator in the development of photography, art, and diagrammatic presentation for their printed features. The Interactive Division continues in that tradition by developing innovative web features that, together with the related print features, have resulted in a new, synergistic model of dual media development.

- ■ Diagrammatic presentations can become the navigational centerpiece of an experiential web presentation, and can deliver far more information than the original static diagrams.

- ■ Web developers should heed Tim Stanton's admonition not to accept discouragement when successive bids don't lead to a contract. Stay in touch with the client. Content-Free bid on three projects before they were contacted to submit a proposal for New York Underground. Perseverance works.

- ■ The Brainstorm is a crucial step towards excellent web development. Honor your ideas.

- ■ A labor of collaboration can be difficult. In order for really terrific work to see daylight, often both the Art Director and the Creative Talent must understand the nature of the process and simply keep going until they "get it."

- ■ Information Architecture is only one, albeit very important, aspect of web development. Similar architectures can be employed to obtain dissimilar experiences. Strong functionality requires a strong foundation, and that is Information Architecture.

- ■ Properly implemented, imagemaps are useful for the development of graphically-based interactive content. One advantage is that imagemaps give designers absolute control over the typography of their navigational devices

- ■ Nearly all web developers can stand to learn a fundamental lesson from the developers of National Geographic Interactive's New York Underground. It is imperative that developers look for ways in which they can harness the intrinsic potentials of the medium to tell their story. The synthesis of architecture, scrolling, diagrammatic presentation, and anchoring to a fragment combine to make this one of the most powerful, savvy stories presented on the web to date. Look for the opportunities within what others might consider the "limitations" of the medium.

http://www.nationalgeographic.com/features/97/nyunderground/

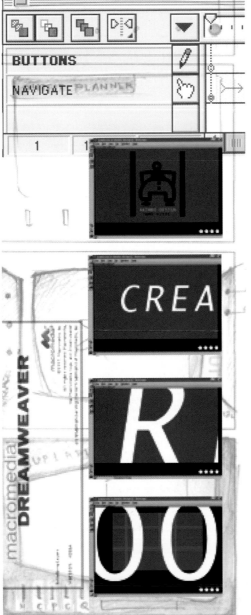

5

Akimbo Design
Designing with Technology

- ■ **Creative Process**
- ■ **Flash Animator**
- ■ **DHTML**
- ■ **Dreamweaver**

http://www.akimbodesign.com The word "akimbo" means to stand with hands on hips, elbows bending outward, in a sort of "harrumph" posture. It is derived from a late Middle English phrase—in a keen bow—which means with a sharp bent. As such, Akimbo is an appropriate name for a company founded by Ben Rigby and Ardith Ibañez, because these two have a sharp bent for transforming new tools and technologies into compelling web design content. This chapter profiles their work with Flash, DHTML, and their design process for the web.

Web Design Firm: Akimbo

Client: Akimbo, San Francisco, California

Original URL: http://www.akimbo.com

Archived URL: http://www.uncom.com/dcw2/

Type of Site: Company Demonstration Site and Portfolio

Server: Pentium 180

Operating System: UNIX BSD

Server Software: Apache

Webmaster: Ben Rigby

Producer: Ardith Ibañez

Art Direction: Ardith Ibañez

Illustration: Ardith Ibañez

Flash Animations: Ardith Ibañez, Ben Rigby

Sound: Ben Rigby

Development and Production Platforms: Mac/PC

Design Software: Macromedia's FreeHand, Flash, Director, Dreamweaver, Adobe Photoshop, Eyecandy, SoundEdit, BBedit, and HomeSite.

Programming: CGI in PERL, Java with Sun's JDK, JavaScript.

Akimbo's Creative Team

Akimbo Design was founded in February, 1997, by Ben Rigby and Ardith Ibañez. Ben occupies the CEO chair while Ardith is the Creative Director. They also employ about seven occasional contractors to do various parts of projects.

Ben graduated from Stanford where he studied science, technology, and society. His curriculum also included a few computer science classes. Following graduation, he worked as Technical Director of The Main Quad (www.mainquad.com), which subsequently merged with Student Advantage. While at the Quad, he did a lot of CGI programming, server management, and related work.

Ardith studied Design at Stanford before moving on to become a senior web designer at Macromedia. While there, she was a member of the team that created their current award-winning site. Before the web, Ardith was a painter and illustrator. (She still paints and illustrates in her "virtual" spare time.) With very little prior knowledge, she learned HTML, Photoshop, FreeHand, and other programs while on the job at Macromedia.

■ note

Ardith Ibañez, the Author

Aside from her founding presence at Akimbo, Ardith is also a co-author of two popular web-related books:

HTML Web Magic ■ Ardith Ibañez and Natalie Zee ■ Hayden Books ■ ISBN 1-56830-355-1

Creating Killer Interactive Web Sites: The Art of Integrating Interactivity and Design ■ Andrew Sather (Editor) ■ Ardith Ibañez and Bernie Dechant ■ Hayden Books ■ ISBN 1-56830-373-4

Akimbo's Design Philosophy

The central tenant of Akimbo's design philosophy is that they always attempt to engage the user through a combination of cutting-edge design and creative implementation of the latest technology. Ben explains it like this, "We compel with strong, bold colors and illustrations as well as an abundance of engaging animation. We create a look that makes viewers wonder, 'Hey! How did they do that?'"

Throughout Akimbo the navigation device, for example, is simply a set of interactive circles, animated in Flash. The circles are an interesting, uncluttered graphical element that relates to the opening dot animation of their splash screen. The look is sophisticated, consistent, and clean. "We like to experiment as much as possible in our designs," Ben continued, "using transparencies, creating different effects with background images, using rich or unusual and interesting graphics."

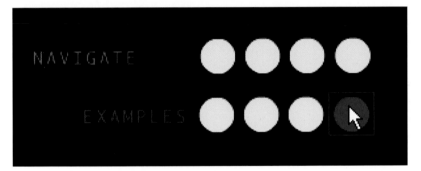

These animated circles, created in Flash, offer a consistent navigation device throughout the Akimbo site. The top set of circles is the default navigation device, the lower set shows the interactive response to a mouseover—prior to clicking.

Technically, the Akimbo team makes a point to minimize the number of connections to the server and to pare file sizes down in order to facilitate fast downloads. Ben said, "We wanted to maintain a stellar site, while at the same time making the download a breeze."

Many of their projects involve JavaScript, Shockwave, DHTML, and a number of interactivities that are driven by CGI. "But for the most part," Ben added, "we try to stick to the technologies that we are sure that our audience can view. We set up our pages so that, in the eventuality that they can't view something (like a Flash animation for instance), they are offered a seamless alternative."

According to Ben, other issues were addressed in the design of the Akimbo site. "We wanted to make navigation so simple, intuitive, and logical that family pets could get around our site. We always have a lot of information that we want to convey to the visitor. Here, one of the challenges was to present all the info in 'mind chunks,' pieces that the mind can easily grasp without getting overwhelmed or bored."

Another challenge that they addressed was to avoid creating a text-heavy site. Ben continued, "We try to express what we have to say in non-textual ways: through the site's design, layout, and the style of the graphics."

■ note

Controlling the Experience

Although Akimbo is dedicated to implementing leading-edge technologies and tools, they routinely offer a "seamless alternative" for visitors who may not be able to view their leading edge content.

For example, for those who didn't have the Flash plug-in, Akimbo's solution was to create an alternate GIF image map navigation bar to supplant the primary Flash-driven navigation bar. Details on this solution will be found in the section titled, "Deconstructing the Akimbo Splash Page Frames" within this chapter.

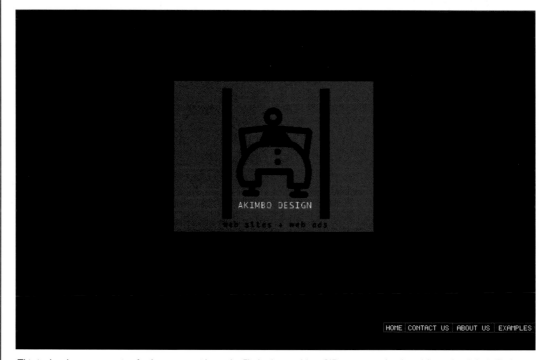

This is the alternate opening for browsers without the Flash plug-in. It's a GIF animation developed from the default Flash animation. Browsers that cannot display the GIF animation will display a static GIF image instead. Note that this page also has static GIF image map in the lower-right corner to replace the Flash-driven interactive navigation bar.

Inspiration and Brainstorming

When asked how Akimbo generates such original sites and design ideas to showcase emerging technologies, Ben responded, "We keep one trillion pencils around the office. Wherever you turn, there is a pencil. In fact I'm planning on constructing a utility belt type of thing that goes all around every wall that will hold pencils and markers in it. We keep sketchbooks on hand so that when an idea strikes, we can write it down. Most importantly, we use a method for brainstorming that was developed by a professor at Stanford University. It involves sitting down for a dedicated hour with the group that's doing the project. That's an hour for writing down every idea that crosses our minds. The key is to defer ALL judgment until the session is over, then we go back and pick through the ideas in the second meeting."

Ben continued, "We focus on design, on pushing web design to places that it hasn't gone before. We are dedicated to design exploration and to creating a challenging and inspiring work environment for ourselves. In order to keep our designs sharp and "cutting edge," we try to remind ourselves of what's going on in the world outside the web, of what matters to real people, people who don't use or haven't heard of the web. As I mentioned, all of us keep sketchbooks to keep the creative juices flowing and to archive cool ideas— both our own and those we derive from popular culture. We find that popular culture is a valuable resource and inspiration. We actually study MTV, movie opening credits, and fashion magazines. These are some of the things that inspire us. Though the web is its own medium, there are many things that we can learn from other media. Things that make us drop our jaws and say, "WOW!" We also make a point to devote time to personal projects and to create extracurricular web sites that haven't a thing to do with clients or business or selling."

Akimbo's Splash Page

The Akimbo opening splash page animation is an exciting, fast-paced demonstration of the power and potential of Flash 2. In only a few short seconds, the visitor not only learns what Akimbo does for their clients, but more importantly, a feeling for Akimbo's style is communicated.

Flash is a vector-based drawing program and animation development tool that creates ultra-compact, resolution independent images and streaming animations. Flash's small files can be transported across the web with astonishing speed, which enables the development of full-screen graphics and interactivity not possible with standard GIF and JPEG content. Flash includes the capability to create polished interactive buttons and images, as well as sound. You'll find several detailed profiles of working with Flash later in this chapter. Here is a breakdown of the processes involved in creating the opening splash page animation for the Akimbo site. This was done using the original, debut version of Flash Animator.

Step 1: Brainstorm

At the beginning of every project, Ben, Ardith, and other team members brainstorm to come up with every possible angle and cool idea. In brainstorming the opening splash page animation for the site, they made lists of adjectives that described their company. They wanted to ensure that whatever design or animation they might create would stay on target. They also decided upon a color palette, choosing different reds accented by a dark gray.

Step 2: Storyboard

Little did they know they'd use many of those actual words in their splash screen movie! After brainstorming, they mapped out a general plan for the animation. What goes first? Last? One of the words chosen to describe their designs was "sexy." Although it's an unusual design adjective, they thought it would grab people's attention, so that word appears first. They also decided to conclude the movie with the logo and company name in order to build momentum for their enterprise via brand recognition.

Step 3: Animate Dots

Ben and Ardith wanted to create an electronic, hi-tech, yet hip look. They figured that dots flashing onscreen would yield a captivating and fun, machine-like look. So Ardith aligned the dots in four columns: three on the left and one on the right. Every couple of frames, different groups of dots appear in different areas of the columns in varied shades of red or gray.

Step 4: Animate the Words

Movie credits have inspired many of Akimbo's animations that involve typography. For this animation, they decided to fade their list of words in and out of the screen. The fade effect was created painstakingly by changing the color of each word or phrase on a frame-by-frame basis. Again, if Ardith were to redo this movie today, she'd make good advantage of Flash 2's new color tweening capability. Instead of needing four versions of one word in four different colors, with Flash 2 she could use just one word. It

would be made it into a Symbol Library item, which would also significantly reduce file size and download time. Then the color change could be induced via Menu: Modify: Element and the colors would have been animated.

One of the words, fast, lent itself to being animated across the screen "like a little roadrunner," Ardith said. They were not terribly concerned with legibility; they just wanted it to look cool. So she made numerous overlaps and timed things so that the animation is slow enough to read some words, yet fast enough to deliver an up-tempo, overall cool techno-beat impression.

Step 5: Animate the Logo

Ardith and Ben also decided to explore ways of playing with the components of their logo. Starting with the parallel bars in the logo, they made it look like the Akimbo man was rising in an open elevator. This part of the animation used layers and tweening to move things up, down, left, and right.

Step 6: Repurpose the Original Movie

When the new Flash 2 became available, Ben and Ardith decided to add something fresh to the homepage splash animation, but they still liked the original dot movie. Luckily, adding a new scene to a Flash Animation is easy with the insert scene feature of Flash 2. The new animation sequence was inspired by the opening credits from the movie *Trainspotting* and was an experiment of sorts.

The primary components of the new sequence contained horizontal lines that move up and down, vertical lines in two colors of red that move side to side, and a modified black "letterbox," which scales horizontally and vertically during the movie.

Step 7: Add and Animate Text

To animate these components, Ardith used the same simple techniques employed in step 4. She moved text left, right, and animated changes in the size and scale of components.

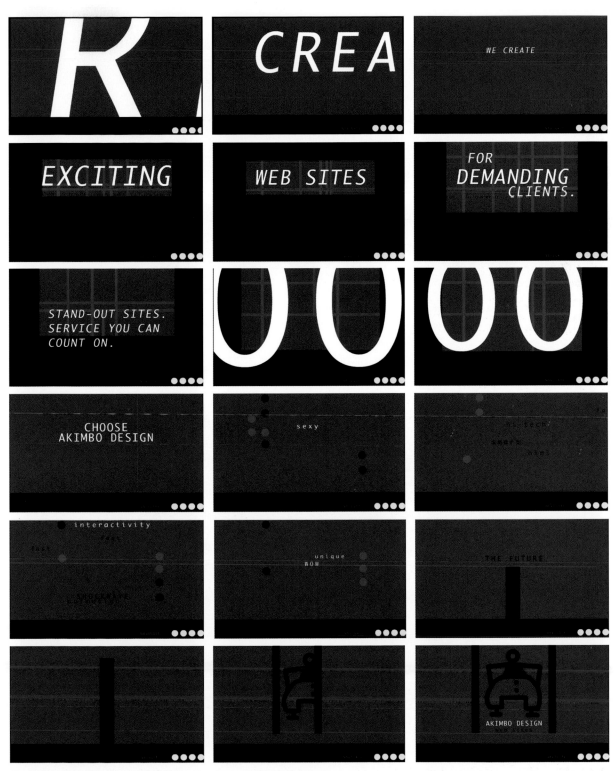

Scenes from Akimbo's opening Splash Page animation, created in Flash Animator.

■ note

The Flash/FreeHand/Illustrator Connection

If you already know Macromedia FreeHand or Adobe Illustrator, it's possible to leverage those skills to develop content and then animate that content with Flash. Both these drawing programs offer versatile drawing tools that are far more extensive than those of Flash. When creating an animation like the Akimbo dots sequence, either FreeHand or Illustrator would have given Ardith precise control over the placement and alignment of her artwork.

In order to generate a Flash animation with content developed in Illustrator, simply save the content as a series of individual Illustrator files (AI or EPS), numbered sequentially, and then import them to Flash from the Menu File: Import. A good important trick is to set the Flash Movie Dimension to equal the dimensions of the Illustrator file before importing. Otherwise, the Illustrator content is clipped. Flash Movie dimensions are easily modified from the Menu Modify: Movie, which launches the Movie Properties Dialog.

Recently, there's been a convergence effort at Macromedia to facilitate swapping content between programs. As a result, FreeHand artwork can now be readily animated into Flash movies without importing it into Flash. (Of course, you may opt to import to Flash and tweak things there, too, but you don't have to.) Animations can be generated from FreeHand files with either the FreeHand 7 Xtra, which ships with both FreeHand and Flash, or with the more advanced FreeHand Animation Power Pack, which is available at http://www.macromedia.com/software/freehand/animpowerpack/.

The Power Pack includes both the new Flash Writer Xtra (which has more features than the FreeHand 7 Xtra) and the Release to Layers Xtra. Flash Writer Xtra provides options to use layers and/or pages as frames of animation. It also delivers improved text options to control whether text arrives in Flash 2 as editable text, vector paths, or is completely omitted. The power of the Release to Layers Xtra is that it enables blend steps to be used as discrete frames in an animation. Support for the browser-safe palette, as well as a URL editor, is also included.

For more information, visit the following URLs: http://www.macromedia.com/software/flash/ http://www.macromedia.com/support/flash/.

Flash Rollovers

Throughout this book, we have examined various methods for delivering interactive rollover buttons. Qaswa used Shockwave, while Bosch, and National Geographic's "New York Underground" used different forms of JavaScript and Java applets.

Flash has many advantages over the other techniques we've profiled so far, in that

- no special code is required

- there is no need for an array

- the buttons themselves don't have to be created in Photoshop or another imaging program, as a result of Macromedia's convergence efforts, the same Flash buttons can be delivered as either Flash, JavaScript, RealSystems, or all three manner of content simultaneously.

This is the default appearance of the Navbar: NAVIGATE is visible with four unmarked buttons adjacent.

Mousing over each button shows the destination of each link. This button takes the visitor to the "Company Info" area of the site. Note how the main window of the FRAMESET reflects the visitor's position at "Mission," which is the opening page of the "Company Info" area.

Flash Interface Overview

It should be noted that all the Akimbo Flash Animations were created in the original version of Flash. The newer version, Flash 2, has many valuable features that were unavailable in the first release. Consequently, there are a number of parts that are now a lot easier to create in different ways, especially transitioning between (inbetweening) the colors.

For further reference, there are many excellent Flash tutorials online. A tutorial titled, "Buttoning up Flash and Interactivity" by Ken Milburn and Janine Warner, authors of Ventana's Flash 2 Web Animation Book, teaches you how to make rollover buttons. You'll find other great tutorials in addition to theirs at: http://www.macromedia.com/support/flash/how/expert/.

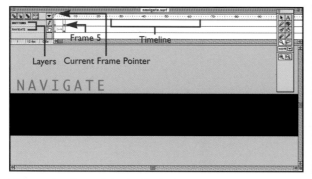

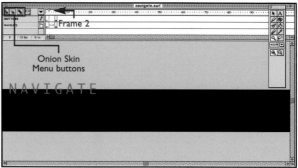

The completed "movie" for the Akimbo Navbar is shown here, open at frame 1. Over the course of five frames, the word "Navigate" is animated down over the black bar. Changing-state buttons appear in the frame 5. Across the top of this window is the Flash Timeline with the Current Frame Pointer. The Current Frame Pointer is the tiny triangle immediately above the notch for frame 1, which is at the extreme left of the Timeline. Note also that there are two Layers showing in this Timeline: BUTTONS and NAVIGATE.

Above the Layer's Names are three buttons on the left that control Onion Skin settings, while the button to the right is the Onion Skin Menu Button. The Onion Skin feature of Flash makes it easy to develop a sequence of frames because it shows dimmed views of prior and subsequent frames. Onion skinning can help an animator see what has already been drawn and better plan for what to draw next. Note here that the Current Frame Pointer triangle on the Timeline has been moved to frame 2 and that the word "Navigate" has begun to animate down over the black bar. Note, too, the Tool Box at the extreme right, floating over the Animation Window.

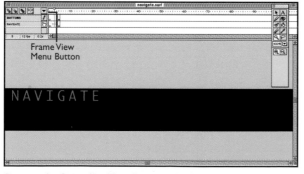

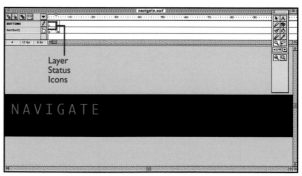

Between the Onion Skin Menu Button and the Timeline Header is a triangular button located topmost in a stack of three buttons, called the Frame View Menu Button. The Frame View Menu Button is used to modify the size of the Frame Views, meaning that the tiny rectangles with dots (and an arrow running through the Navigate Layer's frames) can be resized Small, Normal, Large, and so on. Note that animation has proceeded to the frame 3 and that the word "Navigate" has moved further down over the black bar.

Beneath the Frame View Menu Button are two more buttons (which reside between the Layer Names and the Frames within the Timeline). Both these buttons are the Layer Status Icons for their associated Layers. Clicking one of these buttons opens the Layer Menu for that Layer, which hosts options to change the status of the Layer. Options include Current, Normal, Locked, Hidden, Show All, Hide Others, and Lock Others to name a few. Again, the animation has proceeded to frame 4.

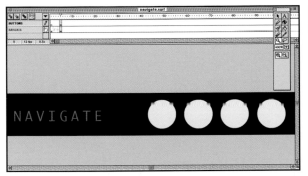

Now the animation has proceeded to frame 5. The word "Navigate" has arrived at its destination over the black bar and the navigation buttons have appeared. These buttons were built independently of this particular animation, saved as symbols and further modified by assigning button behavior to them. The use of symbols within Flash permits a component to be reused throughout the movie, thus drastically reducing the file size of the final movie. This delivers fantastic benefits when animations are transferred over the web. Buttons are a specific type of symbol, as will be shown in the next section.

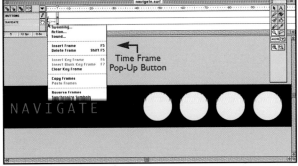

Note that a tiny rectangle (with a dot in the middle of it) appears within each Layer beneath the Current Frame Pointer for each frame as it becomes active. This is the Frame Pop-up Button. Clicking this button opens the Frame Pop-up Menu. (Shown here is the Frame Pop-up Menu for frame 1 of the Navigate Layer.) Many controls for fine-tuning and working with animation frames are located in the Frame Pop-up Menu.

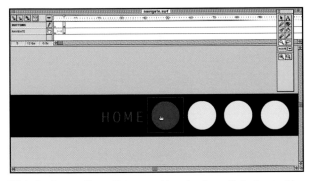

With the Current Frame Pointer positioned at frame 5, the interactivity of the Navbar can be explored. Mousing over various buttons invokes the word that is associated with each button. Mousing over the first button reveals that it has been set to bring up the word "Home." Note that all the type for the words in these Flash animations is set directly in Flash. (It could also have been set in another program, such as Illustrator or FreeHand.) When used within the web site, clicking this button launches that page into the main frame of the frameset. Access to the URL assignment capability (and many other related actions) of Flash is via the Action... option of the Frame pop-up menu.

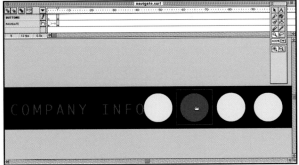

With the Current Frame Pointer still positioned at frame 5, the second button reveals its association with the "Company Info" area of the site. The "Company Info" button is set to launch the main frame of the frame set. Mousing over the third button launches the "Contact Us" area, while the fourth button links to the "Examples" area.

■ step-by-step

Flash Buttons and Symbols

Creating a set of changing-state interactive buttons may seem daunting to anyone who hasn't done it before. This next section profiles the process used by Akimbo for their navigation bar. The technique ranges from setting the graphics up as buttons, to saving the assembly as a symbol, and then assigning a URL and/or action to each button.

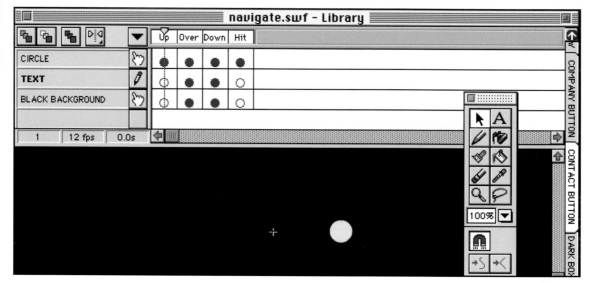

Step 1: The artwork was first created in Flash and then a symbol produced. To set up the symbol, they chose Insert: Create Symbol, which opened the Symbol Properties dialog in order to name the button. The Button Behavior box was checked next, which opened a new scene that was already preprogrammed with the Up, Over, Down and Hit states.

Step 2: A circle was drawn first. At frame 2, Insert Frame was chosen from the Frame Pop-up. Next, from the Frame Pop-up, Insert Key Frame was chosen. Now the graphic (or symbol) was available to edit, change, delete, or substitute. **Note:** there are three layers here, the Up position used only two layers (the background counts!) while the Over position utilized three layers.

Step 3: The Down position was created by clicking frame 3 and choosing Insert Frame, then Insert Key Frame from the Frame pop-up. Again, the graphic was available to be edited. All three layers were utilized here too. This was really not difficult to do!

Step 4: The Hit position used two layers. Again, the procedure for associating the graphic was the same as before. Simply choose Insert Frame followed by Insert Key Frame from the Frame Pop-up.

Frame Tags, Attributes, and Values

Akimbo used frames on their site in a transparent aesthetically pleasing manner. All too often, frames produce a perplexing (and ugly) clutter of scrollbars and obscured content.

Fundamentally, frames permit nesting of HTML pages. They allow you to put pages within pages and have some of the pages change while others don't. Imagine dividing a screen into three vertical sections and putting a different HTML page within each section. This would actually involve four frames, instead of three! The initial frame holds the three internal frames and is called the Frameset. Combining frames with targets enables one region of a frame to launch different regions within a frameset.

What follows are some common tags, attributes and values for frames. The elements, <FRAMESET><FRAME></FRAME></FRAMESET>, are "tags." Other items are either "attributes" or "values."

<FRAMESET>	Initiates the beginning of a FRAMESET
ROWS="n,n"	Defines the ROWS within the FRAMESET, with either a number, percentage (%), or *. Thus, "n" is a numeric "value", "%", or "*."
COLS=""	Defines the COLUMNs within the FRAMESET, using either a number, percentage (%), or *. Thus, "n" is a numeric "value", "%", or "*."
FRAMEBORDER="0"	The variable "0" eliminates BORDERs on the FRAMEs, whereas a value of "1" provides a single pixel BORDER. "NO" or "YES" are also accepted values.
BORDER="FALSE"	Controls the thickness of FRAME BORDERs and must be used in the outermost FRAMESET. It works the same as the FRAMEBORDER. Here, "FALSE" is equivalent to "0" and other variables are numeric.
FRAMESPACING="0"	(Internet Explorer only) The variable"0" dictates that there is no spacing (or padding) between the FRAMES. Essentially, Explorer adds control for BORDER thickness.
<FRAME>	Defines the beginning of a FRAME, within a FRAMESET.
NAME=	Permits the FRAME to be named so that the FRAME can be targeted.
SRC=""	Used in conjunction with the TARGET attribute, a file (graphic or HTML) can open an HTML file within another FRAME of the FRAMESET.

TARGET="name"	Designates which specific FRAME content loads into.
TARGET=""	The following TARGET presets initiate: _blank: a blank new window _self: the same window as the link _parent: the parent frameset _top: the full body of the window
SCROLLING="NO"	Controls FRAME SCROLLING, but it is not consistent across brow-sers. The default value is "auto"; "yes" or "no" are other values.
NORESIZE	Prevents the user from resizing individual FRAMES.
MARGINHEIGHT=1	Controls the height of the space between the frame edge and its contents. The value cannot be less than "1."
MARGINWIDTH=1	Controls the width of the space between the FRAME edge and its contents. The value cannot be less than "1."
FRAMEBORDER="0"	Controls the border of a single FRAME and recognized values are "yes" or "1" and "no" or "0." It is not implemented consistently across browsers.
</FRAME>	This closing container is often omitted and should not be. It defines the end of a FRAME within a FRAMESET.
</FRAMESET>	Defines the end of a FRAMESET.
<NOFRAMES>	Defines what appears in browsers that don't support FRAMES ability.
</NOFRAMES>	Closing container for the NOFRAMES content, which may occur either before or after the FRAMESET tags.

Deconstructing Akimbo's Splash Page Frames

Note that this code is written in what may be regarded as exemplary HTML style. What does that mean? It means that the tags are consistently expressed in all capitals, while the content is consistently expressed in lowercase. This makes it far easier to read and distinguish code from content. Furthermore, the code is symmetrically arrayed on the page in "butterfly fashion." This makes it easy to see the relationships between opening tags and closing tags. Although disorganized code can work just as well as exemplary code (the browser doesn't care), editing code of this quality is much easier—and it's almost a pleasure to read. This should be evident when you begin to read the code which follows.

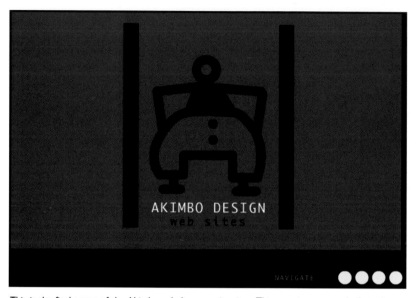

This is the final scene of the Akimbo splash page animation. This page is composed of two borderless frames. The upper (main) frame contains the animation and the lower (navigation) frame contains the Navbar. The navigation bar remains constant, while the upper frame is updated to reflect choices that the visitor may make either within the main frame or the navigation frame.

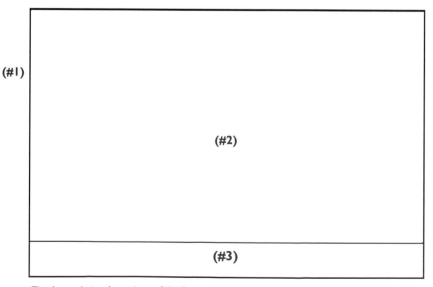

This figure shows the regions of the frameset, labeled #1, #2, and #3. It should help you understand the deconstruction below.

■ code

```
<HTML>
<HEAD>
    <TITLE>¦¦ welcome to akimbo design ¦¦</TITLE>
    <META NAME="description" CONTENT="Akimbo Design creates hip and exciting web sites!">
    <META NAME="keywords" CONTENT="Akimbo Design, web sites, web design, hip, exciting">
</HEAD>
```

■ 1
```
            <FRAMESET ROWS="*,50"
            FRAMEBORDER="0"
            BORDER="0"
            FRAMESPACING="0"
            FRAMEPADDING="0"
            BORDERCOLOR="#990000">
```

■ 2
```
            <FRAME SRC="/site/main.html"
            NAME="main"
            MARGINWIDTH=0
            SCROLLING="auto"
            NORESIZE
            FRAMEBORDER="0"
            BORDER="0"
            FRAMESPACING="0"
            FRAMEPADDING="0">
```

■ 3
```
            <FRAME SRC="/site/navigation.html"
            NAME="navigation"
            SCROLLING="no"
            NORESIZE
            FRAMEBORDER="0"
            BORDER="0"
            FRAMESPACING="0"
            FRAMEPADDING="0">
```

■ 4
```
<NOFRAMES>
<HEAD>
    <TITLE>¦¦ welcome to akimbo design ¦¦</TITLE>
    <META NAME="description" CONTENT="Akimbo Design creates hip and exciting web sites!">
    <META NAME="keywords" CONTENT="Akimbo Design, web sites, web design, hip, exciting">
</HEAD>
    <BODY BGCOLOR="#990000" TEXT="#CCCC99">
<CENTER>
<IMG SRC="/images/logos/stampman.static.gif" WIDTH="180" HEIGHT="209" BORDER="0" ALT="welcome
to akimbo design. more to come...">
```

■ 5
```
<PRE>
<FONT SIZE="-1">
Akimbo Design creates hip and exciting web sites!<BR>
You are using an older browser. <BR>
A site for you folks is<P>

c  o  m  i  n  g  s  o  o  n
</FONT>
</PRE>
```

```
■ 6 </CENTER>
    </BODY>
    </HTML>
    </NOFRAMES>
    </FRAMESET>
    </HTML>

    #2 main.html

■ 7 <BASE HREF="http://www.akimbodesign.com/site/">
    <HTML>
    <HEAD>
        <TITLE>a k i m b o * d e s i g n</TITLE>
    </HEAD>
        <BODY BGCOLOR="#000000" TEXT="#CCCC99" VLINK="white" ALINK="yellow" LINK="black">
    <CENTER>

■ 8 <!-- BEGIN FLASH MOVIE -->
    <!-- Internet Explorer 3.0 will recognize this object tag and download the control if it is not
    already present -->

■ 9     <OBJECT CLASSID="clsid:D27CDB6E-AE6D-11cf-96B8-444553540000"
        CODEBASE="http://active.macromedia.com/flash2/cabs/swflash.cab" WIDTH="100%" HEIGHT="99%">

■ 10    <PARAM NAME="Movie" VALUE="http://www.akimbodesign.com/images/flash/home.spl">
    <PARAM NAME="quality" VALUE="high">
    <PARAM NAME="Loop" VALUE="true">
    <PARAM NAME="bgcolor" VALUE="#990000">

■ 11 <!-- This section will be processed by Netscape 2.0 or later -->

■ 12 <SCRIPT LANGUAGE="JavaScript">

    <!--
    if ( (navigator.mimeTypes &&
    navigator.mimeTypes["application/futuresplash"] &&
            navigator.mimeTypes["application/futuresplash"].enabledPlugin) ||
            (document.cookie && (document.cookie.indexOf("ShockwaveFlash=1") >=
    0)) ) {

■ 13        // Netscape 3.0 with the plug-in installed, use it...
            document.write('<EMBED
        SRC="http://www.akimbodesign.com/images/flash/home.spl"
        PLUGINSPAGE="/shockwave/download/index.cgi?P1_Prod_Version=ShockwaveFlash"
        TYPE=application/futuresplash WIDTH="100%" HEIGHT="99%" LOOP="true"
        QUALITY="high" BGCOLOR="#990000">')
    } else {

■ 14        // They are using Netscape 2.0 or there is no plug-in installed
            // Note we will get here if they have the plug-in w/ Navigator 2.0
            //but there is no way for us to detect this configuration
            // Display an animated GIF here

■ 15    document.write('<TABLE WIDTH=100% HEIGHT=100%><TR>');
    document.write('<TD VALIGN=CENTER ALIGN=CENTER>');
            document.write('<IMG
        SRC="http://www.akimbodesign.com/images/logos/stampman.gif" ALT="main logo
        animation" HSPACE=30 WIDTH=288 HEIGHT=216>')
    document.write('</TD></TR></TABLE>');
    }
```

```
■ 16  </SCRIPT>

■ 17  <!-- Other browsers will simply display this GIF file -->
      <NOEMBED>
      IMG SRC="http://www.akimbodesign.com/images/logos/stampman.gif" HSPACE=30
      WIDTH=288 HEIGHT=216>
      </NOEMBED>
      </OBJECT>
      </BODY>
      </HTML>

      #3 navigation.html
■ 18  <!--If the user doesn't have flash installed, they will see a gif image map navigation graphic and
      never know that they are missing out on the Flash version. Flash is an Active-X component on
      Explorer, while on Netscape it's a plug-in, meaning that it conforms to Netscape's standard for all
      other plugins.
      -->

      <HTML>
      <HEAD>
          <TITLE>a k i m b o * d e s i g n</TITLE>
      </HEAD>
          <BODY BGCOLOR="#000000" TEXT="#CCCC99" VLINK="white" ALINK="yellow" LINK="black">
      <CENTER>

■ 19  <!-- BEGIN FLASH MOVIE -->

      <!-- Internet Explorer 3.0 will recognize this object tag and download the control if it is not
      already present -->

■ 20      <OBJECT CLASSID="clsid:D27CDB6E-AE6D-11cf-96B8-444553540000"
          CODEBASE="http://active.macromedia.com/flash2/cabs/swflash.cab" WIDTH="100%" HEIGHT="73%">
          <PARAM NAME="Movie" VALUE="http://www.akimbodesign.com/images/flash/navigate.swf">
          <PARAM NAME="quality" VALUE="best">
          <PARAM NAME="Loop" VALUE="false">
          <PARAM NAME="Salign" VALUE="tr">
          <PARAM NAME="bgcolor" VALUE="#000000">

■ 21  <!-- This section will be processed by Netscape 2.0 or later -->
      <SCRIPT LANGUAGE="JavaScript">

      <!--if ( (navigator.mimeTypes && navigator.mimeTypes["application/futuresplash"] &&
      navigator.mimeTypes["application/futuresplash"].enabledPlugin) ||
          (document.cookie && (document.cookie.indexOf("ShockwaveFlash=1") >=
      0)) ) {

          // Netscape 3.0 with the plug-in installed, use it...
          document.write('<EMBED
          SRC="http://www.akimbodesign.com/images/flash/navigate.swf"
          PLUGINSPAGE="/shockwave/download/index.cgi?P1_Prod_Version=ShockwaveFlash"
          TYPE=application/futuresplash WIDTH=100% HEIGHT=80% VALIGN=top SALIGN=tr
          LOOP=false QUALITY=best BGCOLOR="#000000">')
      } else {

          // They are using Netscape 2.0 or there is no plug-in installed
          // Note we will get here if they have the plug-in w/ Navigator 2.0
          //but there is no way for us to detect this configuration
          // Display an animated GIF here
          document.write('<IMG USEMAP="#navbar"
      SRC="http://www.akimbodesign.com/images/nav/navigation.gif" WIDTH="220" HEIGHT="15" ALIGN="right">')
      }
```

```
■ 22  </SCRIPT>

■ 23  <!-- Other browsers will simply display this GIF file -->
      <NOEMBED>
      <IMG USEMAP="#navbar"
      SRC="http://www.akimbodesign.com/images/nav/navigation.gif" WIDTH="220" HEIGHT="15" ALIGN="right">
      </NOEMBED>
      </OBJECT>

■ 24  <!--image map for the non-flash gif navigation-->
      <MAP NAME="navbar">
      <AREA SHAPE=rect COORDS="0,1,31,14" HREF="main.html" TARGET="main" >
      <AREA SHAPE=rect COORDS="32,0,100,14" HREF="/site/company/contact.html" TARGET="main">
      <AREA SHAPE=rect COORDS="101,0,60,14" HREF="/site/company/index.html" TARGET="main">
      <AREA SHAPE=rect COORDS="161,0,220,14" HREF="/site/examples/index.html" TARGET="main">
      <AREA SHAPE=default HREF="/site/company/index.html"   TARGET="main">
      </MAP>
      </BODY>
      </HTML>
```

■ deconstruction

#1 home.html

■ **1** FRAMESET initiates the main FRAMES window which will contain all of the proceeding HTML documents. The value of the ROWS attribute "*,50" establishes that the first ROW (*), which contains the "main" FRAME, occupies whatever space remains after the second row takes its allotted height of 50 pixels. The (*) symbol is like a wildcard; it always means whatever space is left over. If the end user stretches his or her browser up or down, the bottom frame will maintain a fixed position of 50 pixels and the top frame will scale. Subsequent attributes establish that the FRAMESET has no FRAMEBORDER, BORDER, FRAMESPACING, FRAMEPADDING, and that the BORDERCOLOR will be the same deep red color used for the animation's background.

■ **2** SRC= "/site/main.html" is the relative URL (see glossary) for the content that will be loaded (initially) in this FRAME. The attribute NAME= "main" specifies the name for this FRAME. Much of the power of FRAMES revolves around the capability to NAME a FRAME and direct pages to open in specific, named FRAMES.

■ **3** This is the second of two FRAMES; the bottom ROW of the FRAMESET, contains the Navbar content throughout the site. No matter where the visitor travels within this site, the bottom FRAME and its contents remain constant. SRC="/site/navigation.html" is the relative URL for the Navbar content. NAME= "navigation" specifies the name of this FRAME. SCROLLING= "auto" tells the browser to only use scrollbars if the contents of the FRAME exceed the FRAME'S specified dimensions.

■ **4** The <NOFRAMES> tag is where alternative content is placed for FRAMES-challenged browsers.

■ **5** The <PRE></PRE> tags ensure that the content is laid out on the page p-r-e-c-i-s-e-l-y as it was entered. It allowed Akimbo designers to use more playful typography, with spaces between the letters "coming soon." It also usually forces most browsers to display a monospaced font (see glossary).

■ **6** The closing tags for this page must include </NO FRAMES> and </FRAMESET>. Note that the NOFRAMES content is preceded by </BODY></HTML>, which closes off the <NOFRAMES> content.

#2 main.html

■ **7** The BASE tag causes relative URLs to proceed from the new URL specified by the BASE tag.

■ **8** Here's a good use of comment tags <!-- and --> to place explanations within an HTML document. Such explanations are hidden from visitors (unless, of course, they access the source code) and are useful guideposts when it comes time to troubleshoot, edit, or update the page.

■ **9** The OBJECT tag is used here instead of either the EMBED tag. In the W3C's official spec for HTML 4.0, the OBJECT tag is favored over the EMBED tag. There are potential problems associated with the use of the OBJECT tag regardless, due to backwards compatibility issues between the browsers, but that's not a problem here because OBJECT tag is implemented only as one of several alternatives for delivering contents for this page. This OBJECT tag is primarily directed at Internet Explorer 3.0, although both the 4.0 Explorer and Navigator browsers should be capable of delivering this content. If the browser is incapable of handling this content, it skips either to line [11] or line [13]. CLASSID is used to provide the name of the file containing the OBJECT. CODEBASE is used to provide the URL for the OBJECT. Together, the CLASSID and CODEBASE are used to identify, locate, and download the desired OBJECT. The WIDTH and HEIGHT attributes are used to specify the dimensions of the content, which is displayed via the OBJECT tag. Here, the OBJECT is a Flash movie.

■ **10** These parameters are used to pass instructions to the OBJECT discussed at [9] above. NAME attributes are used to specify instructions. For example, NAME="Movie" instructs the OBJECT to play the movie that is further defined by the attribute VALUE="http://www.akimbodesign.com/images/flash/home.spl." The NAME parameters are usually specified by the file format; in this case, the file format is a Flash movie (.spl file.) Similarly, NAME="quality" instructs the OBJECT with VALUE="high" to control the quality of the Flash movie. NAME="Loop" instructs the movie to repeat indefinitely.

■ **11** This comment indicates that the following content is directed at Netscape 2.0 or later. The following code is the first of three alternatives that will seamlessly provide content for browsers that could not handle the OBJECT tag at [9].

■ **12** The first line here tells the browser that the following code is Java Script. Subsequent JavaScript code generates an "if" statement to detect support for either Future Splash or Shockwave Flash plug-ins. Note that Future Splash was the original name of Flash Animator before Macromedia acquired the program. Netscape 2.0 with appropriate plug-ins proceeds to the EMBED tag at [13].

■ **13** If the browser is Netscape 3.0 and equipped with the plug-ins, it proceeds to the EMBED tag, driven by the JavaScript document.write. The attributes of the EMBED tag specify the source SRC to be embedded, and the location PLUGINSPAGE of the plug-in (should it need to be downloaded), as well as the TYPE, WIDTH, HEIGHT, LOOP, QUALITY, and BGCOLOR for the movie.

■ **14** Another comment to clarify what's going on as the browser reads the page looking for something it's capable of displaying.

■ **15** Here's the second alternative, again driven by a series of JavaScript document.write instructions. These are simply HTML tags to assemble a TABLE containing a static GIF image.

■ **16** The end of the JavaScript is </SCRIPT>.

■ **17** Now for the third alternative, contained by <NOEMBED> </NOEMBED> tags. Only the lowliest of browsers will display this content—again, the static GIF from [15] above. What's the difference between this and [15]? The previous content is displayed within a TABLE layout, which ensures controlled optimal placement within the FRAME. A standard closing tag follows, as this is the end of this HTML document.

#3 navigation.html

■ **18** This page, navigation.html, supplies the content for the second ROW of the FRAMESET that was initiated at [3], home.html. Navigation.html will remain constant through the visitor's exploration of the site because it is the navigation device. The interactivity of the Navbar is driven by a Flash movie. Again, note how the comment helps to explain what's happening technically on this page. Although the page runs equally well without such comments, as stated above, comments make it easier to understand the code when it's necessary to edit or revise.

■ **19** Most of the code on this page mirrors the code employed on main.html. Refer to [8].

■ **20** With the exception of the specific movie, this code is the same as [9] and [10]. Note that, although this is a navigation device, no URLs are included with this movie. That's because the interactivities—and consequently the URLs—are contained within the Flash movie itself.

■ **21** This code is exactly the same as the code employed at [11] through [15].

■ **22** This is the end of the JavaScript.

■ **23** This differs from the code at [16] only in that this GIF file is employed as an image map. For more information on image maps, refer to Chapter 3, "Bosch Tools."

■ **24** These are the URLs associated with the button areas of the Navbar image map.

An Introduction to DHTML

DHTML, or Dynamic HTML, is one of the hottest new buzzwords in web authoring today. DHTML is not really a single technology; it is a collection of existing HTML and programming techniques when combined, enable more interactivity than HTML currently affords.

DHTML specifically combines: CSS (**C**ascading **S**tyle **S**heets), JavaScript, and a "document object model" that allows the inclusion of other scripting languages, such as Active X or VB Script. Some of the coolest features DHTML offers are:

- User-activated drag and drop capabilities.

- Complex animated mouse events.

- Immediate response.

- Web pages that behave like powerful applications rather than static content.

- Exacting control of the look and behavior of a page across platforms including fonts, color, size, positioning, and layering of content.

- Enhanced continuity throughout a site.

- Ease of updating content.

- Style sheets and layering, which means that content layers can be overlaid and turned on or off subject to a visitor's interaction with the page.

Some of the disadvantages to DHTML are:

- Content has to be preloaded before it displays. Anytime there is a delay on the web, it can spell trouble for a site. End-users are not known for waiting around too long.

- Standards for the components of DHTML are not supported equally between browsers. Netscape and IE support CSS and JavaScript slightly differently. This makes coding DHTML a nightmare.

- Because there are no established standards, many browsers will not be able to display DHTML content properly. DHTML will not become a standard for a long time because of these backwards compatibility issues and the need for two sets of pages—one that supports DHTML and another that does not.

When asked his opinions about the pros and cons of DHTML, Ben responded, "Working with DHTML is a lot more gratifying to us than straight HTML because of the enhanced interactivity and dynamic functionality it offers. DHTML is helping us move more towards a CD-ROM type experience, as opposed to a single "web page" experience."

In terms of the drawbacks due to the long wait times of preloading the content, he replied, "It doesn't seem to me that it's any different than waiting for a QuickTime movie to download. Only once the information is there, then everything is unbelievably fast and responsive. The wait is worth it."

Ben clarified that it is possible to make the wait for DHTML less painful. "It was our choice to make the preloading screen. Without it, the page would load like any other HTML document; you'd see image icons until the images loaded. As long as you didn't put too many images on your page, the load and load time would be pretty much the same as a normal HTML document."

With DHTML, you can control image loading. For example, in the Superfly project, Ben wrote an extensive image loading management system that only loaded the images that were needed. The initial load was around 60K (which is admittedly a bit high for a normal page, but not extravagant). The other 150K of images are not loaded until the user requests them—similar to a series of standard HTML documents.

In regards to the browser compatibility issues, Ben continued, "We aim to make cross-platform sites and shy away from proprietary components like ActiveX, which only works on Internet Explorer. We build sites for both Netscape, Explorer, and non-DHTML compliant browsers."

Superfly Fashions

Ardith had special inroads into Macromedia because she once worked there as a senior web designer! Because of her good connections, Akimbo was included among a select few companies asked to bid on developing a demo showcase for Macromedia's DHTML site at http://www.dhtmlzone.com/. They submitted their Superfly Fashions concept for the site by showing storyboards and samples, and were awarded the contract.

Macromedia's DHTML-zone site is well worth visiting, as it includes lots of educational materials about authoring DHTML content. The Superfly Fashions site is presented as a both a showcase and tutorial. Each screen within the demo includes a full-fledged explanation about how it was made.

Akimbo developed the Superfly Fashions site before any DHTML authoring tools existed and programmed the site entirely from scratch, using HTML and JavaScript. A host of innovative techniques were developed during the process, many of which are fully documented on the site. Today, they might have chosen to program some of it in Dreamweaver, a visual DHTML editor from Macromedia. Dreamweaver is covered later in this chapter.

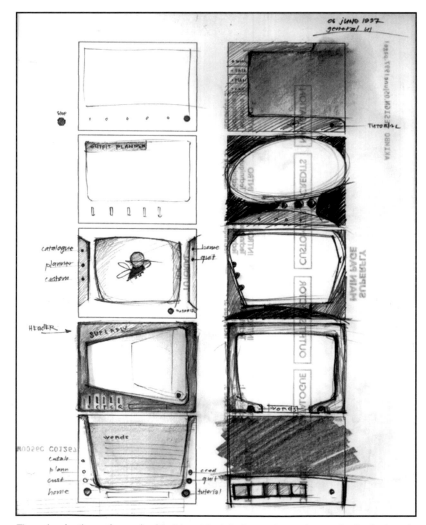

These thumbnails are the result of Ardith and Ben's brainstorming sessions to develop looks and concepts for the Superfly site they developed for Macromedia .

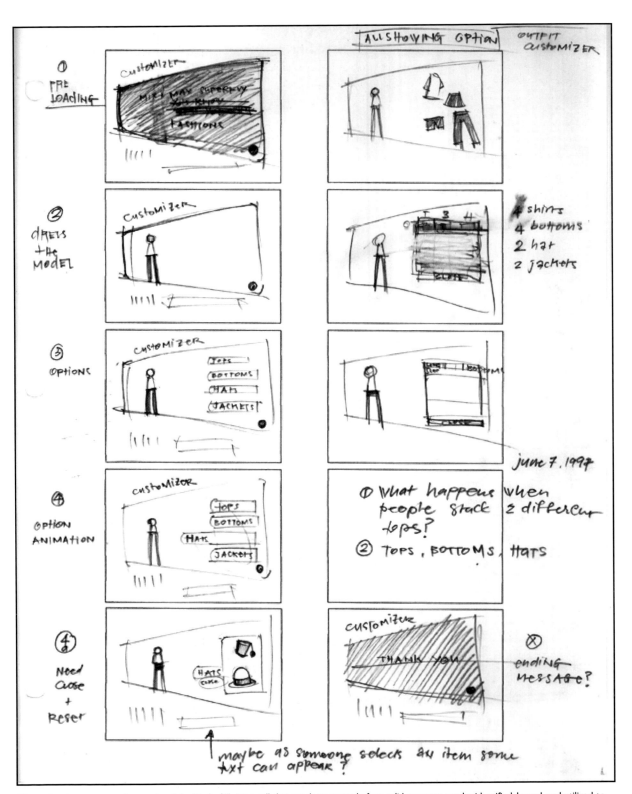

These sketches are a good example of the kind of "letting go" that needs to occur before solid concepts can be identified, honed, and utilized to develop an award-winning site.

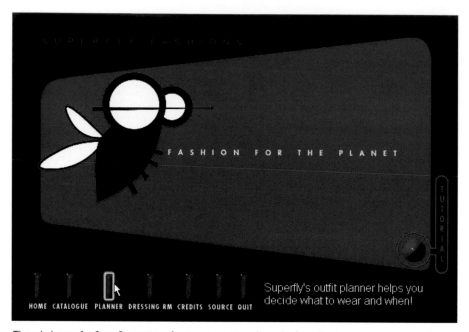

The splash page for Superfly consists of a zippy animation where the Superfly character buzzes around before landing here on the screen. In order to achieve this animation effect, Ben Rigby wrote a Timeline-based movement routine using JavaScript. This involved the JavaScript "layer" feature and moved the art-work from point to point. The JavaScript had to be written two different ways to accommodate Netscape and the other to suit Internet Explorer.

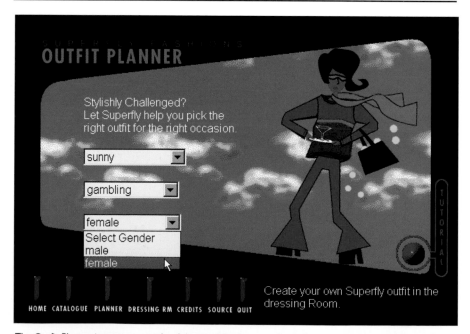

The Outfit Planner is a great example of the precision layout and complex interactivity capabilities made possible with DHTML. Note the Tutorial button to the right side of the screen. If you click the tutorial button a new page appears with a detailed description of the DHTML code used to create it! This site is a great place to obtain an introduction to DHTML.

Visitors to this page can move any item to dress the model by clicking and dragging clothing, wigs, and shoes onto the body shape. This technique was also created using JavaScript and "event capturing." An "event capture" in JavaScript is able to capture the mouse's movements. The browser is able to detect where the mouse is, and if it is pressed down or not. With this type of feedback, the JavaScript is written to detect the mouse's movement, and enabled it to click and drag artwork onscreen.

The catalogue includes wonderful pop-out menus that look as if they're made of transparent color. It's just a GIF which is controlled with JavaScript and CSS! CD-ROM type interfaces are made possible with DHTML which offer a much greater degree of sophistication for web design.

■ **note**

URLs on DHTML and related technologies

DHTML

http://www/whatis.com/dynamich.htm

http://www.w3.org/DOM/

http://home.netscape.com/comprod/products/communicator/features/
Dynamic_HTML.html

http://www.microsoft.com/sitebuilder/features/dynamicom.asp

http://www.dhtmlzone.com/tutorials/superfly/tutorials

CSS

http://whatis.com/styleshe.htm

http://whatis.com/cascadin.htm

http://www.stratcom.com/edge.html

http://www.internetnews.com/wd-news/1997/11/0402-pub.html

http://www.useit.com/alertbox/9707a.html

http://www.microsoft.com/gallery/files/styles/styles-intro.htm

JavaScript

http://www.webcoder.com/index_real.html

http://www.webdeveloper.com/categories/javascript/javascript_js_
tutorial.html

http://www.intricate.com/javascript/tutorial/index.htm

http://www.geocities.com/ResearchTriangle/1828/basic.html

http://home.netscape.com/eng/mozilla/2.0/handbook/javascript/index.html

---

■ **note**

Literature on DHTML and related technologies

HTML 4 Unleashed ■ Rick Darnell (et al) ■ Sams ■ ISBN 1-57521-299-4

Web Publishing with HTML 4 ■ Laura Lemay ■ Sams ■ ISBN 1-57521-336-2

Cascading Style Sheets: Designing For The Web ■ Hakon Wium Lie and
Bert Bos ■ Addison Wesley ■ ISBN 0-201-41998-X

Raggett on HTML 4 ■ Raggett, Lam, Alexander and Kmiec ■ Addison Wesley
■ ISBN 0-201-17805-2

Dreamweaver

Macromedia's Dreamweaver is being promoted as the first visual cross-browser authoring tool. "Cross-browser" means that the product strives to produce code that works on Netscape or Explorer. The product generates code for Cascading Style Sheets, JavaScript, and Dynamic HTML (DHTML) and allows you to write these elements from scratch, or utilize a graphical user interface (GUI) to automatically generate these features. One of the primary breakthroughs that Dreamweaver touts over other HTML editors is its capability to produce "round-trip HTML." This means that HTML is not altered with proprietary tags either on export or import.

Dreamweaver's pages are targeted at the 4.0 browsers of both Netscape and Explorer. The Dreamweaver program is fully integrated with Macromedia's Director, Flash, FreeHand, and Authorware. It also includes a visual FTP interface, and the ability to set up a library of common elements, such as headers and footers. If you modify a library item, it is automatically updated wherever it appeared throughout your site.

■ note

Dreamweaver Sites

http://www.8.ednet.com/products/
content/pcmf/1209/261879.html

http://www.macromedia.com/soft-
ware/dreamweaver/features.html

http://www.macromedia.com/soft-
ware/dreamweaver/dynamic.html

http://www.macromedia.com/soft-
ware/dreamweaver/releasenotes_
fs.html

Akimbo also designed the Elixir Demo for Macromedia's Dreamweaver site. Here the project is opened within Dreamweaver. Counter-clockwise from the upper-left is the Active Page Window, which is the visual workspace where Dreamweaver pages are assembled; the Timelines Window, which is similar to the timeline of either Director or Flash, and is used to control timing and synchronization of animation and events within the DHTML page; the Styles Win-dow, which applies Styles to selected areas of the page; the Launcher Palette, which can launch all the various windows; the Objects Palette, which inserts images, tables, rules, Java applets, ActiveX, plug-ins, and Flash and Director Movies; the HTML Source Window, which displays HTML code as it is generated; the Properties Window, which is used to specify and control the properties of various objects and components of the page, such as fonts, color, and so on.

■ note

Macromedia's Universal Media Initiative

The Universal Media Initiative, constructed by Macromedia, is the company's statement and commitment to adapt all of its authoring tools to support emerging web standards, such as Java and DHTML. Instead of focusing their efforts on software that requires proprietary playback solutions, Macromedia's products deliver multimedia to all platforms without the need for plug-ins.

Through related developments and partnerships, it is now possible to deliver Flash animations as via JavaScript, Shockwave, Flash plug-in, RealSystem 5.0, or as native DHTML Dreamweaver content. Many of these advances are contained within the new Aftershock utility. It generates both HTML and JavaScript that can detect client-browser settings to deliver a Flash movie either as a Flash movie to a browser with the Shockwave plug-in, as a Java movie to a Java-enabled browser without the plug-in, as an animated GIF to older browsers with neither Java nor Shockwave, or as a static GIF to low-bandwidth browsers! For more information regarding the delivery of Flash via Java or Aftershock, refer to the "Flash Player Java edition and Flash Aftershock utility" at http://www.macromedia.com/software/flash.

Additionally, the RealPlayer for Flash is a feature of RealSystem 5.0, which assures reliable delivery of animation, streaming audio, and video, even over slow modem connections. For information refer to http://www.macromedia.com/software/flash/index2.html or http://www.real.com/.

Other results from this initiative include the integration of FreeHand with Flash. The Flash Asset Xtra for Director enhances the capability of Director by providing complete control of Flash files as discrete Sprites within Director—including Lingo control and manipulation of all Flash movie properties. For information about the Flash Asset Xtra, refer to: http://www.macromedia.com/software/xtras/essentials/flash.

For more information about this initiative, visit: http://www.macromedia.com/macromedia/pr/1997/java_universal.html.

What's Next for Akimbo?

Ben shared that Akimbo's next project will be a section that they've been working on for a while: Experiments In Design. "This will be an area of the site where we'll showcase what we can do with the web medium and technology without a time crunch or client restrictions. We're going to go a bit nuts and let our minds range free. For example, Ardith is thinking about doing a site dedicated to how shrimp chips make her feel." This is a section that will show their boundless creativity and technical know-how. At the same time, it will offer them and their future employees an opportunity "to do the things that we've always wanted to do on the web, to go out on a limb with a new idea, to experiment, to have fun with the medium."

He continued, "It's a very exciting time to be developing web sites. With each project we're able to push the limits of design and technology and create sites unlike any predecessor. In fact, DHTML, especially as implemented by Dreamweaver, has enabled us to move closer to our original mission, which is to bring design to the web. We strive to create sites that focus on design rather than new technological tricks and techniques. Dreamweaver enables us to achieve this goal by giving us the ability to hide more of the underlying implementation and to focus on creating unique, intuitive, compelling design."

■ site summary

Akimbo

This chapter walked through the creative process of imaging and programming techniques employed by the forward-thinking Akimbo Design group. The resourcefulness and talent of this team is evident in their cutting-edge work and their interests draw attention to what the future of the web might hold for all of us.

- ■ DHTML is the collective implementation of JavaScript, Cascading Style Sheets, document object models, and new HTML tags and options. These components are technologies. Dreamweaver is a visual authoring tool for generating web sites that employ these technologies. Not only is it the only web authoring tool that handles JavaScript and the only tool that generates cross-browser DHTML, it's also likely to be a pivotal development in the future of the web.

- ■ Flash animator creates ultra-compact, resolution independent vector-base images and streaming animations that result in small files that transport across the web with astonishing speed. Flash includes the capability to create polished interactive buttons and images.

- ■ Artists who are already familiar with Illustrator or FreeHand drawing programs can leverage their skills to create content that can be animated with Flash. FreeHand artists are especially lucky because of the added capability of FreeHand (via the FreeHand Animation Power Pack) to export content to Flash format without ever leaving FreeHand.

- ■ In addition to their leading edge content, Akimbo provides three seamless viewing alternatives—ranging from checking for browser level, providing plug-in accesses, to offering an alternative static GIF. At its best, good site design controls the visitor's experience by implementing alternatives for visitors whose browsers aren't equipped to view the site as it is intended.

- ■ Macromedia's Universal Media Initiative resulted in a convergence of programs and formats between FreeHand, Director, Flash, and Dreamweaver. Among these developments are the Flash Asset for Director, the Aftershock Utility, and the new RealPlayer for Flash, which was developed in partnership between RealSystems and Macromedia. Additionally, these technologies together with Dreamweaver make it easy to deliver the same content to a wide variety of browsers and to generate the requisite code painlessly. This goes a long way to simplify the task of providing seamless alternatives, without the necessity of doing it manually.

http://www.akimbodesign.com

@tlas
Web Magazine

- Collaborative Design
- Combining 3D and 2D
- Cascading Style Sheets
- JavaScript
- Dreamweaver and DHTML

http://www.atlasmagazine.com is the only site that we chose to review both in the original *Deconstructing Web Graphics* and this sequel edition. We can't help ourselves; with each new issue of @tlas the site keeps changing, evolving, taking new risks, and demonstrating new ways to use technology artistically. The site is created from the heart (and for free) by three exceptionally talented individuals: Olivier Laude, Michael Macrone, and Amy Franceschini. This chapter will showcase their work with photography, graphics, Dynamic HTML, and creative uses of the web.

Web Design Firm: @tlas

Client: *@tlas Magazine*

Type of Site: Editorial: (photojournalism and multimedia)

Original URL: http://www.atlasmagazine.com/

Server: Sun Netra

Server Software: Netscape FastTrack Server 3.01

Producers: Olivier Laude, Amy Franceschini, Michael Macrone

Webmaster: Michael Macrone

Programmer: Michael Macrone

Art Director: Amy Franceschini

Creative Director: Olivier Laude

Development and Production Platform: Apple Macintosh

Design Software: Adobe Photoshop, Adobe Illustrator, Infini-D, BBEdit, Macromedia Dreamweaver, BoxTop GIFMation

@tlas' Background Information

@tlas is a non-commercial, web-based magazine that showcases photography, multimedia, design, and using the web to its best advantage. The publication is devoted to growing with technology and showing the world what can be done with new tools, making art for art's sake. @tlas shuns commercialism, predictability, and the clichés of digital art.

The three partners of @tlas are a synergetic and unlikely match. Creative Director Olivier Laude is an extroverted photojournalist who loves to put people and ideas together. He is the glue that holds @tlas together; it was his idea to assemble the team, and he works as a producer/editor/motivator on many of their projects. Michael Macrone is a successful author who makes his living writing about Shakespeare, classical literature, mythology, the Bible and programs the @tlas web site in his alleged spare time. Amy Franceschini was trained as a photographer, though her digital illustration and collage work on @tlas has garnered her assignments from *The New York Times* and MSNBC.

What is most striking about the team, aside from their obvious abundance of talent, is their devotion to artistic integrity. A key part of the synergy of their partnership is their ability to be self-critical and pound hard on the pixels and each other (with the deepest respect, of course!). They don't get paid for their work on @tlas, though attention to their site has brought them paying web design projects from Nike, Autodesk, and Live Picture.

It's one thing to say you're going to create something outside of the box and another to actually achieve true originality. @tlas is unlike anything else on the web, and even though much of what you'll find there might have no apparent purpose other than to surprise, disturb, or inspire, it is exciting that someone on the web is motivated by sheer experimentation and the challenge of a new medium.

Creative Process

It's hard to get a straight answer from any of the @tlas team about who originated which ideas. What becomes apparent is that they all have ideas and talents, and that the object in a brainstorming session is not the ownership of the idea, but the strength of the idea.

The answer to what drives @tlas—technology or art—is blurry. Sometimes the approach is that a new technology looks really cool and they examine what to do with it. Other times the opposite tack is taken, where really cool artwork finds a home with the appropriate technology.

"Michael usually gets really excited about something new, like DHTML," Amy related, "and my first response is often to think it's really lame. Then I go home and my brain sticks like a broken record on the capabilities of what he described to me. Even if my first response is to dismiss it, I almost always rise to the occasion and present Michael with something visually compelling with which to test the new feature. Michael is like a kid in a candy store when it comes to new browser or programming features. He is so amazing. There is virtually nothing I can present to him that he won't figure out a way to make happen."

One thing is apparent when interviewing this team: They all mutually respect each other's ideas and talents and enjoy working together. The work is often frustrating, and real-world issues like paying rent are not absent, but the rewards on this site are creative, not monetary.

@tlas Look and Feel

@tlas' sole designer, Amy Franceschini, was surrounded by artists as a child. Her stepfather was a concrete poet (a style of poetry popularized by the dada movement, which creates visuals out of words and typography) who put out an international biannual magazine of mail art and poetry called *Kaldron*. She remembers receiving a daily stack of submissions from around the world, which she would beg to steal for the walls of her bedroom. Her birth mother and father were very visual people, so she was introduced to different ways of seeing at an early age.

Amy studied photography at San Francisco State's art department from 1990 to 1992. She credits this experience as "invaluable." During art school, she learned about how to capture an emotion or a moment in time and how to tell a visual story. After receiving her degree, she floundered around and eventually got an internship at a small photography magazine called *Photometro*. She worked under the guidance of Henry Brimmer, a designer who graduated from Ulm Design School in Germany. She worked closely with Henry for seven months, reviewing portfolio submissions, editing work, laying out pages, and scanning. She worked in exchange for computer classes, while support-ing herself as a waitress and saving for her own computer.

While learning to use Photoshop, Illustrator, and Quark, Amy was immediately struck that she had finally found the tools to express her ideas in totality. "People at the magazine would look over my shoulder and say 'you're such a good designer,'" she remembers. It was as if she had found the right vehicle for her work, and the outside world gave her immediate confirmation of that truth.

@tlas Logo Design

When asked what Amy had in mind for the @tlas logo, she responded, "Maybe the question should be, what don't you have in mind? When I am designing logos for @tlas, I'm not really thinking of it as a logo, but more of a morsel; something you could almost hold in your hand. The 3D aspect of the logo lends itself to jumping out of the page. I like to embellish the logotype with imagery and smaller type to create a sense of dialog between the elements that tells a story. I try to capture enough of the story in the logo to get people to explore further."

For the logo design, Amy used a combination of software tools. Starting with Illustrator, she created the 2D font. Next, she used KPT Vector Effects to warp the logo in Illustrator. She then imported the vector data into Infini-D and created an extrusion and bevel. She lit the 3D model in Infini-D, picked the right angle, and saved the results as a PICT file, which she brought into Photoshop. From there, she turned the single file into a Photoshop file with 15 separate layers, where she created numerous drop shadows and added extra illustration elements.

■ note

Amy's Inspiration

When asked how Amy gets her inspiration for her art, she listed her heroes. "I am a huge fan of Lari Pittman's paintings. His lavish, graphic, luscious paintings inspire me to push myself and not let time be such a building block in my personal work. He is one of the great masters, in my mind." She is also influenced by Islamic tantric art. "When I think about the fact that those works were created by hand, it blows my mind. All those dots; check it out! My physical surroundings also end up subconsciously in my work all the time, such as shapes from gum wrappers or shapes and colors from the faded products from the Filipino convenience store downstairs!"

When asked where she goes for inspiration, she joked, "To the Filipino convenience store!" Actually, in addition to that she attends as many art exhibits, movies, performances, punk shows, circuses, car shows, air shows, and destruction derbies as she can. "I get visually stimulated by almost anything, but I think it is most important to dump yourself into a situation you normally wouldn't frequent," she added. "That's when I get inspired."

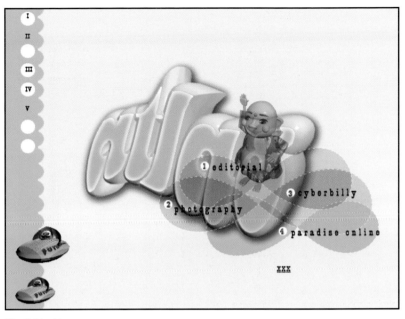

The finished logo.

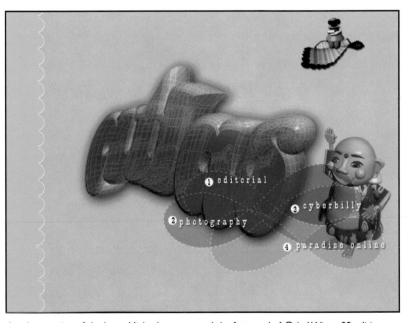

Another version of the logo. Michael programmed the front-end of @tlas' Winter98 edition to load either logo randomly.

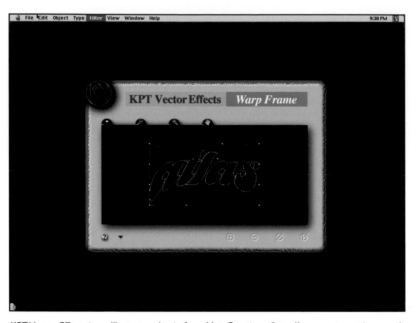

KPT Vector Effects is an Illustrator plug-in from MetaCreations (http://www.metacreations.com) that warps and distorts Illustrator vector information. It's necessary first to convert a font to "outlines" in Illustrator before this filter works.

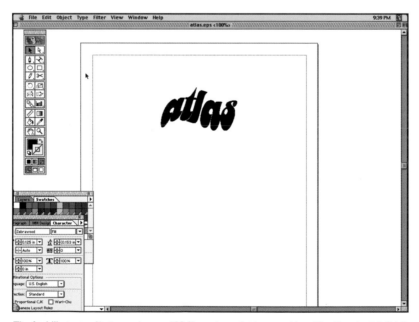

The final Illustrator file is saved as an .EPS file, so it can be imported into MetaCreation's Infini-D.

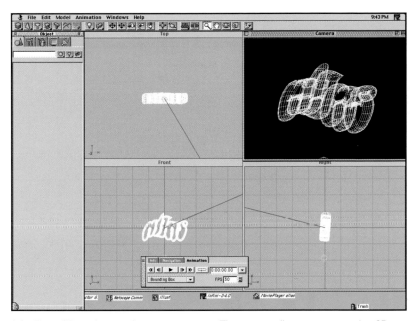

Infini-D is a 3D rendering and animation program. The program allows you to extrude a 2D graphic into a 3D shape. Extrusion is like creating a cookie cutter effect. The front of the artwork is treated as a 2D plane, and the sides are assigned 3D depth and an optional bevel. Amy chose to use a "convex" bevel, which gave the edges a rounded look. In Infini-D, you can either view the logo in wireframe mode (shown here) or as a solid rendered object (shown next). Amy combined both versions in one of her finished logos for @tlas.

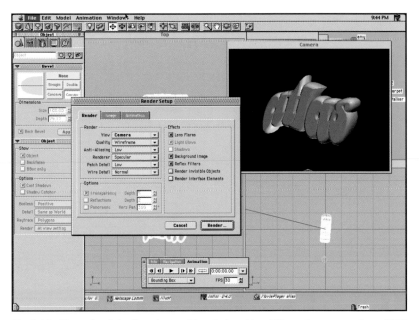

The finished logo after being lit and rotated into final position. This version was saved as a PICT file for further modification in Photoshop.

This screen is the result of all the Photoshop layers being turned on.

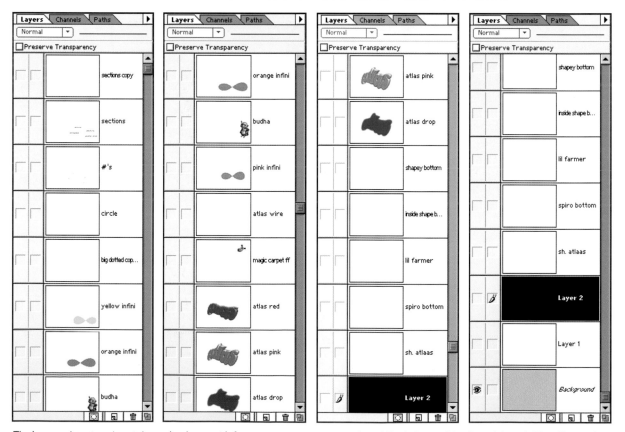

The Layers palette is so long, it has to be shown with four separate screen captures here. Watch the scroll bar in each image! Note: The number of layers affects the file size in Photoshop, but once the image is flattened, it suffers no size penalty over any other single layer image.

These figures show some of the combined layers in Amy's Photoshop document. Each layer is transparent and lays over the next. The final figure on the bottom right shows all the above sampled layers turned on.

Interface Innovations

There are a number of original approaches to interface design issues in @tlas. We will study two areas of the site for this purpose—photography and the site map. Both examples were created using Amy's layered Photoshop techniques and Michael's JavaScript rollovers. The photography section features Olivier's photography.

Typically, Olivier presents Amy with artwork or photography, Amy presents Michael with a layered Photoshop document, and Michael figures out how to get it up on the web.

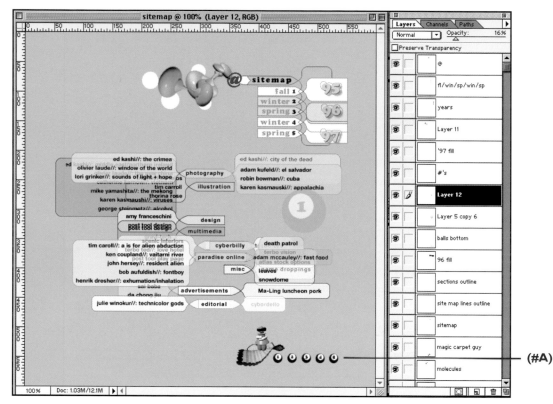

(#A)

This is a screen shot of one of Amy's Photoshop files (75 layers deep!) that was given to Michael to program as a JavaScript rollover. As your mouse rolls over the various issues of @tlas (1-5), different categories light up, showing which magazine issues covered which subjects. The numbered billiard balls **(#A)** at the bottom of the screen offer links to the various magazine issues.

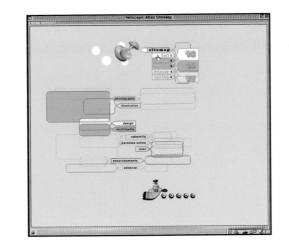

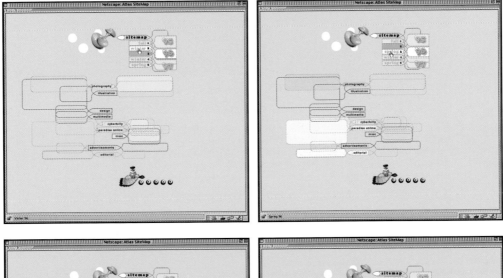

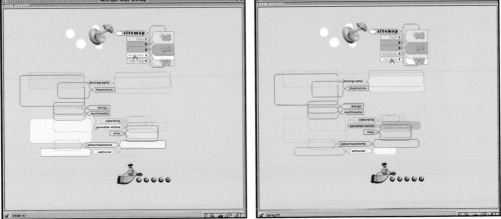

The effect of rolling over each active button creates a dynamic effect, as transparent colored shapes dance around the page, showing the contents of each section.

(#C)

(#A)

(#B)

(#D)

In the Photography section, the rollover buttons update a position on the map of China, **(#A)**, reveal the latitude and longitude of each city **(#B)**, and light up a text button with the name of each city **(#C)**. An additional bar of numbers across the bottom right of each screen indicates if there is more than one image in the series from each respective city **(#D)**.

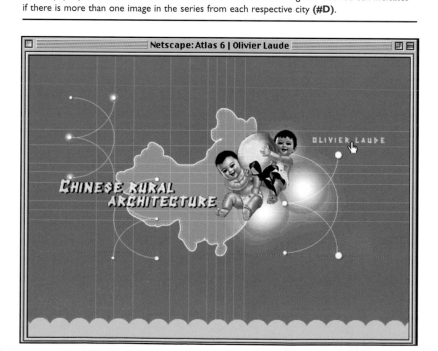

The splash screen to this section opens up in its own browser window (courtesy of JavaScript) and plays a charming animation where all the dots in the image glow and travel along the paths, ultimately lighting up Olivier's name.

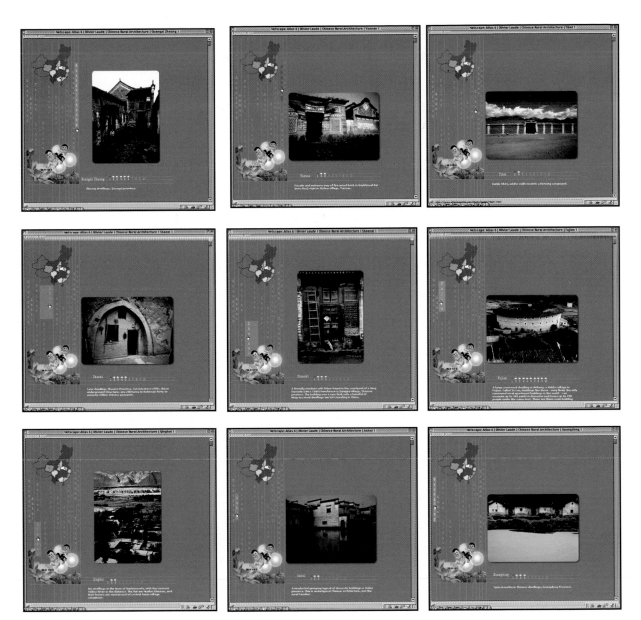

If you look at all the screens together, you can see the moving rollovers, map coordinates, and map locations.

Design Control Issues

If you care about control, the web is perhaps the most unfriendly design medium in the world. Control over positioning, typography, color, and behavior is taken for granted in other digital design mediums, but on the web it's a hard fight to have control over anything.

To gain precise artistic control over the @tlas site, Michael used his programming ingenuity to fight browser and platform discrepancies. Turning to the new features of 4.0 browsers and DHTML, Michael created an innovative strategy to ensure the maximum amount of design control over @tlas' content.

Here are some of the problems that Michael set out to conquer in @tlas:

Font Size: At the system level, Macs and PCs display type very differently. This difference in standards creates a situation where 10-point type on a Mac looks more like 13 or 14-point on a PC. Add the fact that monitors are set to different standards—on Macs 72 ppi (pixels per inch) and PCs 96 ppi—it becomes difficult to feed the same type measurements into a cross-platform compatible site and come up with consistent results.

```
%^!&*&@&*#^      fall '95      *&%!!!$%?^      subscribe      !@(??^&*(!

@ city of the dead     @ window of the world     @ joaquin's town
@ ski vixens           @ name droppings          @ chinese pop posters
                       @ cyberbilly
```

```
%^!&*&@&*#^      fall '95      *&%!!!$%?^      subscribe      !@(??^&*(!

@ city of the dead     @ window of the world     @ joaquin's town
@ ski vixens           @ name droppings          @ chinese pop posters
                       @ cyberbilly
```

Under identical browsers, the fonts on a page can vary sizes simply because of the differences between Macs and PCs.

Monitor Resolution: Monitors are set to many different resolutions, independent of Windows or Macintosh platform differences. A web page looks big on a monitor set to 12 inches and small on a monitor set to 21 inches.

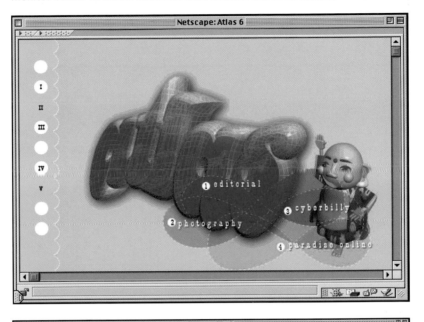

System Fonts: Macs ship with Helvetica; Windows ships with Arial. There are differences between the Mac's Courier and the PC's Courier New. The font names are different, but so are the widths and sizes, making precise layout a nightmare, especially when using precise HTML tables. Type in one typeface might wrap, while in another it would look small and have too many spaces.

Of course, it's impossible to solve all the problems just listed. Michael turned to solutions within HTML 4.0, including CSS (**C**ascading **S**tyle **S**heets) and JavaScript, to ensure that @tlas looked as good as it could under a myriad of different conditions. This section will examine his use of these technologies for the purpose of achieving precise design control.

cyberbilly :

Ted Terbolizard does Atlas. **Log Buddha** premieres: It's Buddha's digitoscope ant farm —it's **channel surfing** the reincarnation highway —it's more than we bargained for—it's **Fermat's theorem with a human face** —it's also **interactive** (excluding tax **and** shipping charge). Futurefarmers explore the latest in bioweb technologies. (OO) \'`\/ " "

cyberbilly :

Ted Terbolizard does Atlas. Log Buddha premieres: It's Buddha's digitoscope ant farm -- it's channel surfing the reincarnation highway -- it's more than we bargained for -- it's Fermat's theorem with a human face -- it's also interactive (excluding tax and shipping charge). Futurefarmers explore the latest in bioweb technologies. (OO) \'`\/ " "

Different fonts not only have different appearances, but the differences in weight and size make precise layout impossible.

Cascading Style Sheets

Before looking at Michael's innovative use of CSS, we thought we'd first offer an overview of style sheets and how they work. This section covers the origins, specifications, and different implementations of CSS.

When the web was first developed, it was never expected to offer precise design control. HTML was created as a portable document language, meaning that it could be viewed and authored from any number of computer platforms or operating systems. It was specifically intended to be customizable by the end user. If an end user had vision problems, the fonts could be altered to display larger; if an end user was color blind, colors could be changed; if an end user was blind, ASCII text could be interpreted by a voice reader. It's actually a pretty wonderful philosophy, as HTML originated with the intent of displaying content for anyone and everyone. In this context, HTML was developed to be a display medium, not a design medium.

Along came web developers who saw the web as a design medium, whether it was intended to be or not. Its capabilities of merging images, sounds, movies, and text combined with hyperlinks made it an attractive multimedia environment. Netscape was the first browser to break a lot of HTML conventions to offer tags that appeased designers. HTML purists and standards organizations went crazy fighting these unstandard tags and they lost. Whether or not the web was invented for the purpose it is being used for cannot change the fact that people want to use it for well-designed content.

The web is ultimately a communication medium. It is proven that visually well-designed content enhances communication. Designers and HTML purists at heart have the same goal: to communicate. OK, so where do style sheets fit into all this philosophizing?

By creating two sets of specifications, one for style sheets and another for HTML, the W3C (**W**orld **W**ide **W**eb **C**onsortium) was able to make a separation between HTML content and style content. Style sheets are a vehicle for design templates that apply to HTML documents in order to describe how to display the content. CSS documents define the properties of tags and elements in HTML.

A style sheet document can be contained within an HTML document. This type of implementation is called an "internal" style sheet. Style sheets can also be independent documents that are self contained. This type of style sheet is called an "external" style sheet. External style sheets are particularly powerful because multiple HTML pages can be set to reference a single external style sheet.

Style sheets can describe precise positioning, precise fonts, precise font sizes, precise colors, and precise type spacing. For this reason, they were chosen as a solution for @tlas' quest for precise design control.

Programming CSS

The structure of a style contains a Selector, a Property, and a Value. The Selector specifies where the style should be applied. It could be used for an existing HTML element, such as H1. In Michael's code, he made up his own names for selectors, such as ".text1" or ".bolder." The curly braces "{" and "}" enclose the body of the style, which contains the Property and the Value. To the left side of the colon is the Property, and to the right side the Value. Semicolons are used to separate multiple sets of Properties and Values.

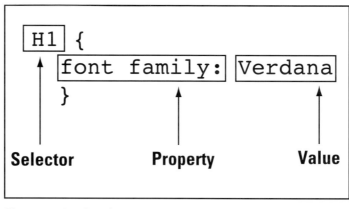

The construction of a style.

In this example, the browser is being instructed to use Verdana at 24 pixels high for the H1 tag:

```
H1   {
     font-family: Verdana;
     font-size: 24px;
     }
```

When creating styles for text, it's necessary to decide what unit of measurement to use for the size values. CSS allows you to use pixels, points, picas, ems, ens, x-height, inches, centimeters, or millimeters. Here's a handy chart for CSS units of measurement:

CSS	Item/Description
px	pixel: A pixel is the distance from one dot to another on a computer monitor.
pt	point: A point is 1/72 inch. How many pixels that translates to depends on the resolution of your screen, but it is one pixel on 72 dpi systems.
pc	pica: 12 points.
em	em: The "body size" of a font. If the font is 12 points, one em is 12 points.
en	en: 1/2 em.
ex	x-height: The height of a lowercase "x."
in	inch: The length of the thumb of King Henry VIII.
cm	centimeter: 1/100 meter.
mm	millimeter: 1/1000 meter.

■ tip

Use Pixels (Most of the Time)

Because of cross-platform differences, a point or a pica might mean very different things on different operating systems. Michael recommends that you use pixels or percentages as your unit of measurement for type in style sheets. This usually ensures consistent results on different systems.

Michael uses pixels when dictating margin and padding positioning with CSS. He claims that working with absolute positioning can turn into a minefield because some of the same terms don't work in IE that work in Navigator. This is another reason for his reliance on separate external style sheets.

There are always exceptions to rules. One of the style sheets Michael wrote for Windows uses points, because when he was playing around with different measurements those results seemed most reliable to him. Some users get angry if you use pixels, because it disables their ability to adjust font size. If you specify sizes in points, they can still use the larger font or smaller font features of their browser. Sometimes points can yield more consistent results, and this unit of measurement still lets end users change their font size, but many artists don't want to let end users do this because it ruins their designs. The decision of which unit of measurement to use in CSS depends, in part, on your artistic and overall goals.

Bottom line: Until you've programmed style sheets for a while and worked with all the value variants, you really can't understand how to troubleshoot all the different factors. Experience, experimentation, and practice are paramount.

Michael's CSS Solution

Michael decided to define the level of control he wanted over his site by dividing the problem areas into four categories: Mac Netscape, Mac IE, PC Netscape, and PC IE. From his experience, he knew that @tlas pages looked different under these four conditions. By creating a style sheet for each platform's browser, he was able to customize the specifications differently to work around each version's distinct characteristics.

Michael made four separate External Style Sheets for this purpose, where he was able to specify position, color, and font information differently for each scenario. He wrote a browser and platform detection JavaScript that produced an on-the-fly link to the proper External Style Sheet. By creating four separate External Style Sheets, Michael was able to harness maximum design control over each browser and platform scenario. We'll examine his code in the next section, which will highlight the differences between the four documents.

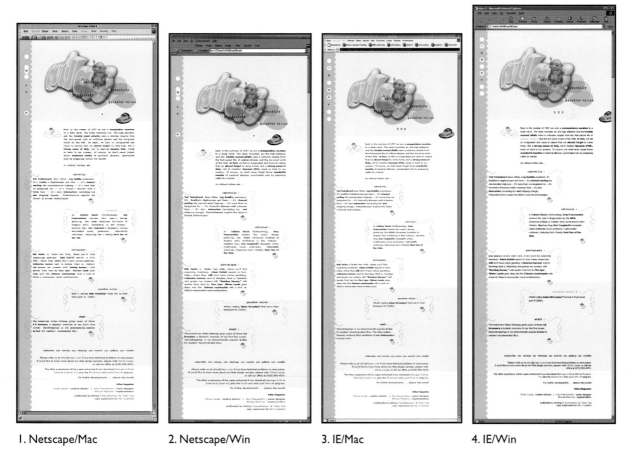

1. Netscape/Mac   2. Netscape/Win   3. IE/Mac   4. IE/Win

The results of four different pages being delivered through linking to two different External Style Sheets. By creating four separate External Style Sheets, Michael was able to harness maximum design control over each browser and platform scenario.

Code Deconstruction

This HTML was used on the site and a JavaScript browser detection script (deconstructed later in the chapter) linked to the appropriate CSS file, depending on platform and browser. (The HTML for this page is 14 pages long! We are simply showing part of the document that references the CSS in this section.)

1.

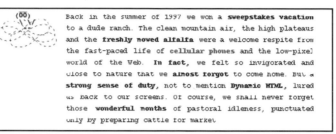

Back in the summer of 1997 we won a **sweepstakes vacation** to a dude ranch. The clean mountain air, the high plateaus and the **freshly mowed alfalfa** were a welcome respite from the fast-paced life of **cellular phones** and the low-pixel world of the Web. **In fact**, we felt so invigorated and close to nature that we **almost forgot** to come home. But a **strong sense of duty**, not to mention **Dynamic HTML**, lured us back to our screens. Of course, we shall never forget those **wonderful months** of pastoral idleness, punctuated only by preparing cattle for market.

Netscape/Mac

2.

Back in the summer of 1997 we won a **sweepstakes vacation** to a dude ranch. The clean mountain air, the high plateaus and the **freshly mowed alfalfa** were a welcome respite from the fast-paced life of **cellular phones** and the low-pixel world of the Web. **In fact,** we felt so invigorated and close to nature that we **almost forgot** to come home. But a **strong sense of duty,** not to mention **Dynamic HTML,** lured us back to our screens. Of course, we shall never forget those **wonderful months** of pastoral idleness, punctuated only by preparing cattle for market.

Netscape/Win

3.

Back in the summer of 1997 we won a **sweepstakes vacation** to a dude ranch. The clean mountain air, the high plateaus and the **freshly mowed alfalfa** were a welcome respite from the fast-paced life of cellular phones and the low-pixel world of the Web. **In fact,** we felt so invigorated and close to nature that we **almost forgot** to come home. But a **strong sense of duty,** not to mention **Dynamic HTML,** lured us back to our screens. Of course, we shall never forget those **wonderful months** of pastoral idleness, punctuated only by preparing cattle for market.

IE/Mac

4.

Back in the summer of 1997 we won a **sweepstakes vacation** to a dude ranch. The clean mountain air, the high plateaus and the **freshly mowed alfalfa** were a welcome respite from the fast-paced life of cellular phones and the low-pixel world of the Web. **In fact,** we felt so invigorated and close to nature that we **almost forgot** to come home. But a **strong sense of duty,** not to mention **Dynamic HTML,** lured us back to our screens. Of course, we shall never forget those **wonderful months** of pastoral idleness, punctuated only by preparing cattle for market

IE/Win

We chose to zoom into a small section of the code, to demonstrate how different style sheets were used for different platforms and browsers.

1.
winter98.css (Macintosh/Netscape for Winter 98)

```
■  1  .text1    { font: 10px/16px Courier, monospace; text-align: justify; margin-top: -2px; }
■  2  .head2    { font: bold 10px/16px Courier, monospace; text-align: right; }
■  3  .head3    { font: bold 16px/16px Courier, monospace; }
■  4  .right    { text-align: right; float: right; margin-top: -14px; }
■  5  .menu     { font: bold 10px/16px Verdana, Arial, Geneva, sans-serif; }
■  6  .stuff    { font: 10px/16px Verdana, Arial, sans-serif; text-align: right; margin-top: -4px; }
■  7  .stuff2   { font: 10px/14px Verdana, Arial, sans-serif; text-align: right; margin-top: -5px; }
■  8  .bolder   { font-weight: bold; }
■  9  A:link    {text-decoration: none; }
■ 10  A.helper:link { color: #ffffff; text-decoration: none; }
```

2.
winter98_macIE.css

```
.text1    {     font: 10px/16px Verdana, Courier, monospace; text-align: left; margin-top: -2px; }
.head2    {     font: bold 10px/16px Courier, monospace; text-align: right; }
.head3    {     font: bold 16px/16px Courier, monospace; }
.right    {     text-align: right; margin-top: -8px; }
.menu     {     font: bold 10px/16px Verdana, Arial, Geneva, sans-serif; }
.stuff    {     font: 10px/16px Verdana, Arial, sans-serif; text-align: right; margin-top: -4px; }
.stuff2   {     font: 10px/14px Verdana, Arial, sans-serif; text-align: right; margin-top: -5px; }
.bolder   {     font-weight: bold; }
A:link    {     text-decoration: none; }
A.helper:link { color: #ffffff; text-decoration: none; }
```

3.
winter98_winIE.css_ (Windows/IE for Winter 98)

```
.text1    {     font: 8pt/13pt Arial, Verdana, monospace; text-align: justify;  margin-top: -2px; }
.head2    {     font: bold 12px/16px 'Courier New', Courier, monospace; text-align: right; }
.head3    {     font:bold 16px/16px 'Courier New', Courier, monospace; }
.right    {     text-align: right; float: right; margin-top: -14px; }
.menu     {     font: bold 8pt/9pt Arial, Verdana, sans-serif; }
.stuff    {     font: 8pt/10pt Arial, Verdana, sans-serif; text-align: right; margin-top: -4px; }
.stuff2   {     font: 8pt/9pt Arial, Verdana, sans-serif; text-align: right; margin-top: -4px; }
.bolder   {     font-weight: bold; }
A:link    {     text-decoration: none; }
A:active  {     text decoration: none; }
A:visited {     text-decoration: none; }
A.helper:link { color: #ffffff; text-decoration: none; }
```

4.
winter98_winNS.css (Windows/Netscape for Winter 98)

```
.text1    {     font: 11px/15px Verdana, Arial, monospace; text-align: justify;  margin-top: -2px; }
.head2    {     font: bold 12px/16px 'Courier New', Courier, monospace; text-align: right; }
.head3    {     font: bold 16px/16px 'Courier New', Courier, monospace; }
.right    {     text-align: right; float: right; margin-top: -14px; }
.menu     {     font: bold 11px/11px Verdana, Arial, sans-serif; }
.stuff    {     font: 11px/15px Verdana, Arial, sans-serif; text-align: right; margin-top: -4px; }
.stuff2   {     font: 11px/14px Verdana, Arial, sans-serif; text-align: right; margin-top: -5px; }
.bolder   {     font-weight: bold; }
A:link    {     text-decoration: none; }
A:active  {     text-decoration: none; }
A:visited {     text-decoration: none; }
A.helper:link { color: #ffffff; text-decoration: none; }
```

■ deconstruction

■ **1** Michael created a style for ".text1," which used the Courier font, specified a 10-pixel high font using 16 pixels of leading (leading is the space between lines of type) and a top margin of two pixels. Notice in the Winter98.HTML where this specification is requested in line [12].

■ **2** The style named ".head2" requested the same as in .text1, except the Courier font is bold and the text alignment is right instead of top.

■ **3** The ".head3" style specified Courier bold at 16 pixels high with 16 pixels of leading.

■ **4** The ".right" style specified how to handle "right justification of text" with a top margin of 14 pixels.

■ **5** The ".menu" style specified that the font be bold, 10 pixels high with 16 pixels of leading, and that it use either Verdana, Arial, or Geneva as a sans serif font. The purpose of including a list of fonts like this is to provide alternatives if the end user's system doesn't have the first font in the list. Here, if the end user did not have Verdana installed, the browser would display the information in Arial or Geneva, depending on which font it could locate.

■ **5** The ".stuff" style specified a 10-pixel high font with 16 pixels of leading and the font Verdana or Arial. The alignment was set for top at four pixels. A negative leading value moves the text up from the default leading setting.

■ **6** The ".stuff2" style specified a 10-pixel high font with 14 pixels of leading, to display in Verdana or Arial and to use right alignment with a margin of 5 pixels.

■ **7** The style ".bolder" specified that whatever font was being used should display in a bold weight.

■ **9** The style "A:link" removes the underline from links. Because a color is not specified, it takes the active link color from the BODY element of the HTML document, not the style sheet document.

■ **10** The style "A.helper:link" is instructed to use white as the color (shown here in hexadecimal as FFFFFF) and to remove underlining on the link.

■ code

Winter98.HTML

- **11** `<TD Width=348 VAlign=top><FONT Face="Courier,Courier New" Size=2>`

- **12** `<DIV Class="text1">Back in the summer of 1997 we won a`

- **13** `<B Class=bolder>sweepstakes vacation</B> to a dude ranch. The clean mountain air, the high plateaus and the`

```
<B Class=bolder>freshly mowed alfalfa</D> were a welcome respite from the fast-paced
life of

<A HREF="#" onClick="popMe(246,332,'fashion','win98/cellphone.html'); return false">

<B Class=bolder>cellular phones</B></A> and the low-pixel world of the Web.

<B Class=bolder>In fact,</B> we felt so invigorated and close to nature that we

<B Class=bolder>almost forgot</B> to come home. But a

<B Class=bolder>strong sense of duty,</B> not to mention

<B Class=bolder>Dynamic HTML,</B> lured us back to our screens. Of course, we shall
never forget those

<B Class=bolder>wonderful months</B> of pastoral idleness,  punctuated only by preparing
cattle for market.

<BR>

<BR> So without further ado ...</DIV></FONT></TD>
```

■ deconstruction

■ **11** Looking at the HTML that references the data next, notice that the <FONT Face= "Courier, Courier New" Size=2> element is used to specify the font, in addition to the style sheet. Michael made the decision to put the FONT tag here so that people who didn't have style sheet-compliant browsers would still get the appropriate type face. Everything you could do with the font tag you can now do with style sheets. The only problem is it won't show up on older browsers or WebTV.

■ **12** The <DIV Class> element was used to invoke the style ".text1," which was defined in the external CSS document in reference [1].

■ **13** Notice other references to the External Style Sheets in the element <B Class=bolder>, which was deconstructed in number [8]. <B> would normally make the type bolder, but in some cases a browser will override the bold tag when using style sheets, so Michael added this redundant style to compensate.

JavaScript Browser Detection

Michael used JavaScript to detect the browser and platform that people were using to access his site. Once he obtained the information about the user, the script determined which CSS document to display.

■ code

```
<HTML>
<HEAD>
<TITLE> Atlas 6 </TITLE>
<META NAME="keywords" CONTENT="Atlas, @tlas,
\@tlas, magazine, photography, photojournalism,
multimedia, design, arts, art, cyberbilly,
Olivier Laude, Michael Macrone, Amy
Franceschini, Terbo Ted, dhtml, Dynamic HTML">
<!-- Copyright (c) 1998 by Atlas Web Design -->
```
■ 1
```
<SCRIPT Language="JavaScript">
<!--
```
■ 2
```
window.onerror = null;
```
■ 3
```
window.defaultStatus='Atlas 6';
self.name = "main";
```
■ 4
```
var uA = navigator.userAgent;
var aN = navigator.appName;
var aV = parseInt(navigator.appVersion);
```
■ 5
```
var ie      = (aN.indexOf('Micr') != -1);
var mac     = (uA.indexOf('Mac') != -1 ||
uA.indexOf('mac') != -1);
```
■ 6
```
if (!mac) {
if (ie) document.writeln("<LINK Rel='stylesheet'
Type='text/css' HREF='./win98_winIE.css'>");
else document.writeln("<LINK Rel='stylesheet'
Type='text/css' HREF='./win98_winNS.css'>");
} else {
if (ie) document.writeln("<LINK Rel='stylesheet'
Type='text/css' HREF='./win98_macIE.css'>");
else document.writeln("<LINK Rel='stylesheet'
Type='text/css' HREF='./win98.css'>");
}
```

■ deconstruction

■ 1 <SCRIPT Language="JavaScript"> could have specified the version of JavaScript (1.1 or 1.2), which sets a level for debugging and error reporting. Michael didn't specify which version he used, because IE complains if you state 1.2 and the end user has enabled debugging. This command turns off error reporting. An end user can't fix the JavaScript error even if it's reported, so if left turned on, error reporting can get annoying.

■ 2 window.onerror = null; states that if there's an error in the script, ignore the JavaScript. This command turns off error reporting. An end user can't fix the JavaScript error even if it's reported, so if left turned on, error reporting can get annoying.

■ 3 window.defaultStatus='Atlas 6'; causes the word Atlas 6 to appear in the status window as the default message. The status window would normally be blank.

■ 4 This snippet of code establishes the following:

```
var uA = navigator.userAgent;
var aN = navigator.appName;
var aV = parseInt(navigator.appVersion);
```

var uA initiates a variable for the user agent. This object contains information about the browser that can be captured by the script. For example, the user agent for Navigator 4.04 for Macintosh Power PC might look like this: "Mozilla/4.04 (M, I, PPC, N)." Mozilla is the user agent for Netscape Navigator. Unfortunately, Internet Explorer uses the word Mozilla to describe itself, even though it behaves very differently from Navigator. Therefore, Michael felt he should get additional information. The next variable is aN, or the application Name, and the variable following that is aV, or application Version, which simply gives the browser version number. This part of the JavaScript queries the browser about the user agent, the application name, and version. By requesting all three variables, Michael was able to sniff out whether the browser was in fact IE or Navigator for Windows or Macintosh.

■ 5 The next snippet:

```
var ie      = (aN.indexOf('Micr') != -1);
var mac     = (uA.indexOf('Mac') != -1 ||
uA.indexOf('mac') != -1);
```

allowed Michael to create a variable for the platforms: Mac, Win95, or WinNT. The script checks to see if these variables are true or false and then performs actions (such as referencing the correct CSS file) based on the true/false-ness of the variables. The next step [6] performs the action based on the result of the variable query.

■ 6 The if and else statements in this section of the code instruct the JavaScript to send the correct CSS to the correct platform and browser.

JavaScript Versus CGI for Browser Detection

Many people who program using Perl and CGI (see Glossary) turn up their noses at JavaScript. Michael used JavaScript for browser detection intentionally, because for his purposes it worked better than using CGI.

A CGI script needs to be executed from the server, instead of the client. Many times, visitors to the @tlas site get the URL from someone else's bookmark file. Let's say you're on a Windows machine, but your friend who has a Mac sent you the URL for the site. If Michael had relied on a CGI, the Windows visitor would get the Mac page, because he would bypass the initial frontdoor URL that the CGI would have detected. By keeping the JavaScript detection code in the HTML instead of on the server, Michael ensured that anyone who comes to the site, regardless of how they obtained the URL, gets the appropriate CSS file.

Michael chose JavaScript because it works in the client (browser) rather than on the server, which allows him to preview his work locally. He doesn't need to connect to his ISP, fire up an FTP client, upload new files, and then preview the results online (at a top rate of around 33.6 Kbps). With JavaScript browser detection, he can, for example, make a really minor change to a style sheet and then preview it instantly on whatever browser he has running. No uploading, no downloading.

Perl-heads have tended to look down on JavaScript, and there are good reasons for that. Early JavaScript was pretty lame, and Perl remains superior at text- and file-handling, but there's a whole world of client-side scripting that Perl can't touch.

In brief, Michael uses JavaScript to deliver the CSS links, rather than CGI to deliver different pages or different chunks of pages, because:

- It includes instant local previews;

- It's less work for the server;

- JavaScript has more browser "objects," not just the user agent, but also the application name and application version, which works better for the task of browser detection;

- It can integrate browser detection with other client scripting routines; Perl can't measure your screen width while it's testing your browser;

- SSI (server-side includes) will not necessarily be available or accessible on the present or future Atlas server;

- Unless Michael uses Perl to write out the entire page, which is the quintessence of local inaccessibility, he could never preview the page offline. A user might always go to a URL directly rather than passing through the CGI script;

- Although Michael learned Perl first, he's much more familiar today with JavaScript. "I can write it off the top of my head, while with Perl I always have to look something up."

DHTML and Dreamweaver

Absolute positioning is possible with a combination of JavaScript and CSS. For the Cyberbilly section of @tlas, Michael used Dreamweaver to create the motion for a flying spaceship that Amy designed.

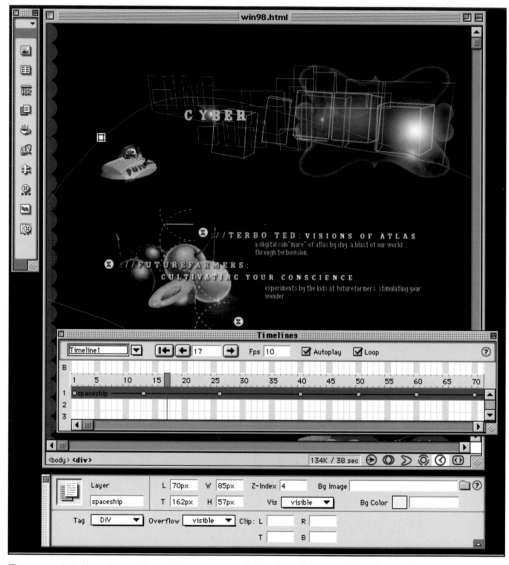

This screen shot shows the interface to Dreamweaver and plots the path for the Cyberbilly spaceship.

Michael used Macromedia's Dreamweaver to generate the code for the flying spaceships movement. Using the timeline feature and keyframes, he was able to draw a boomerang shape onscreen and have the program calculate the JavaScript and CSS code. For this type of functionality, Michael said, "Dreamweaver is a program that you've just gotta have!"

One caveat he mentioned was that you cannot modify the code for the motion once Dreamweaver writes it or you will not be able to reaccess the path. As long as you leave the code alone, you can bring the file back into Dreamweaver at any time to change the shape of the path.

Michael's Views on Programming

Anyone who's dedicated enough to make multiple versions of a site in order to achieve precise design control is clearly passionate about their work. Michael spends a great deal of energy figuring out the workarounds in this medium. His JavaScript work includes conducting endless experiments to ensure no one gets a JavaScript error on @tlas pages. His work with understanding how fonts and size relationships work on cross-platforms and browsers is unparalleled. Michael puts a lot of thought into the end user experience, from both a practical and artistic perspective.

Michael has watched the evolution of the web since the early days of gray backgrounds, through the features of frames, tables, and colored fonts. He's bored with HTML now and spends most of his time working with JavaScript. "Let's face it," he says. "There's very little new stuff one can expect from HTML. All the new innovations are appearing from outside sources, such as style sheets, JavaScript, and DHTML."

He's very enthused about new tools, such as Dreamweaver, but notes, "Dreamweaver is a great tool if you know what you're doing. It doesn't shield you from needing to learn how to program, but it can be a tremendous time saver if you know what you're doing. You still need to troubleshoot this stuff in order to work reliably with it, and no editor can save you from that eventuality."

Interestingly, Michael says he actually spends less time dealing with the code these days and much more time ensuring that the images are compressed properly and look their best. He uses a host of software tools, which include:

GIFmation
http://www.boxtopsoft.com/

DeBabelizer
http://www.equilibrium.com/

photoGIF
http://www.boxtopsoft.com/

GIFWizard
http://www.gifwizard.com/

Teach Yourself JavaScript and DHTML

Michael taught himself how to program CSS, just like he taught himself HTML, JavaScript, and DHTML. Whenever he first hears of a new web programming technique, he searches the web for online tutorials and demonstration sites. Occasionally books are helpful too, but they are often outdated or inaccurate. Here's his list of favorite resources for learning CSS and related technologies.

Cascading Style Sheets: Designing for the Web
Bert Bos and Harkon Lie ■ 256 pages ■ $29.95 ■ Addison Wesley (These authors are part of the W3C committee who developed the CSS spec. It doesn't cover the latest CSS2 specifications, but it's an excellent book for learning the basics.)

Recommended URLs

A list of CSS attributes that work in Internet Explorer.
http://www.microsoft.com/msdn/sdk/inetsdk/help/dhtml/references/css/attributes.htm

An excellent gallery of CSS examples.
http://www.microsoft.com/gallery/files/styles/default.htm

Includes links to helpful sites about DHTML.
http://www.atlasmagazine.com/dhtml/

A helpful tutorial on CSS.
http://webdeveloper.com/categories/html/html_css_1.html

Check out the tutorials on CSS.
http://www.webcoder.com/howto/article.html

The CSS spec from the W3C.
http://www.w3.org/Style/

Resources for CSS absolute and relative positioning.
http://www.w3.org/TR/WD-positioning

A complete list of properties.
http://www.w3.org/TR/WD-CSS2/propidx.html

A complete list of descriptors.
http://www.w3.org/TR/WD-CSS2/descidx.html

■ note

Michael Macrone, the Author

Michael is generous with sharing his ideas and programming techniques. "You almost have to be generous to get deeply into this stuff," he explains. "People like me look at what other people do in order to figure out how to do it ourselves. Part of the spirit of the web is to share freely, and let others stand on your shoulders to get to the next level." He also confesses to having the spirit of a "teacher." That's obvious from his articles in *Interactivity Magazine* on the web.

If you would like to see articles Michael has published, online check out: http://www.atlasmagazine. com/michael/networking.html and *Interactivity Magazine* at: http://www.interactivitymag.com.

Michael's books on other subjects include:

Insight Guides: Crossing America
■ Simon & Schuster ■ 1986

Brush Up Your Shakespeare!
■ Harper & Row ■ 1990

It's Greek to Me! Brush Up Your Classics
■ HarperCollins ■ 1991

By Jove! Brush Up Your Mythology
■ HarperCollins ■ 1992

Brush Up Your Bible!
■ HarperCollins ■ 1993

Eureka! What Archimedes Really Meant and 80 Other Key Ideas Explained
■ HarperCollins ■ 1994

Lessons on Living from Shakespeare
■ Crown ■ 1996

Brush Up Your Poetry!
■ Cader/Andrews & McMeel ■ 1996

Naughty Shakespeare
■ Cader/Andrews & McMeel ■ 1997

What's Next for @tlas

Amy has formed an outside multimedia firm, called Future Farmers: cultivating your conscience. Working in partnership with Stella Lai, a 3D artist and designer, AirKing (music), Pants (programming), the firm (http://www .futurefarmers. com) offers commercial illustration and multimedia design.

The metaphor of "farming" is to reappropriate ideas in order to create artwork, producing a fertility of resourcefulness. The projects of Future Farmers, are playful and provocative and definitely err on the abstract side of the commercial fence.

When we last touched base with the team, Amy was busy with futurefarmers.com, Olivier was off to Equador on a shooting assignment, and Michael was working on a programming assignment for an outside contract. It might seem like none of their minds were on @tlas at all, but this team works best by letting everyone have freedom and flexibility, and then coming together and producing a new issue that is better than the last.

Michael closed with this statement: "@tlas' philosophy is not to necessarily build a site that the people are going to love. We're always going to shove something unexpected their way. Regardless, there are certain lines you have to draw. We don't exist to annoy people or crash their browsers. It's up to us to make the experience of @tlas more about the evocative content than the technology used."

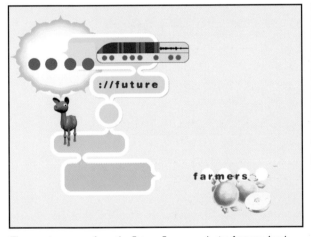

The opening screen from the Future Farmer web site features Amy's design work, Stella's 3D models, AirKing's music, and programming from Pants.

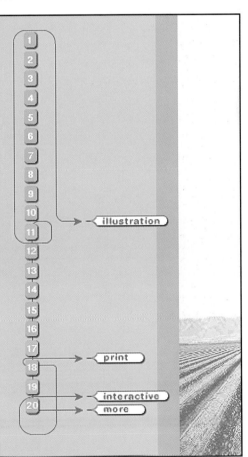

Amy's beautiful interface leads to the collection of commercial work the firm has produced for outside clients, including MSNBC and New York Times Magazine.

■ site summary

@tlas

@tlas is a place to visit when you want to see fresh, inspiring, technologically challenging art. It is a place where personal vision is respected and nurtured, and team members work with each other's ideas and tools. Michael's views about JavaScript and the direction of HTML are prophetic and point to new directions of the web medium. The voices from this site come from the hearts and minds of three individuals who are breaking new ground and walking where few have yet walked. To summarize, this chapter covered:

- The use of JavaScript for browser detection instead of CGI because of its better object handling.

- Amy's use of 3D and 2D graphics shows the influence of Photoshop as an editing tool to create hybrid imagery.

- Understanding how Amy gets ideas and inspiration teaches how her approach makes her artwork personal and individualistic.

- Working with CSS allows for better creative control over typography, despite the fact that browsers and platforms interpret the code differently. Until standards are set, Michael's approach of using multiple External Style Sheets is the only way to ensure optimal results between platforms and browsers.

- Looking at some of the innovative interface designs for @tlas shows the range of possibilities that have not yet been explored on the web.

Web Graphics Appendix
File Formats, Color, Optimization

- **Web Color**
- **Hexadecimal-Based Color**
- **Image Compression**
- **Web File Formats**

This chapter offers background information into many behind-the-scenes web authoring issues, such as web color, hexadecimal color, file formats, and compression. Feel free to read all the nitty gritty details, or skim the material for the exact information you need.

Web Color

In the art world, a discussion about color is about tones, hues, palettes and how humans associate feelings with colors. In the computer world, it is not possible to explain how to work with color without a discussion of video cards, monitors, and mathematics. Furthermore, it's difficult to effectively use computer color without having some understanding of the technical constraints, which are different on the web than in other digital design mediums.

Even if you are new to creating web graphics, you are likely experienced with mature image editing programs, such as Photoshop. Photoshop effectively shields users from the complications of computer color by providing color pickers and color palettes that are intuitive to use. If, however, you use a tool like Photoshop for web graphics, you'll want to first understand web palette management and hexadecimal mathematics. Photoshop was not designed with the web in mind, so it is up to you to understand how to prepare color files so they are web appropriate. This section goes into a technical and practical explanation of web color constraints and describes how to best produce images that will be displayed by web browsers.

How Computers Display Color

Computer monitors display color by using a method that is called RGB color. The monitor screen is composed of an array of tightly packed pixels. Each pixel is composed of a single red, green, and blue dot. The colors that a monitor displays at each pixel are "mixed" onscreen by varying the intensities of these three red, green, and blue color dots. The variation of intensity for each individual dot can range from a value of 0 (which is off) to a maximum value of 255 (which is on). How does this work? Well, red can be "off" (a value of 0), while green can be "half-on" (a value of 127), and blue can be fully "on" (a value of 255); and the resulting pixel appears greenish-blue.

Computer monitors display the number of colors that the computer's video card supports. These colors ranges are referred to as the "bit depth." The most common levels of bit depth supported by video cards and computer monitors are:

- ■ 8-bit   256 colors
- ■ 16-bit   65,536 colors
- ■ 24-bit   16.7 million colors

Dithering Problems in 8-Bit Environments

In order to view 24-bit color, a computer system requires a high-end video card, which costs extra money and is usually installed as an after-market addition. Many computer artists invest in 24-bit video cards (or extra VRAM that enables 24-bit color) because this allows them to see and create images with maximum color fidelity. Unfortunately, average computers consumers don't need or own 24-bit color system because most computers are used for simple tasks such as word processing, databases, or spreadsheets.

The truth is that most of the web-viewing audience using computer systems are only capable of displaying 8-bit color or, at best, 16-bit color. As soon as color is viewed from a system that only supports 8-bit colors, palette management problems emerge. Since both 16-bit and 8-bit systems are limited in the colors they can display, they must dither down any images that exceed 256 colors.

These two examples show a close-up view of the same image with dithering and without.

Dithering is a process where colored images with more than 256 colors are generated by color mixing and thereby simulate colors that can't be displayed. By placing two other colors in close proximity to fool the eye into seeing intermediate colors, blue and red, for example, can be arrayed to create an illusion of purple. Too often, dithering results in an unattractive scattering of pixels as the browser struggles to emulate a color from an exhausted palette. The key to creating graphics without unwanted dithering is to use the same colors that the browser uses, as opposed to using colors that the browser will dither to fit into its fixed palette. This palette is called the browser-safe palette.

What Is Browser Safe?

The browser safe palette is a palette of 216 colors that is uniform across the Mosaic, Netscape, and Explorer browsers, regardless whether they are viewed on the Mac or PC platforms. Use the Browser Safe palette to avoid color shifting and to ensure greater design (color) control, especially because the majority of viewers browse the Net on computers that are limited to 8-bit color.

Because the Mac and PC platforms both handle their color palettes differently, the browsers don't have the same colors available to them across all platforms, which results in inconsistent, unreliable color—but the discovery of Browser Safe Color solves this problem.

The Browser Safe palette contains only 216 out of 256 possible indexed colors because there are 40 colors that vary between Macs and PCs. Those 40 variable colors are eliminated to achieve a reliable cross-platform palette—otherwise, unsightly dithering is the consistent result.

In September 1995, Lynda Weinman and Bruce Heavin identified these 216 colors that are uniformly available across platforms in the major browsers: Mosaic, Netscape Navigator, and MS Explorer. Lynda Weinman published their results in January of 1996 in her book titled *Designing Web Graphics*.

As Lynda explains at her site, "This is the actual palette that Mosaic, Netscape, and Internet Explorer use within their browsers. This palette is based on math, not beauty." What she means is that the colors were not chosen but were extrapolated from a color cube that makes an evenly engineered dispersion of each of the three colors (red, green, and blue) through all possible combinations within the limits of a six by six cube.

This is a cube where the zero point of the x,y,z axis represents zero intensity for all three colors. At the opposite corner of the cube is the convergence of the sixth, or maximum intensity (x6,y6,z6), for all three colors.

Thus, the absence of color, or a value of 0, for all three colors results in black. Similarly, the maximum intensity, which is a value of 255, for all three colors blends to make white. The intervening shades and blends are described within the spaces of the cube described by this x,y,z axis between the diagonally-opposed black and white corners.

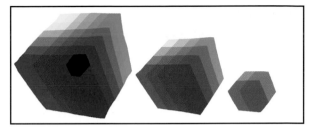

The front of the color cube and its inner cubes that decrease in intensity. Image courtesy of Bruce Heavin.

Although there is an absolute logic to this math, it does not (unfortunately) translate into the subjective beauty of an artistic palette. These colors were not chosen for their aesthetic usefulness: there's a dreadful lack of important flesh tones, a lamentable lapse in useful grays, a paucity of truly pleasing or otherwise useful shades, and so on.

The Browser Safe palette (together with a wealth of information) is available at http://www.lynda.com/hex.html. If you download her palettes, you'll have versions that are organized by hue (color) and value (darks and lights). Photoshop 4.0 now comes equipped with the web safe palette, so it is easier to create images that use these colors in the first place. If you use this, the browser will not dither your images and they will look much more professional when viewed by end-users who have to see the web through 8-bit system-tinted glasses.

Monitor and System Calibration

Neither science and theory, nor the use of the right palette stuff will give good viewing results unless a viewer's monitor is calibrated to accurately display the color and contrast of the images it receives. Calibration is a big issue that goes well beyond the scope of this book. **Photoshop 4 Artistry** ■ Barry Haynes and Wendy Crumpler ■ New Riders ■ ISBN 1-56205-759-6, has an excellent section on monitor and system calibration.

An interesting place to visit which has an online calibration checkup is at: http://www.zonezero.com/calibration/english.html.

Hexadecimal Based Color

Hexadecimal math is the method of notation used for describing individual colors within HTML code. If you view the source of web pages, or look at the code deconstructions in this book, you'll see odd looking numbers inside the <BODY> tag that describe color, such as #FF0066 or #339900. You are looking at the hexadecimal notation for RGB color values.

The hexadecimal notation system allots two places for each of the three color channels: R, G, and B. Thus, in hexadecimal 00FFCC: 00 occupies the red channel, FF occupies the green channel, and CC occupies the blue channel. This is another level of complication due to the necessity of describing colors not only for the monitor to digest, but also for the scripting languages to manipulate!

Hexadecimal is used in HTML to specify colored text, lines, background, borders, frame cells, and frame borders. Each color within an indexed 256-color palette can be described in Hexadecimal. The table below shows the corresponding values between hexadecimal and customary integer values.

Corresponding integer and hex values

16 integer values:	0 1 2 3 4 5 6 7 8 9 10 11 12 13 14 15
16 hex values:	0 1 2 3 4 5 6 7 8 9 A B C D E F

990033 R:153 G:000 B:051	FF3366 R:255 G:000 B:102	CC0033 R:204 G:000 B:051	FF0033 R:255 G:000 B:051	FF9999 R:255 G:153 B:153	CC3366 R:204 G:051 B:102	FFCCFF R:255 G:204 B:255	CC6699 R:204 G:051 B:153	993366 R:153 G:051 B:102	660033 R:102 G:000 B:051	CC3399 R:204 G:051 B:153	FF99CC R:255 G:153 B:204	FF66CC R:255 G:102 B:204	FF99FF R:255 G:153 B:255	FF6699 R:255 G:102 B:153	CC0066 R:204 G:000 B:102
FF0066 R:255 G:000 B:102	FF3399 R:255 G:051 B:153	FF0099 R:255 G:000 B:153	FF33CC R:255 G:051 B:204	FF00CC R:255 G:000 B:204	FF66FF R:255 G:102 B:255	FF33FF R:255 G:051 B:255	FF00FF R:255 G:000 B:255	CC0099 R:204 G:000 B:153	990066 R:153 G:000 B:102	CC66CC R:204 G:102 B:204	CC33CC R:204 G:051 B:204	CC99FF R:204 G:153 B:255	CC66FF R:204 G:102 B:255	CC33FF R:204 G:051 B:255	993399 R:153 G:051 B:153
CC00CC R:204 G:000 B:204	CC00FF R:204 G:000 B:255	9900CC R:153 G:000 B:204	990099 R:153 G:000 B:153	CC99CC R:204 G:153 B:204	996699 R:153 G:102 B:153	663366 R:102 G:051 B:102	660099 R:102 G:000 B:153	9933CC R:153 G:051 B:204	660066 R:102 G:000 B:102	9900FF R:153 G:000 B:255	9933FF R:153 G:051 B:255	9966CC R:153 G:102 B:204	330033 R:051 G:000 B:051	663399 R:102 G:051 B:153	6633CC R:102 G:051 B:204
6600CC R:102 G:000 B:204	9966FF R:153 G:102 B:255	330066 R:051 G:000 B:102	6600FF R:102 G:000 B:255	6633FF R:102 G:051 B:255	CCCCFF R:204 G:204 B:255	9999FF R:153 G:153 B:255	9999CC R:153 G:153 B:204	6666CC R:102 G:102 B:204	6666FF R:102 G:102 B:255	666699 R:102 G:102 B:153	333366 R:051 G:051 B:102	333399 R:051 G:051 B:153	330099 R:051 G:000 B:153	3300CC R:051 G:000 B:204	3300FF R:051 G:000 B:255
3333FF R:051 G:051 B:255	3333CC R:051 G:051 B:204	0066FF R:000 G:102 B:255	0033FF R:000 G:051 B:255	3366FF R:051 G:102 B:255	3366CC R:051 G:102 B:204	000066 R:000 G:000 B:102	000033 R:000 G:000 B:051	0000FF R:000 G:000 B:255	000099 R:000 G:000 B:153	0033CC R:000 G:051 B:204	0000CC R:000 G:000 B:204	336699 R:051 G:102 B:153	0066CC R:000 G:102 B:204	99CCFF R:153 G:204 B:255	6699FF R:102 G:153 B:255
003366 R:000 G:051 B:102	6699CC R:102 G:153 B:204	006699 R:000 G:102 B:153	3399CC R:051 G:153 B:204	0099CC R:000 G:153 B:204	66CCFF R:102 G:204 B:255	3399FF R:051 G:153 B:255	003399 R:000 G:051 B:153	0099FF R:000 G:153 B:255	33CCFF R:051 G:204 B:255	00CCFF R:000 G:204 B:255	99FFFF R:153 G:255 B:255	66FFFF R:102 G:255 B:255	33FFFF R:051 G:255 B:255	00FFFF R:000 G:255 B:255	00CCCC R:000 G:204 B:204
009999 R:000 G:153 B:153	669999 R:102 G:153 B:153	99CCCC R:153 G:204 B:204	CCFFFF R:204 G:255 B:255	33CCCC R:051 G:204 B:204	66CCCC R:102 G:204 B:204	339999 R:051 G:153 B:153	336666 R:051 G:102 B:102	006666 R:000 G:102 B:102	003333 R:000 G:051 B:051	00FFCC R:000 G:255 B:204	33FFCC R:051 G:255 B:204	33CC99 R:051 G:204 B:153	00CC99 R:000 G:204 B:153	66FFCC R:102 G:255 B:204	99FFCC R:153 G:255 B:204
00FF99 R:000 G:255 B:153	339966 R:051 G:153 B:102	006633 R:000 G:102 B:051	336633 R:051 G:102 B:051	669966 R:102 G:153 B:102	66CC66 R:102 G:204 B:102	99FF99 R:153 G:255 B:153	66FF66 R:102 G:255 B:102	339933 R:051 G:153 B:051	99CC99 R:153 G:204 B:153	66FF99 R:102 G:255 B:153	33FF99 R:051 G:255 B:153	33CC66 R:051 G:204 B:102	00CC66 R:000 G:204 B:102	66CC99 R:102 G:204 B:153	009966 R:000 G:153 B:102
009933 R:000 G:153 B:051	33FF66 R:051 G:255 B:102	00FF66 R:000 G:255 B:102	CCFFCC R:204 G:255 B:204	CCFF99 R:204 G:255 B:153	99FF66 R:153 G:255 B:102	99FF33 R:153 G:255 B:051	00FF33 R:000 G:255 B:051	33FF33 R:051 G:255 B:051	00CC33 R:000 G:204 B:051	33CC33 R:051 G:204 B:051	66FF33 R:102 G:255 B:051	00FF00 R:000 G:255 B:000	66CC33 R:102 G:204 B:051	006600 R:000 G:102 B:000	003300 R:000 G:051 B:000
009900 R:000 G:153 B:000	33FF00 R:051 G:255 B:000	66FF00 R:102 G:255 B:000	99FF00 R:153 G:255 B:000	66CC00 R:102 G:204 B:000	00CC00 R:000 G:204 B:000	33CC00 R:051 G:204 B:000	339900 R:051 G:153 B:000	99CC66 R:153 G:204 B:102	669933 R:102 G:153 B:051	99CC33 R:153 G:204 B:051	336600 R:051 G:102 B:000	669900 R:102 G:153 B:000	99CC00 R:153 G:204 B:000	CCFF66 R:204 G:255 B:102	CCFF33 R:204 G:255 B:051
CCFF00 R:204 G:255 B:000	999900 R:153 G:153 B:000	CCCC00 R:204 G:204 B:000	CCCC33 R:204 G:204 B:051	333300 R:051 G:051 B:000	666600 R:102 G:102 B:000	999933 R:153 G:153 B:051	CCCC66 R:204 G:204 B:102	666633 R:102 G:102 B:051	999966 R:153 G:153 B:102	CCCC99 R:204 G:204 B:153	FFFFCC R:255 G:255 B:204	FFFF99 R:255 G:255 B:153	FFFF66 R:255 G:255 B:102	FFFF33 R:255 G:255 B:051	FFFF00 R:255 G:255 B:000
FFCC00 R:255 G:204 B:000	FFCC66 R:255 G:204 B:102	FFCC33 R:255 G:204 B:051	CC9933 R:204 G:153 B:051	996600 R:153 G:102 B:000	CC9900 R:204 G:153 B:000	FF9900 R:255 G:153 B:000	CC6600 R:204 G:102 B:000	993300 R:153 G:051 B:000	CC6633 R:204 G:102 B:051	663300 R:102 G:051 B:000	FF9966 R:255 G:153 B:102	FF6633 R:255 G:102 B:051	FF9933 R:255 G:153 B:051	FF6600 R:255 G:102 B:000	CC3300 R:204 G:051 B:000
996633 R:153 G:102 B:051	330000 R:051 G:000 B:000	663333 R:102 G:051 B:051	996666 R:153 G:102 B:102	CC9999 R:204 G:153 B:153	993333 R:153 G:051 B:051	CC6666 R:204 G:102 B:102	FFCCCC R:255 G:204 B:204	FF3333 R:255 G:051 B:051	CC3333 R:204 G:051 B:051	FF6666 R:255 G:102 B:102	660000 R:102 G:000 B:000	990000 R:153 G:000 B:000	CC0000 R:204 G:000 B:000	FF0000 R:255 G:000 B:000	FF3300 R:255 G:051 B:000
CC9966 R:204 G:153 B:102	FFCC99 R:255 G:204 B:153	FFFFFF R:255 G:255 B:255	CCCCCC R:204 G:204 B:204	999999 R:153 G:153 B:153	666666 R:102 G:102 B:102	333333 R:051 G:051 B:051	000000 R:000 G:000 B:000								

The Browser Safe Color Palette includes the hexadecimal and RGB values for all 216 Browser Safe colors. This can be downloaded from Lynda Weinman's site at http://www.lynda.com/hex.html.

■ note

Hexadecimal Resources

Another way to decipher and/or find the hexadecimal for an RGB color is through the use of a hex calculator. Win95 includes a Calculator, found in the Accessories group. To access this feature; select Scientific, then Hex, input your RGB values, and the corresponding hex will be calculated. Mac users can download Cicinelli's hex calculator from ftp://ftp.amug.org/pub/mirrors/info-mac/sci/calc/calculator-ii-15.hqx.

■ note

ColorSafe

In 1995, Don Barnett and Bruce Heavin created a range of custom-mixed Browser Safe colors by building patterns composed of some Browser Safe colors that fool the eye into seeing a more desirable color. Because they were built out of the Browser Safe palette, these were essentially blocks of pre-planned dithers that produce a superior palette while retaining cross-platform, cross-browser color consistency. These palettes were displayed in the DreamWorks chapter of Lynda Weinman's original *Deconstructing Web Graphics*.

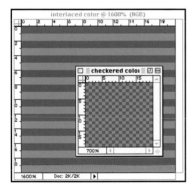

A close up of predithered patterns, which use browser safe color. When reduced to 100%, the pattern is not visible, but the illusion of a secondary color is achieved.

This idea may have lead to the development of a valuable software tool, ColorSafe, which generates custom colors on-the-fly via the same logic. Color-Safe (MAC and Win95) is available directly from BoxTop software at http://www.boxtopsoft.com/.

A good, unbiased review and tutorial of ColorSafe can be found at http://www.ruku.com/colorsafe.html.

■ note

Browser Safe Is NOT for Photographs

The Browser Safe Palette helps images that are composed of flat color, such as graphics, logos, cartoons, and many illustrations. Browser Safe colors do not need to be used on color photographs. The browser actually does an excellent job of dithering down photographs, where it adds a lot of unwanted dots and noise to flat color images.

Making Fast, Small Web Graphics

The following sections describe many factors related to creating small, fast web graphics. Some of the topics include image file size, resolution, bit depth, compression types, and file formats. This is a big subject with lots of components, but the payoff is you'll be able to create faster and better looking graphics.

Image File Size and Resolution

Image file size is defined by how much disk space the file uses. File size is determined by three factors. The first factor is the dimensional size of the image in pixels. The dimensional size coupled with the resolution of the image determines the file size at a given dimension.

An image with the dimensional size of 1" by 1" at 72 pixels per inch yields a far smaller file size than the same image 1" x 1" at 300 pixels per inch. You should always keep web graphics at screen resolution, which is 72 pixels per inch. If you create images at a higher resolution, they appear magnified on the screen and take up too much space to be efficient.

When the dimensional size and resolution remain constant, file size can be further reduced by using compression. Compression types vary depending on the file format in use. First, let's look at the different compression types in the next section.

Lossy and Lossless Compression Types

Two flavors of compression are used by web graphics file formats: lossy and lossless. Lossless compression does not discard detail, while lossy compression discards detail to obtain a smaller file size. When you compress an image via a lossy method and then subsequently decompress (or open) it, the image you open will be different from the original image you had prior to compression. Given the same scenario with a lossless compression method; the image you decompress will be exactly the same.

Web File Formats

Although many image file formats can be used on the web, GIF and JPG are the most common. This appendix will give you an overview of these two popular formats, because they are the file types that are used throughout the web and in the deconstructed examples inside this book. Many new file formats are being developed for the web, but they are outside the scope of this book.

GIF

GIF is an acronym for **G**raphics **I**nterchange **F**ormat that is pronounced with a "j" sound, as in "jiffy." This format has a restricted palette that cannot exceed 256 colors and employs a lossless compression scheme. In practice, the GIF format is only truly lossless when the subject image doesn't have to undergo bit depth reduction to become a GIF. This is because once the palette is reduced image quality is lost, even if the compression method inclurs no quality loss.

The GIF format is optimal for use with graphics and illustrative images such as cartoons, logos, and line drawings. The GIF format excels with reliable control of limited colors and offers excellent compression for large areas of solid color. Its features also include transparency and animation. Due to the constraints of 256 colors, GIF doesn't usually work well for detailed photographic images; it should only be used for photographs when either transparency or animation is necessary. Implemented properly, GIFs can be Browser Safe because a GIF image must be "indexed" and must include a CLUT, which leads us to our next section.

CLUTs and Indexed Images

The fundamental difference between the GIF and JPG formats is that a GIF file is limited to storing no more than 256 colors, whereas the JPG can store 16.7 million colors. This is because GIF images are indexed images. Any 8-bit (or lesser bit depth) image is referred to as indexed and must contain a palette. Why?

The GIF format is designed to store color information in a color map. Among other things, this color map is called a CLUT, or **C**olor **L**ook **U**p **T**able. It may also be called an index of color, color index, palette, or lut. It is also often referred to as a pain.

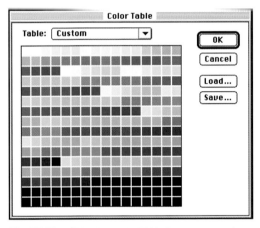

The CLUT or **C**olor **L**ook **U**p **T**able for an image with a custom palette. The CLUT for an indexed image is accessible in Photoshop via the menu Image: Mode: Color Table.

A CLUT could be compared to a set of paint buckets that may number as few as two but cannot exceed 256. Each pixel of a GIF image is mapped to a single bucket for its color. Thus, if the color contained by bucket #72 is changed (or remapped) from tomato red to orange orange, then all pixels within the image that are assigned to bucket #72 (and which formerly displayed tomato red), now show up as orange orange. Technically, the buckets in this analogy are referred to as slots in the CLUT.

A 3-Bit CLUT

Slot # Color	Name	RGB Value	HEX Value
0	aqua	000 255 255	00FFFF
1	blue	000 000 255	0000FF
2	fuchsia	255 000 255	FF00FF
3	lime	000 255 000	00FF00
4	red	255 000 000	FF0000
5	white	255 255 255	FFFFFF
6	yellow	255 255 000	FFFF00
7	black	000 000 000	000000

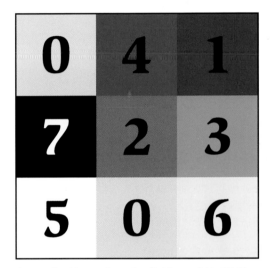

A example of how an image is called from a 3-bit CLUT. This hypothetical example has only nine pixels. Each pixel in this image is numbered to signify how a CLUT is referred to in the GIF file format to describe the color slot, and hence the color, for each pixel. The pixels are indexed to numbered slots (or buckets) within the CLUT, which contains the color information in RGB. Corresponding hex values are included in this chart.

We looked at monitor bit depths earlier in this chapter. Images have bit depths too. Here's a handy chart for the common bit depth ranges.

Bit Depth Ranges

Image Bit depth	Bits per Pixel	# Possible Colors
3-bit	3 bits/pixel	= 8 colors
4-bit	4 bits/pixel	= 16 colors
5-bit	5 bits/pixel	= 32 colors
6-bit	6 bits/pixel	= 64 colors
7-bit	7 bits/pixel	= 128 colors
8-bit	8 bits/pixel	= 256 colors

◾ note

How Are GIFs Compressed?

When an image exceeds 256 total colors, all of the existing colors have to be remapped (on the basis of their frequency of appearance within the image) to an indexed CLUT. When an image contains less than 256 colors, its file size is reduced. The file size or the compressibility of the GIF format is also influenced by whether the image contains dithering when the image is converted to indexed color.

Assuming you have started with a 256 color image, GIF compression looks for horizontal runs of the same color and replaces repetitive enumeration of pixels with groupings of same colors, which results in a smaller file size.

GIF compression works best on horizontal runs of the same exact color. A GIF of the American Flag, for example, compresses much better when it is horizontal (as when on a flag pole and held out by a strong wind) than if it is draped lengthwise. Why? Because the long runs of same color in the stripes of the flag are optimal for GIF compression when the flag is horizontal. When the flag is vertical, the horizontal runs of same color are very short. Thus, if the flag is oriented diagonally, intermediate compression results. The file would not be as small as the horizontal flag but far smaller than the vertical flag. Similarly, zebras and striped horses are more compressible when standing on their heads than on their feet.

What this boils down to is that if you create images with large amounts of flat color, use less colors than 256, and keep dithering down to a minimum, your GIF files will be much smaller and download more quickly.

GIF Animation

The most recent implementation of the GIF format, GIF89a, provides the capability for streaming animations composed of a sequence of individual GIFs, much like a flipbook.

Further resources for GIF Animation are located at:

http://iawwww.epfl.ch/Staff/Yves.Piguet/clip2gif-home/GifBuilder.html

http://www.mindworkshop.com/alchemy/gifcon.html

http://www.uncom.com/dcw2/tnt/gif/animation

http://iawwww.epfl.ch/Staff/Yves.Piguet/clip2gif-home/GifBuilder.html

◾ note

Further Resources

The intent of this Web Graphics Appendix is to be definitive rather than exhaustive, so if you want to delve further into this subject I recommend three helpful resources:

Designing Web Graphics 2 ◾ Lynda Weinman; New Riders ◾ ISBN 1-56205-715-4. This volume is the perfect adjunct for nearly every topic within this book.

Coloring Web Graphics 2 ◾ Lynda Weinman and Bruce Heavin ◾ New Riders ◾ ISBN 1-56205-818-5. This entire volume is devoted to the subject of web color and includes helpful tips about color theory and an assortment of indispensable web color palettes for use in many imaging programs.

Photoshop Web Techniques ◾ J. Scott Hamlin ◾ New Riders ◾ ISBN 1-56205-733-2. This book offers a clear discussion of color math and many practical methods for the application of color on the web. This appendix is indebted to several of J. Scott Hamlin's approaches.

Saving a GIF in Photoshop

Unlike saving a JPG, saving to the GIF format entails a number of variables and options. The following section enumerates these variables and offers tips and techniques useful for saving small GIF files.

The Indexed Color dialog is accessed from the Image:Mode menu.

The Indexed Color Dialog has three interrelated sets of variables controlling color, color depth, and dithering for the image that is being indexed. All of these factors affect quality and file size.

The Palette Options are used to specify which palette is used or what kind of palette is used on an image. The Exact palette setting is determined by the colors within the Image and is only available if the image contains no more the 256 colors. The System palettes, for both Mac and PC, are preset palettes that are useful for multimedia, but not particularly useful for the web. The Web palette is the same as the browser safe 216-color palette described earlier. The Uniform is a mathematical sampling of the range of colors in the image. The Adaptive palette is a different sampling based on the frequency of appearance of colors found in the image. Custom permits the user to load a palette that has been saved. Previous reuses a palette from a prior conversion.

Color Depth options vary dependent on the type of palette chosen in the Palette Options, as some palettes have more variability than others. Shown here are the possible Color Depths for the Web palette. You can also enter any value between 1 and 256 yourself.

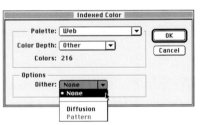

The options for Dither are None (which is preferable), Diffusion, and Pattern. If a dither must be applied to an indexed image to smooth a gradient or flesh tone, Diffusion is the only dither option.

GIF File Size versus Quality Tips

Here are a few tips, tricks, and facts that will help you with GIF graphics:

- Shaving bandwidth usually involves experimentation. Always save the file down to the lowest bit depth which yields unacceptable results, and then go back up one bit depth for the "keeper."

- A slight reduction of image dimensions may permit the retention of higher bit depth (to obtain a higher color quality) while still obtaining a tolerable file size.

- It may be possible to obtain a smaller file size by selecting the smallest tolerable bit depth and using the adaptive palette. The trade-off is that images with flat color should use the Web palette or they will dither once viewed on 8-bit systems.

- If the GIF image has 256 or less colors, it can be saved with an exact palette.

- Selecting Areas of Influence: An adaptive palette can be influenced to give priority to certain areas of color within an image by selecting them with the Lasso or other selection tool, and sustaining this active selection prior to the conversion via Image: Mode: Indexed Color.

- Dithering is a process where absent colors are simulated by placing two other colors in close proximity to fool the eye into seeing those absent colors. For example, blue and red can be arrayed to create an illusion of purple. Dithering is useful on images that contain glows, drop shadows, or blurs.

- Dithering should be avoided unless the undithered image is unacceptable such as, for example, when the image has large areas of gradated color or flesh tones.

- Dithering reduces compressibility of an image because the dither breaks up the runs of same color that GIF uses to obtain compression.

- When there is room for artistic license, a subtle use of Photoshop's artistic filters—such as dry brush strokes and posterize, or the sketch filters, such as conte crayon—often both reduces the number of colors and also creates color clusters that translate to enhanced compressibility.

- On an 8-bit system, no matter how finely the adaptive palette is tuned to the images, the browser remaps the image to the Browser Safe palette.

■ note

Further resources for GIF:

http://www.theimage.com/web/graphic/gifvsgif/gif1A.html

http://www.mindworkshop.com/alchemy/gifcon.html

http://www.boxtopsoft.com/

http://www.uncom.com/dcw2/tnt/gif/animation

http://www.uncom.com/dcw2/tnt/gif/transparency

JPEG

JPEG is an acronym for **J**oint **P**hotographic **E**xperts **G**roup. The JPEG format is the format of choice for most high-color photographic imagery displayed on the web because it supports 24-bit color with 16.7 million colors. JPEG compression excels at retaining smooth gradations as well as subtle tonal and color changes. It also employs a lossy compression scheme that causes little noticeable image degradation when properly implemented. The JPEG format is not Browser Safe, however, because this lossy compression scheme tends to shift color and JPEGs cannot store or retain 8-bit palettes.

Thus, an image created with Browser Safe color and subsequently saved as a JPEG will not match a companion image that has also been created with Browser Safe color and been saved as a GIF. Nor will the JPEG match an HTML-specified Browser Safe background, although the above described companion GIF will match exactly.

Interlaced GIFs and Progressive JPGs

Both GIF and JPEG provide a means for an image to be viewed initially in a blurry fashion that subsequently sharpens as the image continues to download. With GIFs, this is called interlacing. With JPEGs, it is called progressive. The advantage to using this style of JPEG or GIF is if you want the image to load more quickly, giving the end-user a chance to choose to wait or leave the page. Interlaced graphics are not advisable for navigational elements because they sometimes fail to finish loading, thus leaving the visitor stuck.

Saving a JPEG in Photoshop

Saving a JPEG image is really quite easy. Compared to the array of tricks and trade-offs involved with GIFs, JPEG is a no-brainer.

The standard JPEG dialog box is invoked when the default Photoshop JPEG format is selected from the menu File: Save As. In the Image Options area of the dialog, quality is determined by choosing between the Highest (10) and the Lowest (1). This controls the degree image degradation, where more degradation obtains greater compression results. (Unlike GIF, that's all you really need to know about JPG compression.) Beneath compression, three Format Options provide for generic JPEG, which are Baseline; Baseline Optimized, which yields smaller files with cleaner compression resulting in less artifacts; and Progressive, which initially opens the image in a blur that sharpens as the image continues to download.

■ **note**

Further resources for JPG:

http://www.theimage.com/web/graphic/jpgvsjpg/gif2A.html

http://www.boxtopsoft.com/

http://www.uncom.com/dcw2/tnt/jpg

■ notes...

Contact Appendix
Talent Directory

■ the team

Lynda Weinman
lynda.com, L.L.C
423 E. Ojai Ave. 107-506
Ojai, CA 93023
805.646.7076
http://www.lynda.com
lynda@lynda.com

**Bruce Heavin
Illustration**
Bruce Heavin
423 E. Ojai Ave. 107-506
Ojai, CA 93023
805.640.9607 fx
http://www.stink.com/bruce/

Alink Newmedia
Ali Karp
332 N. Oakhurst Dr. Studio B
Beverly Hills, CA 90210
310.858.7370
alink@earthlink.net

Jon Warren Lentz
PO Box 396
Carlsbad, CA 92018
jwlpsi@uncom.com
http://www.uncom.com
http://www.uncom.com/decon2

Robert Reinhardt
Technical Editor
206 Beatrice Street
Toronto, Ontario
M6G 3G1 Canada
nakedboy@fine-art.com

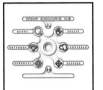

I. **Qaswa** 19
Design and Function
http://www.qaswa.com/

Ammon Haggerty
Qaswa Communications
S.S. Vallejo, Varda Landing
Sausalito, CA 94965
415.331.0580
415.331.0580 fx
ammon@qaswa.com

2. **Cooper-Hewitt** 43
Museum on the Web
http://www.si.edu/ndm/

Elisabeth Roxby
elisabeth@roxx.com
http://www.roxx.com

Dynamo
Art Technology Group
http://www.atg.com

Julie H. Keisman
jkeisman@ix.netcom.com

Cooper-Hewitt
National Design Museum
Smithsonian Insitution
2 East 91st St.
New York, NY 10128
212.849.8300

3. **Bosch Power Tools** 73
Well-Tooled Elegance
http://www.boschtools.com

Heath Greenfield
Cramer-Krasselt
225 N. Michigan Ave.
Chicago, IL 60601
312.616.2601
312.616.2334 fx
Heath_Greenfield@c-k.com

Stuart Cohn
Upshot (Senior Art Director)
225 W. Wacker Drive
Chicago, IL 60606
312.943.0900
312.943.9699 fx
stuartcohn@upshotmail.com

Level 9
5 State Street
Montpelier, VT 05602
802.229.2005
802.223.0452 fx
http://www.l9.com

John Taylor
San Francisco, CA 94123
jatee@sirius.com

Tim Stanton
950 Superba Ave.
Venice, CA 90291
310.306.6470
310.574.2869 fx
tstanton@infonorth.com or
t.stanton@worldnet.att.net

The Amazing Don Foley
8222 Stonewall Dr.
Vienna, VA 22180
703.849.1707 ph/fx
don@foleymedia.com

Trevor Elliott
24301 SE 261st Place
Maple Valley, WA 98038
310.306.6470
310.577.2869 fx
t@contentfree.com

4. **National Geographic** 105
Synergy of Print and Web
http://www.nationalgeographic.com/features/97/nyunderground/

5. **Akimbo** 125
Designing with Technology
http://www.akimbodesign.com

Akimbo Design
2503 Bryant St.
San Francisco, CA 94110
415.642.4230
415.642.4232 fx

6. **@tlas** 157
Web Magazine
http://www.atlasmagazine.com

@tlas
1201-B Howard St.
San Francisco, CA 94103
415.553.4074
415. 552.6328 fx

Amy Franceschini
PO Box 410232
San Francico, CA 94141
415.552.2124
ame@sirius.com
http://www.futurefarmers.com
http://www.atlasmagazine.com

Olivier Laude
Creative Director
olivier@sirius.com

Michael Macrone
macrone@well.com
http://www.well.com/~macrone/

Glossary
Description of Terms

#

8-bit graphics: A color or grayscale graphic or movie that has 256 colors or less.

8-bit sound: 8-bit sound has a dynamic range of about 48 dB (decibels).

16-bit graphics: A color image or movie that has 65,536 colors.

16-bit sound: Standard CD-quality sound. 16-bit sound has a dynamic range of about 96 dB.

24-bit graphics: A color image or movie that has 16.7 million colors.

32-bit graphics: A color image or movie that has 16.7 million colors, plus an 8-bit masking channel.

µ-law: µ-law is a sound file format used by UNIX platforms. These files have the .au file extension.

a

active navigation: Point-and-click navigation, where the enduser guides the information flow.

adaptive dithering: A form of dithering in which the program looks to the image to determine the best set of colors when creating an 8-bit (or smaller) palette. See **dithering**.

additive color: The use of projected light to mix color. This is the type of color we see on video monitors.

aliasing: In bitmapped graphics, the jagged boundary along the edges of different colored shapes within an image. See **anti-aliasing**.

alpha channel: A masking channel used in 32-bit graphics that can include 8-bit transparency information. In Photoshop, an alpha channel is a masking channel that can be stored permanently with an image file for compositing purposes.

animated GIF: A single GIF file with multiple images and information for displaying them sequentially.

anti-aliasing: A technique for reducing the jagged appearance of aliased bitmapped images, usually by interpolating the color and value of pixels at the boundaries of adjacent colors.

artifacts: Image imperfections, usually caused by compression.

attribute: A modifier to an HTML tag (for example, <TAG ATTRIBUTE>).

authoring tools: Creation tools for interactive media.

AVI: **A**udio-**V**ideo **I**nterleaved. Microsoft's file format for desktop video movies.

bit depth: The number of bits used to represent the color of each pixel in a digital image. Specifically, bit depth of 1 = 2 colors (usually black and white); bit depth of 2 = 4 colors; bit depth of 4 = 16 colors; bit depth of 8 = 256 colors; bit depth of 16 = 65,536 colors; bit depth of 24 = 16,777,216 colors. (See **Chapter 6**)

bitmapped graphics: Also called raster graphics. Bitmapped graphics are images that have a specific number of pixels. As such, they are fixed into a particular grid of so many vertical and horizontal lines of pixels. This grid is called a "raster," and images that are fixed to such a grid are said to be "rasterized." The GIF and JPEG images that you commonly use on the Web are bitmapped. See **vector graphics**.

b

browser: Also called user agent. An application that enables you to access World Wide Web pages. Most browsers provide the capability to view web pages, copy and print material from web pages, download files from the web, and navigate throughout the web.

browser-safe colors: The 216 colors that do not shift between platforms, operating systems, or most web browsers.

c

cache: A storage area that keeps frequently accessed data or program instructions readily available so that you do not have to retrieve them repeatedly.

CERN: The European Laboratory for Particle Physics (formerly **C**onseil **E**uropèenne pour la **R**echerche **N**uclèaire). A joint project of the European Economic Community, where the World Wide Web was first conceived.

CGI: **C**ommon **G**ateway **I**nterface. The programmatic interface between a web server and other programs running on that server. Commonly used for extending the interactivity of a web site.

Cinepak: Cinepak is a form of very high compression for movies. The compression type is called "lossy" because it causes a visible loss in quality.

client: A computer that requests information from a network server. See **server**.

client pull: Client pull creates a slideshow effect with HTML text or inline images. It is programmed within the <META> tag.

client side: Client side means that the web element or effect can run locally off a computer and does not require the presence of a server.

client-side imagemap: A client-side imagemap is programmed in HTML and does not require a separate map definition file or a live web server to operate.

CLUT: **C**olor **L**ook**U**p **T**able. An 8-bit or lower image file uses a CLUT to define its palette.

color mapping: A color map refers to the color palette of an image. Color mapping means assigning colors to an image.

color names: Some browsers support using the name of a color instead of the color's hexadecimal value.

container: An element that encloses other objects, for example, <HEAD> </HEAD> is a container.

compression: Reduction of the amount of data required to re-create an original file, graphic, or movie. Compression is used to reduce the transmission time of media and application files across the Internet.

compositing: The process of combining images. Often implies masking, in that a masked image might be "composited" over another image.

contrast: The degree of separation between values.

d

data rate: The data rate is the amount of data per second of real-time media. It is commonly used for both sound and movies.

data streaming: The capability to deliver media in real-time, much like a VCR, rather than having to download all the information before it can be played.

decibel (dB): The measure of relative intensity between two signals, usually used in measuring sound. Decibels are a logarithmic measurement, where twice the power is equal to 3 times as many dB.

dithering: The positioning of different colored pixels within an image to approximate colors that are not in the available palette. A dithered image often looks noisy, or composed of scattered pixels. See **adaptive dithering**.

document: Any individual object (text, image, media) on the web.

dpi: **D**ots **P**er **I**nch. A common measurement related to the resolution of an image. See **screen resolution**.

dynamic range: The measure of the listenable range of sound that is above the level of background noise and below the level of distortion. The larger the number, the better the quality of the sound.

e

element: An object in an HTML file.

entity: Special characters (such as ©, ®, or @) that are defined by ASCII character combinations (such as &#169, &#174, or &#64).

extension: Abbreviated code at the end of a file, usually used to identify the type of file. For example, a JPEG file may have the .jpg extension.

f

fps: **F**rames **P**er **S**econd. A movie contains a certain number of frames per second; if there are fewer frames, the motion will be more jerky and the file size will be smaller.

frames: Frames offer the capability to divide a web page into multiple regions, with each region acting as a nested web page.

FTP: **F**ile **T**ransfer **P**rotocol. An Internet protocol that enables users to remotely access files on other computers. An FTP site houses files that can be downloaded to your computer.

g

gamma: Gamma measures the contrast that affects the midtones of an image. Adjusting the gamma lets you change the brightness values of the middle range of gray tones without dramatically altering the shadows and highlights.

gamut: A viewable or printable color range.

GIF: A bitmapped, color graphics file format. GIF is commonly used on the web because it employs an efficient compression method. See **JPEG**.

GIF89a: The most current GIF specification.

guestbook: A type of form that allows endusers to enter comments on a web page.

h

hexadecimal: The base-16 number system often used in scripts and code. Hexadecimal code is required by HTML to describe RGB values of color for the web.

HTML: **H**yper**T**ext **M**arkup **L**anguage. The common language for interchange of hypertext between the World Wide Web client and server. Web pages are written using HTML. See **hypertext**.

HTTP: **H**yper**T**ext **T**ransfer **P**rotocol is the protocol that the browser and the web server use to communicate with each other.

hue: Defines a linear spectrum of the color wheel.

hyperlink: Linked text, images, or media.

hypertext: Text that is linked to documents on the web.

i

imagemaps: Portions of images that are hypertext links. Using a mouse-based web client such as Netscape or Mosaic, the user clicks on different parts of a mapped image to activate different hypertext links. See **hypertext**.

inline graphic: A graphic that sits inside an HTML document instead of the alternative, which would require that the image be downloaded and then viewed by using an outside system.

interlaced GIFs: The GIF file format that allows for "interlacing," which causes the GIF to load quickly at low or chunky resolution and gradually come into full or crisp resolution.

ISP: **I**nternet **S**ervice **P**rovider.

j

Java: A programming language developed by Sun Microsystems that is cross-plat-form compatible and supported by some web browsers.

Java applet: A Java-based mini-application.

JavaScript: A scripting language that enables you to extend the capabilities of HTML. Developed by Netscape. No relation to Java (except the name).

JPEG: **J**oint **P**hotographic **E**xperts **G**roup; also the graphic format that they developed. JPEG graphics use lossy compression technique that can reduce the size of the graphics file by as much as 96 percent. See **GIF**.

l

links: Words or graphics in a hypertext document that act as pointers to other web objects. Links are generally underlined and may appear in a different color. When you click on a link, you can be transported to a different web site that contains information about the work or phrase used as the link. See **hypertext**.

lossless compression: A data compression technique that reduces the size of a file without sacrificing any of the original data. In lossless compression, the expanded or restored file is an exact replica of the original file before it was compressed. See **compression**.

lossy compression: A data compression technique in which some data is delib-erately discarded in order to achieve massive reductions in the size of the com-pressed file. See **compression**.

m

mask: The process of blocking out areas in a computer graphic.

MIME: **M**ultipurpose **I**nternet **M**ail **E**xtensions. An Internet standard for transferring nontext-based data such as sounds, movies, and images.

monospaced font: A typeface in which each character takes the same amount of horizontal space. This style of type is requested with the HTML code <TT> or <PRE>.

MPEG: **M**oving **P**ictures **E**xperts **G**roup. Also the name of a high-quality media format for both audio and video.

o

object: Any distinct component of HTML, such as a tag, attribute, image, text file, and so on.

p

passive navigation: Animation, slideshows, streaming movies, and audio. Basically, anything that plays without the enduser initiating the content.

perl: **P**ractical **E**xtention and **R**eporting **L**anguage. A popular language for CGI.

plug-in: Plug-ins are supported by some browsers and extend the capability of standard HTML. Examples of plug-ins include Shockwave, Flash, QuickTime, and so on.

PNG: (pronounced "ping") **P**ortable **N**etwork **G**raphics. PNG is a lossless file format that supports interlacing, 8-bit transparency, and gamma information.

PostScript: A page description language used for printing text and graphics on laser printers and other high-resolution printing devices.

PP: (also **IPP**) (**I**nternet) **P**resence **P**rovider. Usually a web-hosting service.

ppi: **P**ixels **P**er **I**nch. A common measurement related to the resolution of an image. See **screen resolution**.

proportional font: A typeface in which each character takes up a different width.

progressive JPEG: A type of JPEG that produces an interlaced effect as it loads, much like interlaced GIFs.

provider: Provides Internet access. See **ISP**.

q

QuickTime: System software developed by Apple Computer for presentation of desktop video.

r

resolution: Image resolution is measured by **dots per inch (DPI)** or **pixels per inch (PPI)**. Web images must be viewed at screen resolution, where images destined for print can be printed at much higher resolutions on high-resolution printing devices.

resolution independent: Vector graphics (Illustrator, CorelDraw, and Freehand are some examples of programs that generate vector graphics) are resolution independent, because the same file will print at different resolutions, depending on the device it is viewed on or printed on.

raster graphics: See **bitmapped graphics**.

rollover: A type of navigation button that changes when the enduser's mouse rolls over it.

s

sample rate: Sample rates are measured in kilohertz (KHz). Sound-editing software is where the initial sample rate settings are established. Standard sample rates range from 11.025 KHz, 22.050 KHz, 44.10 KHz, to 48 KHz. The higher the sample rate, the better the quality. The sample describes its highs and lows. See **data rate**.

sampling resolution: Sampling resolution affects media quality, just like dpi resolution affects the quality of images.

saturation: Defines the intensity of color.

screen resolution: Screen resolution, measured in dots per inch, generally refers to the resolution of common computer monitors. 72 dpi is an agreed upon average, although you will also hear of 96 dpi being the resolution of larger displays.

search engine: A type of application commonly found on the web that enables you to search by keywords for information or URLs.

server: A computer that provides services for users of its network. The server receives requests for services and manages the requests so that they are answered in an orderly manner. See **client**.

server push: Server push is the method of requesting images or data from the server and automating the image or data playback. It involves CGI and the presence of a live web server.

server side: Server side means any type of web page element that depends on being loaded to a server. It also implies the use of a CGI script.

server-side imagemap: A server-side imagemap requires that the information about the imagemap be saved within a "map definition file" that needs to be stored on a server and accessed by a CGI script.

single pixel transparency: Sometimes also referred to as a single pixel GIF, a technique for creating space in HTML with an image file that is only composed of a single pixel. The pixel is typically colored the same as the background so it blends in, or it is created with GIF transparency. The single pixel can be stretched horizontally or vertically by using HEIGHT and WIDTH attributes in HTML code.

splash screen: The main menu screen or opening graphic to a web page.

sprite: An individual component of an animation, such as a character or graphic that moves independently.

t

tables: Tables create rows and columns, as in a spreadsheet, and can be used to align data and images.

tag: An HTML directive, enclosed in "<" and ">".

texture map: 2D artwork that is applied to the surface of a 3D shape.

transparent GIFs: A subset of the original GIF file format that adds header information to the GIF file, which signifies a defined color will be masked out.

true color: The quality of color provided by 24-bit color depth. 24-bit color depth results in 16.7 million colors, which is usually more than adequate for the human eye.

u

user agent: see **browser**.

URL: Uniform **R**esource **L**ocator. The address for a web site.

v

value: The range from light to dark in an image.

vector graphics: Images that are stored as lines and curves instead of pixels. Vector graphics can be rendered in various sizes, resolutions, and media without losing information. See **bitmapped graphics**.

Video for Windows: A multimedia architecture and application suite that provides an outbound architecture that lets applications developers access audio, video, and animation from many different sources through one interface. As an application, Video for Windows primarily handles video capture and compression and video and audio editing. See **AVI**.

w

WYSIWYG: (pronounced wizzy-wig) **W**hat **Y**ou **S**ee **I**s **W**hat **Y**ou **G**et. A design philosophy in which formatting commands directly affect the text displayed onscreen so that the screen shows the appearance of printed text.

Index

Symbols

A

<deconstructing web graphics>

Web Design Case Studies and Tutorials

Deconstructing Web Graphics profiles top web designers and programmers in order to demystify and analyze how they make decisions, solve complex issues, and create exceptional web sites. Adding her own voice and digital design teaching experience to the book, best-selling author Lynda Weinman selects from her list of favorite designed web sites. She walks you through how to read and understand the source code for each page, breaks down all of the technical elements, and describes the inside details straight from the designers and programmers who created the pages.

This conversational and information-rich guide offers insight into web design that is not found through any other means. Profiles of successful web designers, programmers, photographers, and illustrators allow them to share their tips, techniques, and recommendations. You'll bring your own web design skills to a higher level through studying their experiences and the step-by-step tutorials and examples found in *Deconstructing Web Graphics*.

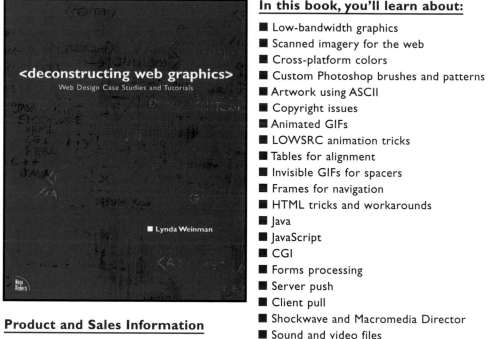

In this book, you'll learn about:

- Low-bandwidth graphics
- Scanned imagery for the web
- Cross-platform colors
- Custom Photoshop brushes and patterns
- Artwork using ASCII
- Copyright issues
- Animated GIFs
- LOWSRC animation tricks
- Tables for alignment
- Invisible GIFs for spacers
- Frames for navigation
- HTML tricks and workarounds
- Java
- JavaScript
- CGI
- Forms processing
- Server push
- Client pull
- Shockwave and Macromedia Director
- Sound and video files
- VRML

Product and Sales Information

Deconstructing Web Graphics by Lynda Weinman
ISBN:1-56205-641-7 ▪ $44.99/USA ▪ 250 pages
Available at your local bookstore or online
Macmillan Publishing ▪ 1-800-428-5331
- http://www.lynda.com
- http://www.mcp.com/newriders

■ testimonials

Deconstructing Web Graphics

"As an experienced web developer, I find most HTML books repeat the same basic information. However, this book is very different. It has seamlessly blended design and programming. By reading this book carefully and implementing the examples, you can learn many of my secret tips and tricks, which I have learned by trial and error, over the last three years. A must-have for any serious web developer." —Steve

"Your books have been invaluable to me in my journey from print to web design. After understanding and testing all the recipes in *Designing Web Graphics.2*, I really started to cook with *Deconstructing Web Graphics*. Truly, that book is the frosting on the cake: information and inspiration all in one package. I implore you to write another and another; I'll be first in line to buy them. As an illustrator, book designer, and sometime writer, I'd like to offer kudos to Bruce Heavin and Ali Karp as well as to you for keeping the flags of quality flying high." —Ray

"I'm just e-mailing you to thank you for writing the books you have. I've purchased *Deconstructing Web Graphics* and *Coloring Web Graphics*, and as a traditional print-based designer, these have helped me greatly in understanding color space and layout control for the web. Keep up the excellent work!" —Elizabeth

"Bought *Deconstructing Web Graphics*. Took a quick browse and had it stolen from my truck the next day. So I bought another. Great book. And thanks for the handy color palette." —Steve

Cara, Lynda: Sto leggendo il tuo libro ed sono affascinata con lui, voglio felicitarti per quest'opera. Brava! Quando lo finisca ti scrivero, ed arrotondare i miei commenti. Ok? Per cortesia vorrei ricevere indirizzi, cosi belle come il tuo dal punto di vista grafico per navigare, grazie mille! Arrivederci." —Silvia

"I now have almost all of Lynda's books and continue to be amazed and inspired by what she has to teach, for teach is what she does. And as we all remember our favourite teachers…they were inspirational. I appreciate this book's breadth as well as variety. I ALWAYS learn something from her books, but this one is actually FUN. As an interface designer for web-based applications, I appreciate her approach and accumulating knowledge into one place. Thank you Lynda Weinman!" —Amazon Books Reader

"Just dropping you a note to say how much I enjoyed your books. The format is great and very inspiring. Not only are the case studies in *Deconstructing Web Graphics* enlightening and informative, but all the background info makes it a damn good read too!!! Keep up the great work." —Vu

<coloring web graphics.2>

Master Color and Image File Formats for the Web

The purpose of this book is to help artists, programmers, and hobbyists understand how to work with color and image file formats for web delivery. Web browsers and different operating systems handle color in specific ways that many web designers aren't aware of. This updated second edition includes information about Photoshop 4.0, Illustrator 7.0, DitherBox, and DeBabelizer Pro.

A color palette of 216 browser-safe colors is identified and organized to help web designers confidently select successful cross-platform color choices and combinations. The book includes sections on color theory and understanding web color file formats, as well as step-by-step tutorials that explain how to work with browser-safe colors in Photoshop 4.0, Paint Shop Pro, Photo-Paint, Painter, FreeHand, and Illustrator 7.0. The cross-platform CD-ROM includes hundreds of suggested color combinations for web page design, as well as hundreds of palettes and browser-safe clip art files.

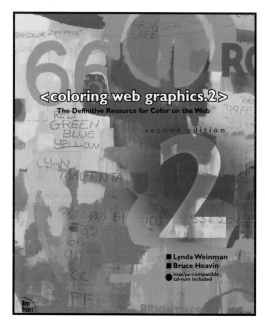

In this book, you'll learn about:

- Creating colors in your artwork that won't shift or dither across multiple platforms
- Choosing web-appropriate color schemes for your page designs
- Creating browser-safe hybrid variations
- Using Photoshop, Paint Shop Pro, Photo-Paint, FreeHand, Illustrator, and Director to manage web-specific color

The cross-platform CD-ROM includes:

- Browser-safe color palettes
- Browser-safe color swatches for Photoshop and other imaging programs
- Browser-safe colors organized by hue, value, and saturation
- Browser-safe color clip art for web use
- Electronic versions of color swatches grouped as they are in the book
- Sample HTML pages with recommended color groupings
- Sample patterns, backgrounds, buttons, and rules

Product and Sales Information

Coloring Web Graphics.2
By Lynda Weinman & Bruce Heavin
ISBN:1-56205-818-5 ▪ $50.00/USA ▪ 314 pages
Available at your local bookstore or online
Macmillan Publishing ▪ 1-800-428-5331
- http://www.lynda.com
- http://www.mcp.com/newriders

■ testimonials

Coloring Web Graphics

"I wanted to let you know that as a multimedia professional, your books (I own and have read all three) have been a source of great inspiration. Although the folks I work with are not quite as interested as I am in cutting-edge design issues for web and CD-ROM, I have relied upon your books as an invaluable resource for my production work as an Assistant Art Director and for my personal artwork. Also, a special thanks to Bruce for those color swatches, which have to be the single most exciting breakthrough for web designers." —Cheryl

"I bought your book, *Coloring Web Graphics* (Korean Edition). It is the best book of web design reference. (Just I think so. :-)) My distress was almost unbearable. I had worried about what color is safe on cross platform for a long time. Your book was the answer." —Hoon

"Oooh !! Lynda you are famous in Morocco more than I am. All people here are talking about this flower that has a pure prettiness in her pen and brain. Really I want to know all your books and I want also to be near of your bright ideas that make the person feel that the earth is the better place to live." —Bassaz

"I have some difficulty to read books in English because I'm Brazilian. But, I need to say, your book is great!" —Eddie

"Just wanted to tell you that I think your books are great. I'm currently a bookseller at Borders Books and Music in St. Louis, and I always recommend your books as great web design source. I just wanted to compliment your great work and tell you I try and support your books whenever I possibly can! Take care and keep up the good work!" —Mike

"I was getting these dots on my gifs. Then my partner in our "fledgling" web thing lent me your *Deconstructing Web Graphics* and *Coloring Web Graphics* books. How did someone write two entire books on exactly what I wanted to know? I have selected you to be my inspiration in order to expand my 10-year-old graphic design business into web graphics. All the clients want it. And why not make it beautiful while I'm at it. Thanks much." —Felice

"Am currently reading *Coloring Web Graphics* and am finding it most interesting and helpful. Hope to get your newest book soon, too! I appreciate reading someone who is an art professional (I am not) as it should help me to apply better graphic and color design to pages I develop. Thanks for sharing your ideas, both in print and here on the web!" —Gary

"*Coloring Web Graphics.2* contains answers to questions I have had for several years. It is a visual and well written index for web design work. Hundreds of suggestions for color and link combinations. Software includes test samples, swatches, cluts. This is a "must have" for web designers on any level." —Amazon Reader

"When this book calls itself "the definitive resource for color on the web," they aren't pushing hype. This book covers graphic file types, color theory and relationships, using color on multiple platforms and with various browsers. Coated stock is used throughout to demonstrate color principles and design elements. Advice on how to transfer expertise from printed page to web page and how to work around web constraints make this book particularly valuable. And thank goodness for discussion of how to make the smallest possible web files for fast downloading. Includes a CD-ROM for MAC and Windows with palettes, browser-safe clip-art, examples and samples. For all user levels." —Amazon Internet Books Editor

<designing web graphics.2>
How to Prepare Media and Images for the Web

Completely updated and expanded to include the latest on file formats, file sizes, compression methods, cross-platform web color, and browser-specific tehcniques, *Designing Web Graphics.2* is the definitive graphics guide for all web designers. If you are already working in the digital arts, in print or video, looking to transfer your skills to the web, this is the book for you. Step-by-step instruction in a conversational and easy to read style from a fellow artist/designer will help you understand the best methods and techniques for preparing graphics and media for the web.

Written in a conversational and user-friendly tone, *Designing Web Graphics.2* has received rave reviews from both experienced web designers and newcomers to the field. It's the bestselling book on this subject and is being used by web designers all over the world, including those from Hot Wired, Adobe, and Discovery Online.

In this book, you'll learn about:

- Creating small and fast web graphics
- Browser-safe colors for cross-platform use
- GIFs, JPEGs, and PNGs through the use of comparison charts that help you pick the best compression method
- Scanning tips (Photoshop 4.0 techniques)
- Sound, animation, and interactivity
- Creating navigation bars, rollover effects, and linked graphics
- Step-by-step tutorials for programming Photoshop 4.0 action palettes
- Practical applications for JavaScript, Shockwave, CGI, and plug-ins
- Embedding inline music, animation, and movie files
- Animated GIF creation techniques (how to control size, speed, and color palettes)
- Creating GIF and PNG transparencies for the web
- Web TV specs and authoring tips
- Updated typography section

Product and Sales Information

Designing Web Graphics.2 by Lynda Weinman
ISBN:1-56205-715-4 ■ $55.00/USA ■ 500 pages
Available at your local bookstore or online
Macmillan Publishing ■ 1-800-428-5331
- http://www.lynda.com
- http://www.mcp.com/newriders

■ testimonials

Designing Web Graphics.2

"Wow! *Designing Web Graphics.2* is an amazing book. A friend of mine loaned it to me, but I know I will be buying my own copy since it seems like a great reference. I like your writing style and have to grin at your daughter's pictures (someday she'll be embarrassed I guess, if she isn't already.) I am recommending you to anyone who asks me for web graphics help." —Graham

"About six months ago, I finished an interactive media course, which barely scratched the surface of HTML. After I finished, an arts organization said to me, "We like your work, how about writing a website for us? You can write them, can't you?" So I went out and got *Designing Web Graphics.2*. I can't thank you enough for the clear, human, and inspiring approach of the book. It's probably one of the main reasons I now have a full-time job in interactive media. Thank you for all the help!" —Martha

"I decided to go out in search of a book, or something, to help me learn at least enough about web graphics so that I wouldn't be ashamed to show my face(?) online again after putting up my site. I'm sure you've heard this story a thousand times, so one more time couldn't hurt. I spent the better part of the next evening going through all of the books on HTML and graphics, trying to find something that would help. Then finally, on the bottom row of the last shelf (this is actually true, and not just for the drama of it), there was your book, *Designing Web Graphics*. Tears of joy streamed from my eyes. (Okay, that's not actually true, but I was very happy). I drove home and spent the rest of the night devouring chapter after chapter. In all seriousness, it is a really beautiful book. Not only does it explain everything that one needs to become a better web graphics designer, but it is actually very well designed itself, and a pleasure to read and look at as a book. I think that it is very funny how many books on web graphics are designed as if they were computer books and not graphics books. Thankfully, as I mentioned before, you have written a beautiful book, which is a pleasure to read, in addition to being useful, and that's what I really wanted to write and say. Thank you very much for writing it, and I look forward to reading your other books." —David

"About two weeks ago I managed (with great difficulty!!) to buy your book *Designing Web Graphics* here in South Africa. As I'm sure you are aware, the value of our rand is absolutely worthless! So your book was rather expensive, but then I just had to have it, and I must say I've not been disappointed and it has been worth every cent. I now see that you have published a few books on the web and have a second book coming out. This is a bad case of a junkie needing his next fix! So I shall be hurrying off to the bookshop and begging them to order me your second book!! Once again thanks for such an excellent book…a friend of mine had discovered it (as she knew that I was looking for it) in a bookshop one weekend and had hidden it behind all the other books. It was the only copy that I could find in Johannesburg!" —Adious

"Just a note to say what a great book *Designing Web Graphics.2* is. Non-geeky, readable info well-presented and easy to follow. An inspiration for self learners on site design. Also nice web sites that do not take three days to download demanding plug-ins. Keep up the good work." —Alan

"Thanks for another great, practical, pleasure-to-read-and-apply book. I loved the first edition and I'm fast falling for the second edition. I am a partner in a small, but prosperous, info design consulting firm. I would never refer to myself as a visual design professional, but we often find ourselves doing visual prototypes of content design on behalf of our clients. I have found your books of enormous help and I appreciate your immersion in digital environments—it shows! I also appreciate the fact that your recommended resources cover a wide range of publishers, something other authors are often not so generous about. You certainly have helped this "reluctant designer"

<preparing web graphics>
Learn to Make Fast, Cross-Platform Compatible, High-Quality Web Graphics

Understanding how to prepare web graphics properly is key to learning how to make web pages look good and perform responsibly. This lower cost alternative to *Designing Web Graphics.2* is appropriate for web publishers who aren't graphic artists. *Preparing Web Graphics* explains the mechanics of web graphics creation, preparation, and delivery. Lynda Weinman supplies the tips and tricks to create graphics that endure the irregularities of different browsers, platforms, and monitor settings.

Using Photoshop 4.0 to produce the bulk of the instructions and corresponding full-color examples, Weinman teaches web publishers how to make fast-loading images without sacrificing quality. She shares her comprehensive knowledge of web graphics engineering This includes working with transparent GIFs, low-bandwidth graphics, anti-aliasing, dithering, color mapping, setting color palettes, compressing images, using browser-safe colors, and creating browser-safe artwork. It also includes working with background tiles, navigation images, typography, web animation, and more.

In this book, you'll learn about:

- Hardware and software for getting started
- Graphics that download quickly—without sacrificing quality
- What happens to graphics when viewed from multiple platforms, browsers, and operating systems
- Successfully working with transparent images and avoiding halos and fringing
- Creating seamless tiles, efficient animated GIFs, and enhancements such as custom rules and bullets
- Follow step-by-step Photoshop 4.0 tutorials for designing web-specific images
- Working with image-based typography, using custom fonts and HTML alignment techniques

Product and Sales Information

Preparing Web Graphics by Lynda Weinman
ISBN:1-56205-686-7 ▪ $39.99/USA ▪ 238 pages
Available at your local bookstore or online
Macmillan Publishing ▪ 1-800-428-5331
- http://www.lynda.com
- http://www.mcp.com/newriders

■ testimonials

Preparing Web Graphics

"I'm writing to thank you for your extraordinary book, *Preparing Web Graphics*. I can't recall any other "how-to" book I've used that would inspire me to write the author(s) a note of thanks. Please humor me while I list the things I love about your book: **1)** You have a clear and logical style of writing that is graceful as well, few people in any discipline have this gift, as this writer-editor well knows. The text is highly readable and yet avoids that irritating colloquial-cutesy-condescending style used in some computer primers. **2)** I know many intelligent, competent people who seem incapable of transmitting their knowledge to others. You, on the other hand, are a born teacher: You have not forgotten where you started, and you know that others need to start there as well; you are gracious enough to begin at the beginning. However, you do not look down upon your audience. Instead, you present the information as if you understand that, while others may not write computer programs and might need courses from time to time to understand certain aspects of computers, we do have our own areas of expertise and are not blithering idiots because we don't always intuit computer knowledge. **3)** The information you present in your breathtakingly clear fashion is actually useful. Every page contains the information I need and have been looking for. I haven't even finished the book and I'm already writing this message. My only complaint so far is that the book's title is something of a misnomer. You give far more information than the phrase *Preparing Web Graphics* would imply: The discussion of text-based vs. text-based HTML vs. WYSIWYG HTML editors is a (very helpful) case in point. **4)** Oh, yes—and the design of the book is beautiful, too. Love that orange cover and the clean design of the pages and the various illustrations series that illuminate exactly what the novice needs to know and would really love to understand. In short, you have a new fan. If your other books are as extraordinary as this one, I'll be buying those, too. I'm already recommending *Preparing Web Graphics* to anyone who will listen. Thanks!" —Andra

"I just purchased your book *Preparing Web Graphics* and found it to be very insightful. I especially liked that you repeated certain steps over and over. Yes, I am a visual person and designer and need it beaten in me to get it." — Crystel

"Every Saturday my daughter Joelle and I park ourselves at the local Barnes & Noble for a few hours. She shoots off to the kids section, whilst I stroll down computer-book row—the geek that I am. After a few hours, on my last run back to the shelves for "whatever catches my eye," I see your books prominently displayed on the end-cap. Hmm. Nice cover. Okay, I pick it up and browse. "Hey, this looks pretty good!" So I drag myself over to the kids section (where Joelle, my seven-year-old is knee-deep in pop-up books), park myself in a corner of the Winnie-The-Pooh stage and start reading. This book couldn't have been better for me. I'm a computer geek by trade (Sr. System Engineer) with a wide background in PCs, Macs, and the Internet. I've always had an interest in the artsy-fartsy things in life, yet I haven't been schooled in art. I'm skilled at Photoshop and have always wanted to make a really great site, but getting started was always the problem. *Preparing Web Graphics* was a great book, and my #1 resource and inspiration for getting started." —Brian

"I just wanted to take a sec and write you a note to commend you on your wonderful books. I literally taught myself everything I know about web design and HTML (not to mention Photoshop) from reading and re-reading the pages of your fine tomes. I know that often the best reward for hard work is feedback from your audience, so I wanted you to know that your books are first rate and have made a big impact (though I sincerely hope you are making lots of money too, 'cause you deserve it, sister!)" —Jodi

<creative html design>

A Hands-On HTML 4.0 Web Design Tutorial

It's easy to make web pages with today's new WYSIWYG editors, but those programs don't teach you how to make fast-loading graphics, write accurate HTML that will endure for future browsers, or the necessary techniques involved in preparing your site for the web. Written by two of the industry's foremost experts, this definitive tutorial teaches you not just how to make a web page, but how to design web sites that are cross-platform compatible and work effectively within the web's distinct constraints.

Creative HTML Design walks you through all the phases of site design—from selecting an ISP and uploading files, to more advanced techniques like adding animation and rollovers. Step-by-step tutorials for Photoshop 4.0 and Paint Shop Pro teach how to design using "safe" colors, make distinctive background tiles, align your graphics, use tables and frames, include JavaScript rollovers, use CSS, as well as numerous other design and HTML features.

Product and Sales Information

Creative HTML Design
By Lynda Wienman and William E. Weinman
ISBN:1-56205-704.9 ▪ $39.99/USA ▪ 434 pages
Available at your local bookstore or online
Macmillan Publishing ▪ 1-800-428-5331
▪ http://wwwcgibook.com
▪ http://www.mcp.com/newriders

In this book, you'll learn about:

- How to build a finished web site with real-world examples and exercises
- How to write and read HTML
- Choosing an Internet service provider or presence provider
- Creating speedy GIF, JPEG, and PNG files
- Working with safe, cross-platform colors that will not shift in web browsers
- Designing distinctive background tiles, with and without visible seams
- Typographic principles and type tricks for the web
- Cascading Style Sheets
- Creating artwork and code for JavaScript rollovers
- Using tables to align text and graphics
- How to use frames aesthetically and effectively
- Using forms aesthetically so they fit the look of the rest of your site
- Adding animation and sound
- Organizing your pages on a server using relative URLs and SSI
- Troubleshooting automatically generated WYSIWYG HTML
- A complete HTML 4.0 reference

The cross-platform CD-ROM includes:

- All the necessary files for the tutorials in this book
- JavaScript rollover code and many other customizable scripts

■ testimonials

Creative HTML Design

"It has been a long time since I fell so totally in love with a subject. I first purchased your book *Designing Web Graphics.2* and instantly recognized the value of the book. Now, with *Deconstructing Web Graphics* and *Creative HTML Design*, the book you co-authored with your brother, Bill, I have a nearly complete reference set designed to take me toward my goal of learning to design web sites. I even purchased his book *The CGI Book*. What I like best about your books is, first of all, they are packed with solid information and CLEAR instructions on how to use the material. Certainly unknown in the field of computers. Secondly, I like how you personalize your books. You bring your family, your father, your brother, and your daughter into the material and in a totally comfortable way introduce us to them all. Your acceptance of self is very evident in your books and your web site. I like it. I think you have achieved a first in the publication of computer instruction manuals. You have managed to introduce emotion into a somewhat dry material. I think your skill as a designer has overflowed a bit and shows us how technical material should be presented. I hope you do very well with your endeavors and know that I plan to purchase every book you have written just to complete my set. I think you have a lot to say, and I intend to keep myself at the cutting edge by reading it. You've done a great job, Lynda." —Heather W.

"Your new book just arrived, and it is a winner! <G> For the first time, I think I can actually learn HTML and not have to depend upon Adobe PageMill to create two new web sites and rework my old (very inactive) one. I also have *Deconstructing Web Graphics*, *Coloring Web Graphics*, and *Designing Web Graphics.2*. Now, if I could just figure out how to use all these resources you and Bill have provided." —Heidi

"I'm a huge fan. I just added *Creative HTML Design* to my web library (it sits beside *Deconstructing Web Graphics* and *Designing Web Graphics.2*). Your books are by far the best on the market. I am a student who has spent two years working in the professional design arena. I have referred many experienced art directors and designers who have never worked with the web before to your books–several ran out and bought *Designing Web Graphics.2* the day I showed it to them. In addition to the great content, the look and feel of your books is top notch." —Rob

First of I wanted to say I just bought your book *Creative HTML Design*, and I love it. I've read it cover to cover, well almost. I just finished Chapter 15, but I'm almost done. I have done a few web sites already, some of which don't follow all your tips, but they were designed before I read your book so... we learn more all the time and I hope to incorporate many of your great ideas. —Susan